Cross-Strait Relations and Inter-Korean Relations

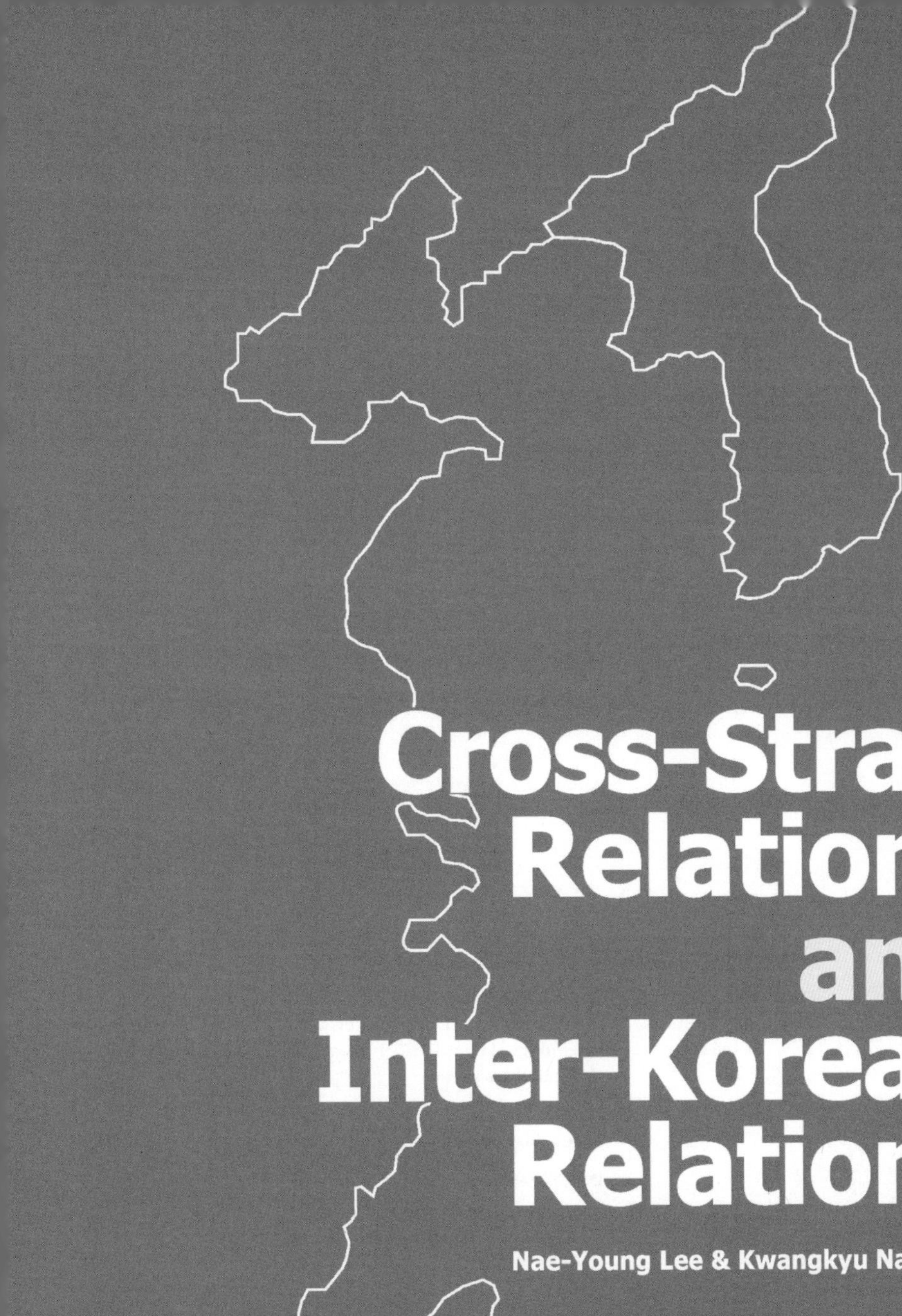

Cross-Strait Relations and Inter-Korean Relations

Nae-Young Lee & Kwangkyu Nam eds.

Cross-Strait Relations and Inter-Korean Relations

First Published 2016
by the Asiatic Research Institute at Korea University
145 Anam-ro, Seongbuk-gu, Seoul 136-701, Korea
www.asiaticresearch.org

price : 16,000won

ISBN 978-89-90769-85-5

Emerson Niou is Professor of Political Science at Duke University. He is the co-author of *The Balance of Power*, Cambridge University Press, 1989. His publications include: "A Theory of Economic Sanctions and Issue Linkage," with Dean Lacy, *Journal of Politics*, 2004; "Term Limits as a Response to Incumbency Advantage," with Kongpin Chen, *Journal of Politics*, May 2005; "External Threat and Collective Action," with Guofu Tan, *Economic Inquiry*, 2005; "Economic Interdependence and Peace: A Game-Theoretic Analysis," *Journal of East Asian Studies*, 2007; "Strategic Voting in Plurality Elections," with Daniel Kselman, *Political Analysis*, 2010.

Nae-Young Lee is a professor of political science department at Korea University and director of Center for Public Opinion Research of the East Asia Institute. Professor Lee was the former Director of the Asiatic Research Institute at Korea University. Professor Lee received both his B.A. and M.A. from Korea University and received his Ph.D. in political science from University of Wisconsin-Madison. He served as a MacArthur fellow of Global Studies Program at University of Wisconsin-Madison, research fellow at Sejong Institute, and a visiting scholar in the Warter H. Shorenstein Asia-Pacific Research Center at Stanford University. He has been a columnist to major newspapers in Korea and he was a Vice President of the Korean Association of International Studies. In 2014, He was a visiting scholar at the Institute of East Asian Democracy of National Taiwan University. His research interests are Korean politics, electoral politics, public opinion, and East Asian political economy. He authored or edited about 15 books and published numerous journal articles and book chapters. His recent publications include 〈*National Identity and Regional Perceptions in East Asia*〉 (Seoul: the Asiatic Research Institute, 2014) 〈*Changing Korean Voters 5*〉 (Seoul: the East Asia Institute, 2013), 〈*Koreans, Who are We: Exploring Korean Identity by Public Opinion*

Survey〉 (Seoul: the East Asia Institute, 2011), "What Determines Korean Perception and Attitude on National Unification?," *Peace Studies*, Vol. 21(1) (2014), "The 18th Presidential Election and Retrospective Voting," *Review of Party Politics*, Vol. 12, No. 2 (2013), "Conceptualization and Measurement of Soft Power in East Asia," in Sook Jong Lee and Jan Melissen, eds. *Public Diplomacy and Soft Power in East Asia* (New York, Palgrave, 2011), "The Automobile Industry," in Byung-Kook Kim & Ezra Vogel. eds. *The Park Chung Hee Era: The Transformation of South Korea* (Cambridge, Harvard University Press, 2011).

Eunju Chi is research professor in the Peace & Democracy Institute at Korea University. She received her Ph.D. in the department of political science and international relations from Korea University. Her research interests are comparative politics, party politics, democratization, and Taiwanese politics. She is the author of *Independence Issues and Party Politics in Taiwan* (2009, in Korean), *Another Chinese, Taiwan* (2015, in Korean). Her work has appeared in *Asian Survey, Asian Perspective, Government & Opposition, Korean Journal of International Relations, Korean Political Science Review, Korea Obsever and Peace Studies*. Her recent publications include "Two-Party Contests and the Politics of Electoral Reforms: The Case of Taiwan," *Government and Opposition* 49 (2014), "Unequal Democracies in East Asia: Rising Inequality and Government Responses in South Korea and Taiwan," *Asian Survey* 48 (2012, with Hyeok Yong Kwon), "Economic Issues, Party Realignment, and China Factor: the Case of Taiwan," *Korean Journal of International Relations*, 55 (2015).

Chi-Hsiung Chang is research fellow, Institute of Modern History, Academia Sinica. He received his Ph.D. Sociology , The University of Tokyo (Japan). Associate

Research Fellow, Institute of Modern History, Academia Sinica (1989-1996). He also served Research Fellow, Institute of Modern History, Academia Sinica (1996-), Visiting professor, Graduate School of Arts and Sciences, The University of Tokyo (1996-1997), Director, North Eastern Asia Research, Academia Sinica (1998-2002), President, Society of Overseas Chinese Studies, R.O.C. (1998-2002), Visiting professor, Institute for Research in Humanities, Kyoto University (2000), Professor, Graduate School of Humanities and Sociology, Department of Chinese Philosophy, The University of Tokyo (2007-2008), Visiting professor, Institute of Modern History, Chinese Academy of Social Sciences (2011). His publications include: 『海峽兩岸在亞洲開發銀行的中國代表權之爭: 名分秩序論觀點的分析』, 中央研究院東北亞區域研究, 2010; "中華民國(台灣)參與WHO/WHA會籍的'國際名分'認定 - '加盟模式'觀點的分析," 中央研究院近代史研究所, 2009; "法理論述 vs. 事實論述: 中華民國與國際奧委會的會籍認定交涉, 1960-1964," 臺灣史研究, 2010; "Conflict between the Eastern and Western Principles of International Order: Negotiations over Status and Order between China and Siam in the Last Years of the Qing Dynasty and the Early Republican Period," Social Sciences in China: A Quarterly Journal, 2007.

Edward I-hsin Chen, who earned his Ph.D. from Department of Political Science at Columbia University in 1986, is currently teaching in the Graduate Institute of American Studies (GIAS) at Tamkang University. His specializes in international relations theories, globalization and international political economy, American foreign policy, and decision-making process of U.S. policy toward China and Taiwan. His English articles include "U.S. Role in Future Taipei-Beijing Relations" in King-yuh Chang, ed., *Political Economic Security in Asia-Pacific* (Taipei: Foundation on International & Cross-Strait Studies, 2004); "A Retrospective and Prospective Overview of U.S.-PRC-ROC Relations," in *Views & Policies: Taiwan Forum*, Vol. 2, No. 2, December 2005

(A Journal of Cross-Strait Interflow Prospect Foundation in Taipei); "The Decision-Making Process of the Clinton Administration in the Taiwan Strait Crisis of 1995-96," in King-yuh Chang, ed., *The 1996 Strait Crisis Decisions, Lessons & Prospects* (Taipei: Foundation on International & Cross-Strait Studies, 2006); and "From Balance to Imbalance: The U.S. Cross-Strait Policy in the First Term of the Bush Administration," in Quansheng Zhao and Tai Wan-chin, ed., *Globalization and East Asia* (Taipei: Taiwan Elite, 2007).

Tung-Chieh Tsai is now a Professor at Graduate Institute of International Politics and Director at Center for Contemporary China Studies and Center for Comprehensive Japan Studies in National Chung-Hsing University. He has gotten his Ph.D (1999) degrees in International Politics from National Cheng-Chi University. The area of specialization of him includes international relations, East Asian studies, Chinese Foreign Policy, and Cross-Strait Issues. His main publications include *China's New Diplomacy* (2008 & 2011), *A Global Journey of Democracy* (2009), *Political Economy of East Asian Regional Development* (2007) , *Contending Issues in Political World* (2005), *The Diplomatic Strategies and Foreign Relations of Taiwan and Mainland China* (2001), *Diplomatic History of Contemporary China* (2000 & 2010), and over one hundred papers are presented at various domestic and international seminars, conferences, and academic journals.

Jung-hyun Park is currently Research Professor at the Asiatic Research Institute, Korea University. Dr. Park earned his Ph.D. in modern Chinese history from Korea University. His Ph.D. research analyzed the rural society of Jiangnan, China, in the 1920-30's. His areas of research interests include bilateral relations between Korea and China, territorial sovereignty in Northeast Asia and a foreign trade network in East Asia. His publications include *The*

Statistics and Analyses of Chinese Foreign Trade, 1868-1948 (co-author, Hanyaipyung Press, 2010), *Modern Chinese Foreign Trade and East Asian Economy* (co-author, Northeast Asian History Foundation, 2008) and *A Study on Modern Chinese Rural Society* (Korea University Press, 2004). "Anti-Communist Policy and a Recapture of Mainland Plan of Taiwan in the 1950s" (2012, Korean), "Changes in Foreign Trade and Trade Network in Japanese-Occupied Areas during the Sino-Japanese War" (2011, Korean).

Kwangkyu Nam, Resarch Professor of the Asiatic Research Institute at Korea University, He is also director of Maebong Institute for One Korea. He received his Ph.D., Dept. of Political Science, Korea University. His areas of research cover the fields of modern Korean Politics, Inter-Korean Politics, foreign policy. His publications include 2014. *The Foundation of Republic of Korea* (2015, co-author), *Nationalism and Post-nationalism in South Korea* (2014, co-author), "A Study on the Transformation for the Unification of the Korean Peninsular in North Korea," (2014), "Research on the Identity between the Provisional Government and the People's Republic (1945.8-11)," "The U.S.-USSR Joint Commission and U.S. and USSR's Policy for an Interim Government in Korea." (2009).

Contents

Preface

This book is an outcome of the research project which was conducted by the Center for Taiwan Studies(CTS) at the Asiatic Research Institute(ARI), Korea University. The Center for Taiwan Studies was founded in April 2009 to serve as a research hub for Taiwan studies in Korea. This project was launched in 2011 with a research grant from Chiang Ching Kuo Foundation(CCKF) in Taiwan. With financial support from Chiang Ching-kuo Foundation, the Center for Taiwan Studies at the ARI organized the joint research team consisting of ten experts from Korea and Taiwan and conducted collaborative research. Research team members from both countries have diverse disciplinary specialties such as history, political science, international relations, and sociology. After one year of collaborative research, the final papers were presented in the conference held at the National Chengchi University of Taiwan in March 2012. Since then, most of papers were revised, some were published as journal articles, and finally these papers are published as a book. We offer sincere apology for long overdue publication of this book.

As the title of the book indicates, this book aims to examine and compare Cross-Strait relations and inter-Korean relations. Both Taiwan and South Korea share meaningful similarities as divided countries throughout the cold-war and post cold-war periods. In both South Korea and Taiwan, perception and policy toward North Korea and China has been the major source of constituting national identity. In addition, how to deal with North Korea and China has been a main issue of political conflict in both countries.

For Taiwan, mainland China has been perceived as brothers sharing cultural heritage and historical bonds. At the same time, mainland China has been considered as a powerful villain who has threatened the survival of Taiwan. Imbalance of the population size and economic and military power between China and Taiwan has created the sense of insecurity and anxiety of Taiwan people. Yet the rapid rise of the Chinese economy during the last twenty years has provided Taiwan an ample opportunity to benefit from it. Therefore, the perception and policy towards China has been sharply divided by major political parties. Identity issue has been the most salient cleavage in Taiwan politics during the last twenty years. The competing concept of national identity-Taiwanese vs. Chinese- has been diluted as people having multiple identities increased. However, increasing homogeneity of national identity does not necessarily reduce its significance. The saliency of national identity as a major source of political cleavage in Taiwan was reduced but remained strong. Moreover, Taiwan people are sharply divided by their preference on Taiwan's relations with mainland China. The division over unification versus independence has remained a salient issue which differentiates the position of the KMT from the DPP.

The relationship between Taiwan and mainland has been improved substantially during the first term of the Ma Ing-ju government. In the realm of trade, signing of economic cooperation framework agreement (ECFA) in 2010 was a milestone for economic cooperation. However, in the last few years many Taiwanese, especially DPP supporters, have negative views of the economic integration between Taiwan and China. They fear that the rapid progress of Cross-Strait economic cooperation, which was accelerated during the Ma Ying-jeou government, may undermine Taiwan's economic autonomy and sovereignty. The DPP also criticizes the ECFA because the economic benefits of the ECFA was limited to the big business and export sectors. The increasing anti-Chinese sentiment was vividly expressed in the Sunflower Student Movement which occurred in March 2014.

The landslide victory for the DPP in the January 2016 presidential and parliamentary elections inevitably affects the direction of Cross-Strait relations. While disappointment over the bad performance of the Ma Ying-jeou government, sluggish economy, high unemployment rate, and rising housing price were the main causes for the defeat of the KMT, public's negative evaluation over Ma's pro-China policy also contributed to the KMT's crushing defeats. Even though the new President Tsai Ing-wen has pledged to maintain peace and cooperation with China during the campaign, the independence-leaning DPP and its supporters anticipate new policy toward China. China's Taiwan Affairs Office expressed opposition any move towards independence after the elections. Thus it remains to be seen whether power shift in Taiwan ushers in a new era of Cross-Strait relations.

In South Korea, perception and policy towards North Korea has fluctuated over the years, depending on the nature of inter-Korean relations. In addition, there has been differing views and position according to political parties and age groups regarding the perception and policy towards North Korea. During the Cold War era from the 1950s to the late 1980s, most of South Koreans, while sharing compatriotic feeling with the people of North Korea, had a deep suspicion and fear of the North Korean regime and its belligerent stance against South. North Korea was considered as a sworn enemy which could threaten the security of South Korea any time by military provocation. Yet the demise of the Cold War international order, increasing power disparity between the two Koreas, and democratization of South Korea created profound change in Korean attitude towards North Korea. The failure of the North Korean regime and widening power disparity between the two Koreas also changed Korean attitude toward North Korea. South Koreans began to see North Koreans as poor, starving brothers in need of help. The majority of South Korean public perceived that the failed North Korean regime could not be a serious threat to South Korea due to power disparity between the two Koreas.

Moreover, democratic transition in 1987 made peaceful coexistence with North Korea politically acceptable within South Korea. In 1998, President Kim Dae Jung pursued a new policy initiative, known as the Sunshine Policy. In June 2000, the Sunshine Policy achieved its greatest success when President Kim Dae Jung travelled to Pyongyang for an unprecedented summit with North Korean leader Kim Jong Il. After the summit, the two Koreas developed official dialogue channels and various socio-cultural exchange programs flourished.

After ten years of efforts to pursue reconciliation and cooperation, inter-Korean relations returned to the period of mutual distrust and animosity during the last decade. In particular, the revelation of the nuclear weapons program by North Korea created a strong sense of betrayal against North Korea and the engagement policy has been criticized as a naïve and improper policy among many South Korean public. Under last eight years of Lee

Myung-bak and current Park Geun-hye presidency, inter-Korean relations have been deteriorated. The sense of mutual distrust has increased and inter-Korean dialogue has been almost stopped. Continuing military provocations, nuclear tests, and missile launch by North Korea heighted the security concerns of South Koreans and hindered possibility of resuming inter-Korean dialogue.

This book is valuable mainly because it is a product of research collaboration between Korean and Taiwan scholars. Moreover, it is very interesting that inter-Korean relations and cross-Strait relations are compared by Korean and Taiwan scholars in four chapers of this book. From four comparative chapters, readers can notice diverse views and policy suggestions on cross-Strait relations and inter-Korean relations. Considering that both countries face common challenge and policy dilemma as divided countries, we expect that this book provides scholars as well as policy makers in Taiwan and South Korea with important policy lessons regarding future directions of cross-Strait relations and inter-Korean relations.

Moreover, we hope that this book contributes to boosting up Taiwan Studies in South Korea. South Korea and Taiwan share similar historical experiences such as remarkable economic growth and successful democratic consolidation. Both countries also face common challenge and policy dilemma as divided countries. How to deal with North Korea and Mainland China has been the most crucial policy agenda in both countries. Nevertheless, it is a pity that Taiwan studies have been paid minor attentions in Korean academic communities, especially in social science. We sincerely hope that this book contribute to enhancing further academic exchange and cooperation among scholars and experts of both countries.

We would like to express sincere gratitude to Dr. Yun-han Chu, President of Chiang Ching Kuo Foundation for financial support for this project. We also appreciate for encouragement and support of Lee Jong-Wha, Director of the ARI for this project. We are also thankful for Professor Lee Ming, Director of the Center for Korean Studies at the NCCU for hosting the conference held at the National Chengchi University in 2012. Finally, we appreciate efforts and patiences of all chapter contributors as well as numerous participants of the conference and workshops.

2016. 4

Nae-Young Lee,
former Director of the ARI & Professor
at Department of Political Science, Korea University

Kwangkyu Nam,
Research Profossor at the ARI, Korea University

The China Factor in Taiwanese Politics

Emerson Niou (Professor, Duke University)

Ever since the Chinese Nationalist Government retreated to Taiwan in 1949, the threat from the Chinese communist regime has been a grave and constant concern for the people of Taiwan. At the time, the fall of Taiwan to the Chinese communist force appeared imminent and unavoidable. Fortunately for Taiwan, immediately after the Korean War broke out in June 1950, President Harry Truman sent the 7th fleet to the Taiwan Strait to guard against military confrontation in that region. And in 1954 the United States signed a defense treaty with the Republic of China, the Sino-American Mutual Defense Treaty, to safeguard Taiwan's security and survival.

The treaty, however, was terminated in January 1980, one year after the United States and the People's Republic of China established diplomatic relations in order for the two countries to form a strategic partnership against the Soviet threat. In an effort to provide Taiwan with some level of security commitment, the United States Congress passed the Taiwan Relations Act (TRA) in 1979, stipulating that the United States will "consider any effort to determine the future of Taiwan by other than peaceful means, including by boycotts or embargoes, a threat to the peace and security of the Western Pacific area and of grave concern to the United States". Although the TRA is not a clear and firm security commitment to defend Taiwan, a policy often referred to as "strategic ambiguity", it has been successful thus far in deterring China from attacking Taiwan using military options.[1]

The precarious security balance was shaken by a new political force, the Taiwan independence movement, as a result of Taiwan's democratization in the 1980s. In 1986 the Democratic Progressive Party (DPP) was established, a party whose goals are primarily to create a Taiwanese national identity, reject unification with the People's Republic of China (PRC), obtain international

---

1_For more on US strategic ambiguity policy, see Benson, Brett V. and Emerson M. S. Niou, "Comprehending Strategic Ambiguity: US Policy Toward Taiwan Security," unpublished manuscript, Duke University, 2000, downloadable from http://taiwansecurity.org/IS/IS-Niou-0400.htm. See also, Hickey, Dennis V. *US-Taiwan Security Ties: From Cold War to Beyond Containment Westport*, Connecticut: Praeger Publishers, 1994.

recognition as a sovereign state, and, at least for some, establish the Republic of Taiwan. The independence movement has consequences beyond Taiwan's domestic politics because China has consistently vowed to use military force against Taiwan if it declares formal independence.

The shift in political power in Taiwan's domestic politics after the 2000 presidential election, with the DPP candidate displacing the Kuomintang (KMT) for the first time in Taiwan's history, created greater uncertainties for China over Taiwan's official policy on the "one-China" issue. From 2000 to 2008, President Chen Shui-bian took a number of bold steps in the direction of independence. For example, in July 2002 he declared that there is "one country on each side of the Taiwan Strait."[2] And, on February 27, 2006, he formally announced that the National Unification Council would "cease to function" and its guidelines would "cease to apply", a deviation from the "Four No's and One Without" policy that he stipulated in his 2000 and 2004 inauguration speeches.

In 2008 KMT regained political power by defeating the DPP in both the legislative and presidential elections. In his inaugural address, President Ma Ying-jeou laid out his promise in dealing with cross-Strait relations: there would be "no reunification, no in-

2_Chen's statement was made on August 3, 2002 at the 29th annual meeting of the World Taiwan Fellow Townsmen Federation held in Tokyo, Japan.

dependence and no war" during his tenure as President. However, his policies have been viewed by critics as largely pro-PRC and part of a long-term scheme to steer Taiwan toward "eventual unification."[3]

In addition to the independence movement, tensions in the Taiwan Strait in recent decades have been further confounded by steadily increasing economic integration between China and Taiwan. Trade between China and Taiwan has increased at an impressive rate. Since 2003, China has become Taiwan's largest trading partner. Taiwan's exports to China (including Hong Kong) grew 37.1 percent in 2010 to US$114.78 billion, which constitutes 41.8 percent of Taiwan's total exports.[4] In addition to raw trade

---

3_For example, during a media interview on March 16, 2011, DPP chairwoman Tsai Ing-wen questioned President Ma's national identity by mentioning the inscription on the urn containing his late father's ashes. The inscription reads, "Dissolving Taiwan Independence Movement, Supporting Gradual Unification." For more background information on Taiwan's domestic politics, see Hsieh, John Fuh-sheng and Emerson M. S. Niou, "Salient Issues in Taiwan's Electoral Politics", in *Electoral Studies* 15:2 (1996), pp. 219-30; Lin, Tse-min, Yun-han Chu, and Melvin J. Hinich, "A Spatial Analysis of Political Competition in Taiwan", *World Politics* 48:4 (1996), pp. 453-81; Rigger, Shelley *Politics in Taiwan: Voting for Democracy* Routledge, 1999; Niou, Emerson M. S. and Philip Paolino, "The Rise of the Opposition Party in Taiwan: Explaining Chen Shui-bian's Victory in the 2000 Presidential Election", *Electoral Studies* 22:4 (2003), pp. 721-40; Nious, Emerson M. S. "Understanding Taiwan Independence and Its Policy Implications," *Asian Survey*, 44:4 (2004), pp. 555-67, July/August.

4_Taiwan External Trade Development Council (TAITRA)

volume, estimates of Taiwan investment on the mainland, both officially approved by Taiwan authorities and investment made by Taiwan firms through third parties, range from $150 billion to over $300 billion, making Taiwan the largest investor in China.[5]

To further integrate the two economies, China and Taiwan signed a historic trade pact, the Economic Cooperation Framework Agreement (ECFA), on June 29, 2010, which cuts tariffs on 539 Taiwanese exports to China and 267 Chinese products entering Taiwan. The ECFA aims to bring about liberalization of cross-Strait trade in products and services, avoiding Taiwan's regional economic marginalization and paving the way for expanded trade relations with the Association of Southeast Asian Nations (ASEAN) and other major trading partners.

The booming economic relationship between China and Taiwan makes economic sense. The two trade partners are in close geographical proximity to one another, have complementary comparative advantages, and share a common language and socio-cultural roots. However, does it make political sense? Many scholars argue that economic interdependence could help ameliorate tensions and promote interstate peace.[6] The proponents of

---

5_US Department of State, http://www.state.gov/r/pa/ei/bgn/35855.htm

6_For reviews of this literature, see Mansfield, Edward D. and Jon C. Pevehouse, "Trade Blocs, Trade Flows, and International Conflict," *International Organization* 54 (2000):

this view argue that interdependence results from trade partners' mutual emphasis on maximization of gains from trade, which will be lost if conflict interrupts the trade relationship. Less interdependent countries will derive greater utility from conflict because their opportunity costs are lower due to lower import and export levels. However, as countries boost trade levels and become increasingly interdependent, more is at stake in terms of welfare gains lost when conflict increases the cost of trade and ultimately threatens the cessation of trade altogether. In short, according to the liberal argument, economic interdependence between China and Taiwan should help ameliorate tension and potential conflicts in the Taiwan Strait.

A contrary position claims that the economic relationship between China and Taiwan places Taiwan in a politically vulnerable position with respect to China and may threaten Taiwan's national security. Dependence scholarship has long cautioned that asymmetries in economically integrated dyads are likely to create incentives for the less dependent actors to exploit their bargaining leverage to manipulate the more dependent party.[7] Proponents of

---

775-808; Barbieri, Katherine and Gerald Schneider, "Globalization and Peace: Assessing New Directions in the Study of Trade and Conflict," *Journal of Peace Research* 36 (1999): 387-404; and McMillan, Susan M., "Interdependence and Conflict," *Mershon International Studies Review* 41 (1997): 33-58.

7_Most notably, Hirschman 1945 and Gilpin 1977. See also related arguments by realists

the economic dependence position point to cross-Strait trade and investment asymmetries to support their concern that Taiwan is becoming too economically dependent upon China in a way that will give China crucial leverage on politically important issues.[8] Indeed, as early as 1985, a Chinese Communist Party United Front Department document made the following statement: "we can definitely, step by step, lead Taiwan's industries to rely on our market as long as we adopt well-organized and well-guided measures. Continuing to develop these efforts would effectively lead us to control the operation of Taiwan's economy that would speed up the reunification of the motherland."[9] And, according to Qian Qichen, former foreign minister of China, Beijing's strategy has been "to blockade Taiwan diplomatically, to check Taiwan milita-

---

who argue that states, which are concerned also by the mutual threat posed to each other, will be wary of any increase of the relative capabilities of any other state including relative gains from trade (Grieco, 1988; Gowa, 1994; and Waltz, 1979).

8_See, for example, Dent, Christopher, "Navigating Taiwan's Foreign Economic Policy," *Issues and Studies* 37 (2001): 1-34; Jefferson, Gary H., "Like Lips and Teeth: Economic Scenarios of Cross-Strait Relations," in Gong, Gerrit W., ed. *Taiwan Strait Dilemmas: China-Taiwan-US Policies in the New Century*, CSIS Press, 2000, pp. 97-116; Deng, Ping, "Taiwan's Restriction of Investment in China in the 1990s," *Asian Survey* 40 (2000): 958-981.

9_Wu, Hsin-hsing *Bridging the Strait: Taiwan, China, and the Prospects for Reunification* Hong Kong: Oxford University Press, 1994, 171, quoted in Bolt, Paul J., "Economic Ties Across the Taiwan Strait: Buying Time for Compromise," *Issues and Studies* 37 (2001): 80-105.

rily, and to drag along Taiwan economically."[10]

During former President Lee Teng-hui's administration, 1988-2000, Taiwan restricted trade with China to try to prevent becoming too economically dependent and politically vulnerable. In 1996, Lee introduced the "patience-over-haste" (jie-ji-yong-ren) investment policy. The policy prohibits some forms of mainland investment altogether, bans major infrastructure projects, limits Taiwanese investment in the mainland to 20-30 percent of total investments, and requires that Taiwan's businesses not make single project investments in excess of $50 million. Taiwan does not import mainland goods, which contributes to Taiwan's substantial trade surplus, and it forbids direct shipping and communication links with the mainland, so Taiwanese investors and traders must operate through third parties. Also, under President Lee's administration, Taiwan initiated the "go south" strategy to stall the mass exodus of Taiwanese businesses to the mainland by offering incentives to invest in Southeast Asia instead.

During President Chen's administration, despite the political tension between China and Taiwan on the "one-China" question,

---

10_This is allegedly a direct quote taken by the Hong Kong media from Qian's speech at an undisclosed national working meeting among Taiwan affairs officials held in Fuchian (December 1993), quoted in Chu, Yunhan, "The Political Economy of Taiwan's Mainland Policy," *Journal of Contemporary China* 6 (1997): 229-258.

〈Figure 1〉

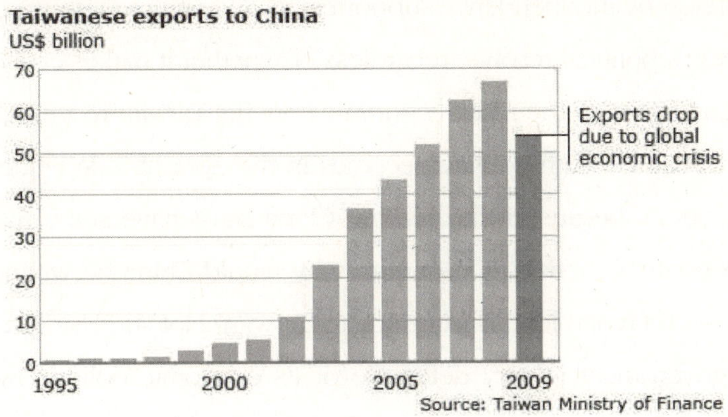

trade between the two sides continued to grow at an impressive rate. Taiwan's exports to China increased more than 10 times between 2000 and 2008 (see 〈Figure 1〉). Given Chen's political background, supporters of Taiwanese independence believed that Chen would not yield to China's coercion if China decided to use its economic leverage for political purposes. Thus, the economic liberation toward China during his tenure was not seen as politically motivated. But it is a different story for President Ma Ying-jeou's government.

Ma, a mainlander, often faces the charges by the Taiwan independence supporters that his eventual goal is to unite Taiwan with China and that he has the intention to "sell out" the former to the latter. Consequently, any policy adopted by his administration toward improving Taiwan's trade relations with China is interpreted by independence supporters as an instrument to weaken Taiwan's political resolve, regardless of whether it makes economic sense. In fact, the more economic benefits Taiwan receives, the more suspicious the policy becomes in the eyes of independence supporters, because it means that China must have some malignant political motives. Otherwise, why would China be willing to give such favorable terms of trade to Taiwan? Not surprisingly, the Ma government is very defensive of its economic policy toward China. For example, in a policy paper issued by the administration to garner popular support for the ECFA, in addition to arguing that the ECFA would be vital for Taiwan's economy in anticipation of political attacks from the DPP, it also had to argue that: "This is not a question of leaning toward Mainland China, nor does it constitute a selling out of Taiwan. This is a necessary economic strategy in competing with other countries." [11]

Based on our discussion thus far, the China factor in Taiwanese politics can be characterized by two types of threat: first, the threat of China using military force to attack Taiwan if the latter declares formal independence, and second, the threat of China using its economic leverage to compel Taiwan to concede

---

11_"Background Information on ECFA: Helping People Do Business to Improve Taiwan's Competitiveness." Mainland Affairs Council, Executive Yuan, March, 2010.

politically. In this paper I study the effects of these two types of threat on Taiwanese politics, with a focus on the (at that time) forthcoming 2012 presidential election. The paper is presented according to the following outline: in Section 1, I use survey data to measure public opinion in Taiwan on the independence and the unification issues and show that many people's preferences are susceptible to manipulation by China; in Section 2, I explore people's perception of the China threat in Taiwan and their confidence in the US security commitment; in Section 3, I study people's attitudes toward trade with China; and in Section 4, I conduct a systematic analysis of the effects of these two types of threats from China, the deterrence and compellence effects, on people's intended vote choice in the forthcoming 2012 Presidential election. The data used in this paper is based on the 2011 Taiwan National Security Survey.[12]

12_The 2011 Taiwan National Security Survey was conducted by the Election Study Center of the National Chengchi University, Taipei, Taiwan, from Feb 24-27, 2011 with a total sample size of 1,104. The principal investigator of the survey is Emerson Niou, Professor of Political Science, Duke University.

I . Preferences on the Taiwan Independence Issue

Given the importance of the independence issue on both Taiwan's domestic politics and the security balance in the Taiwan Strait, it is understandable that surveys have been conducted regularly to track shifts in public sentiment on this issue in Taiwan.[13] The standard approach has generally been to represent respondents' preferences on a 6-point scale. The wording of the question and the distribution of preferences are thus:

> Regarding the relations between Taiwan and Mainland China, there are a number of different views presented on this card. Which position best represents your view on this issue?
>
> 1. to seek independence from China quickly (4.4%)
> 2. to maintain the status quo now and seek independence later (18.5%)
> 3. to maintain the status quo indefinitely (28.1%)
> 4. to maintain the status quo now while deciding what to do later (37.3%)
> 5. to maintain the status quo now and seek unification later (8.0%)

13_For an overview of the evolution of survey questions on the Taiwan independence issue, see Rigger, Shelley "Social Science and National Identity: A Critique", *Pacific Affairs* 72: 4 (1999-2000), pp. 537-52; Rigger, Shelley "Maintaining the Status Quo: What It Means, and Why the Taiwanese Prefer it", *Cambridge Review of International Affairs*, 14, 2 (2001): pp. 115-23.

6. to seek unification with China quickly (1.4%)

7. no answer (2.3%)

The design of this question attempts to separate those in the status quo category who in fact have a first preference either for independence or unification but have, for some unspecified reason, reservations about the timing. This measure of preferences is based on the assumption that preferences on the independence-unification issue can be represented on a uni-dimensional spectrum. Why do people in Taiwan have difficulty deciding between independence and unification? What factors might influence respondents to move away from the status quo and toward either independence or unification? The common sense answer is that since Taiwan and Mainland China have been divided by civil war, the division is only temporary and the two sides will reunite when Mainland China becomes more compatible with Taiwan economically, socially, and politically. But after more than six decades of separation, unification with Mainland China looks to be an ever more challenging, if not impossible, task. Given the contrast between life in Taiwan and life in the mainland, people in Taiwan have no positive incentive to unite with the PRC. As a result, many people are attracted to the idea of Taiwan becoming an independent country, but only if China does not use force to stop that from happening.[14]

To arrive at a complete understanding of the conditionality of preferences, we should abandon the assumption that respondents' positions can be located somewhere along a one-dimensional policy spectrum between independence and unification. Instead, we should ask respondents to state the conditions under which they would move away from the status quo and toward either independence or unification, and vice versa. That is, we should incorporate a multidimensional approach.

The 2011 Taiwan National Security Survey includes four questions to explore precisely this form of conditionality of preferences on independence versus unification:

Q1. If the act of declaring independence will cause Mainland China to

---

14_An earlier attempt to explore the conditions under which respondents would move away from the status quo toward either independence or unification can be found in the following papers: Wu, Naiteh "National Identity and Party Support: The Social Basis of Party Competition in Taiwan", B*ulletin of the Institute of Ethnology*, Academia Sinica, 74 (1993), pp. 33-61; Wu, Naiteh "Liberalism and Ethnic Identity: Searching for the Ideological Foundation of Taiwanese Nationalism", *Taiwanese Political Science Review* 1:1 (1996), pp. 5-40. Alternative methods to measure respondents' preferences on the independence-unification issue can be found in Hsieh, John F. and Emerson M. S. Niou, "Measuring Taiwanese Public Opinion on the Taiwan Independence Issue: A Methodological Note," *China Quarterly*, 181:1 (2005), pp. 158-168, March; and Niou, Emerson M. S. "A New Measure of the Preferences on the Independence-Unification Issue in Taiwan", *Journal of Asian and African Studies*, 40:(1-2) (2005), pp. 91-104.

attack Taiwan, do you favor or not favor Taiwan independence?

Not Favor: 60.8% Favor: 30.5% NA: 8.7%

Q2. If the act of declaring independence will not cause Mainland China to attack Taiwan, do you favor or not favor Taiwan independence?

Not Favor: 18.4% Favor: 74.1% NA: 7.5%

Q3. If great political, economic, and social disparity exists between Mainland China and Taiwan, do you favor or not favor Taiwan unifying with China?

Not Favor: 76.5% Favor: 16.4% NA: 7.1%

Q4. If only small political, economic, and social disparity exists between Mainland China and Taiwan, do you favor or not favor Taiwan unifying with China?

Not Favor: 56.4% Favor: 36.4% NA: 7.2%

Based on responses from Q1 and Q2, respondents can be classified into three categories (see ⟨Table 1⟩): (1) supporting independence even if it will provoke China to attack (33.9 percent),[15] (2) supporting independence only if China will not attack (45.8 percent), and (3) not supporting independence regardless (19.7 percent).[16]

15_Not included are those who supported independence even if war might break out between China and Taiwan but did not support independence if no war were to break out.

16_To simplify presentation, we removed respondents who failed to indicate a clear preference on either Q1 or Q2.

〈Table 1〉 Preferences on Independence

Independence Even If War with China	Independence If No War		
	Not Favor	Favor	Total
Not Favor	19.7%	45.8%	65.5%
Favor	0.6%	33.9%	34.5%
Total	20.3%	79.7%	100.0%

Number of observations: 966
Data Source: The 2011 Taiwan National Security Survey

〈Table 2〉 Preferences on Unification

Unification Even If 2 Sides Are Not Compatible	Unification If the Two Sides Are Compatible		
	Favor	Not Favor	Total
Favor	11.9%	6.0%	17.9%
Not Favor	26.8%	55.3%	82.1%
Total	38.7%	61.3%	100.0%

Number of observations: 990
Data Source: The 2011 Taiwan National Security Survey

Second, on the questions of unification, Q3 and Q4, respondents can be classified into the following three categories (see 〈Table 2〉): (1) supporting unification even under unfavorable conditions (11.9 percent), (2) supporting unification only under favorable conditions (26.8 percent), and (3) not supporting unification under any circumstances (55.3 percent).

An interesting finding from these empirical results is that for many people, a preference for uniting with Mainland China or becoming an independent country is largely dependent on the costs of achieving one goal or the other. If the costs of uniting with

〈Table 3a〉 Preferences on Taiwan Independence and Intended Vote Choice in the 2012 Presidential Election

Vote Choice in 2012	Attitude on Taiwan Independence			
	No Independence	Independence Only If No War	Independence Even If War	Row Total
Ma Ying-jeou	30.3%	55.0%	14.7%	40.6%
DPP Candidate	7.2%	29.4%	63.4%	29.1%
NA	17.9%	50.2%	32.0%	30.3%
Column	19.8%	46.1%	34.1%	100% (959)

Mainland China or becoming an independent country are perceived to be low, then these goals are preferred, while if they are perceived to be too high then the status quo becomes the more attractive option.

People's attitudes on independence and unification clearly correlate with their intended vote choice in the forthcoming 2012 presidential election in Taiwan. The respective supporters of the incumbent President, Ma Ying-jeou, and the candidate nominated by the DPP also diverge in their views on the independence and unification issues.[17] 〈Table 3a〉 shows that only 14.7 percent of Ma's DPP supporters support Taiwan independence even if it means war with China, but 63.4 percent of the DPP candidate supporters share this view.

17_When the survey was conducted in February 2011, the DPP had not yet nominated its presidential candidate.

〈Table 3b〉 Preferences on Unification and Intended Vote Choice in the 2012 Presidential Election

Vote Choice in 2012	No Unification	Attitude on Unification with China		
		Unification Only If Similar	Unification Even If Different	Row Total
Ma Ying-jeou	42.9%	37.2%	19.8%	39.6%
DPP Candidate	76.8%	16.9%	6.3%	29.3%
NA	62.3%	28.4%	9.3%	31.1%
Column	58.9%	28.5%	12.6%	100% (929)

〈Table 3b〉 shows that 19.8 percent of Ma's supporters support unification with China even if the two systems are not compatible, but only 6.3 percent of the DPP supporters share this view.

II. Perceptions of China's Military Threat to Taiwan and the credibility of the US Security Commitment

With almost one half (45.8 percent) of the people in Taiwan willing to support independence if it will not provoke China to attack, it is not surprising that China refuses to renounce the use of force against Taiwan. In February 2000, Beijing released a white paper on the Taiwan issue. Underscoring China's threat to retain a coercive option to achieve its goals with respect to Taiwan, the white paper spells out China's position on the "one-China" principle and threatens the use of force if Taiwan becomes independent or resists negotiations for unification indefinitely.[18] On March 14, 2005, the PRC 10th National People's Congress passed the Anti-Secession Law, which, according to PRC officials, provides legal justification for China's use of force to prevent Taiwan's secession and compel unification after all avenues for peaceful unification have been exhausted.[19]

To improve its chances of achieving successful coercion of Taiwan, China has been actively increasing its military strength. China's military build-up is occurring on two levels. First, by amassing conventional weaponry designed to combat Taiwanese military forces, the PRC compels Taiwan to engage in a costly arms race that threatens to break Taiwan financially, which can be demonstrated by the build-up of its short-range surface-to-surface missile force based in China's Fujian province. Second, the PRC is building up its nuclear arsenal to counter the US. If the PRC can

---

18_Taiwan Affairs Office of the State Council website, "The One-China Principle and the Taiwan Issue," Taiwan Affairs Office and the Information Office of the State Council, People's Republic of China, 21 February 2000, http://www.gwytb.gov.cn:8088/detail.asp?table=WhitePaper&title=White%20Papers%20On%20Taiwan%20Issue&m_id=4.

19_For an explanation of China's draft Anti-Secession Law authorized by the Standing Committee of the National People's Congress, see *Zhaoguo Wang, Vice Chairman of the Standing Committee of the National People's Congress* "Explanations on Draft Anti-Secession Law," Third Session 10th National People's Congress and Chinese People's Political Consultative Conference, 8 March 2005, http://www.china.org.cn/english/2005lh/122118.htm.

make it too costly for the US to intervene in the conflicts in the Taiwan Strait, then China can resort to forceful means to compel Taiwan to unify with China.

The credibility of China's threat, however, might be affected by the United States' security commitment to Taiwan. The United States agrees that the Taiwan Strait dispute is a Chinese domestic issue to be resolved by Chinese on both sides of the Strait. Regardless of how the dispute is resolved, the United States insists that it must be done so peacefully.[20] This policy allows the United States mobility to intervene in the conflict but resists specifying the conditions under which United States will become involved.

In the 2011 Taiwan National Security Survey, respondents were asked whether they think Mainland China will or will not attack Taiwan if Taiwan declares independence: 58.4 percent expressed that they believed China would resort to force if Taiwan declared independence, 32.5 percent did not believe so, and 9.1 percent did not respond. The survey also asked respondents if they think the United States will help defend Taiwan if China attacks: 59.8 percent of the respondents responded positively, 28.2

20_Hickey, Dennis V. "America's Two-Point Policy and the Future of Taiwan," *Asian Survey* 28, no. 8 (1988): 881-896, explains in detail the background and implications of the US policy that insists that the Taiwan Strait dispute be settled peacefully and domestically.

〈Table 4a〉 Perception of China Threat and Preferences on Taiwan Independence if Confident of U.S. Support

Preferences on Taiwan Independence	Perception of China Threat		
	No Worry	Worry	Row Total
No Independence	35 44.9%	43 55.1%	78 13.8%
Conditional	80 31.0%	178 69.0%	258 45.6%
Independence	111 48.3%	119 51.7%	230 40.6%
Column Total	226 39.9%	340 60.1%	566 100%

percent negatively, 12 percent had no opinion.

We find several interesting correlations when we cross-tabulate respondents' level of worry about China's threat with their positions on the Taiwan independence issue and control for the respondents' level of confidence in U.S. support. First, the survey data clearly indicates that Taiwanese concerns about China's threat vary as they grow more or less concerned about the US commitment to defend Taiwan: 60.1 percent of the respondents who have confidence in US support think that China will attack Taiwan if Taiwan declares independence (see 〈Table 4a〉), while 76.6 percent of the respondents who do not have confidence in the United States think China will attack (see 〈Table 4b〉). Second, among those who have confidence in the US security commitment, 40.6 percent prefer independence 〈Table 4a〉, but among those who have no confidence in the US security commitment, only 20.1 percent prefer independence 〈Table 4b〉.

〈Table 4b〉 Perception of China Threat and Preferences on Taiwan Independence if Not Confident of U.S. Support

Preferences on Taiwan Independence	Perception of China Threat		
	No Worry	Worry	Row Total
No Independence	24 27.9%	62 72.1%	86 31.4%
Conditional	23 17.3%	110 82.7%	133 48.5%
Independence	17 30.9%	38 69.1%	55 20.1%
Column Total	64 23.4%	210 76.6%	274 100%

Tables 4a and 4b reveal that perceptions of China's threat are to some degree a function of what people in Taiwan perceive the level of US commitment to be, and that Taiwanese support for independence varies according to the degree of worry about China's threat. Those who perceive the US commitment level as high are more likely to be less concerned about China's threat and more likely to support independence. Conversely, those who worry about US commitment to Taiwan tend to fear China's threat more and are less willing to support independence.

III. Who Favors Trade with China?

People in Taiwan have different views on Taiwan's trade relations with China. Some believe that Taiwan should bravely go westward to take advantage of the Chinese economy as long as

Taiwan is resolute on defending its national sovereignty. However many people are worried that Taiwan's economic dependence on China renders it vulnerable to coercion from the PRC, especially when the KMT is in power. That is, the asymmetrical nature of cross-Strait trade might endanger Taiwan's security because China will become more willing to use its economic leverage to extract political concessions, and because Taiwan becomes more risk averse as its economic dependence increases.

To understand the distribution of people's attitudes toward trade with China, we asked respondents the following question:

> Some people believe that to improve Taiwan's economic growth and to help Taiwanese make more money, Taiwan should strengthen its trade and economic relations with Mainland China; however, others believe that to protect Taiwan's national security, Taiwan should not have a strong trade and economic relations with China. Which position on this issue do you support?

Among the 1104 respondents, 45.2 percent favors increasing trade with China, while 41.8 percent holds the opposite view, and 13 percent has no response. The survey also shows a strong correlation between attitude on the trade issue and one's intended vote choice in the 2012 presidential election. 〈Table 5a〉 shows an overwhelming majority, 78.7 percent, of those who would vote for Ma Ying-jeou in 2012 favors strengthening trade and economic re-

〈Table 5a〉 Intended Vote Choice in the 2012 Presidential Election and Attitudes on Trade

Vote Choice in 2012	Attitude on Trade		
	Security	Trade	Row Total
Ma Ying-jeou	21.3%	78.7%	41.0%
DPP Candidate	79.9%	20.1%	29.0%
NA	53.8%	46.2%	30.0%
Column	48.0%	52.0%	100% (960)

〈Table 5b〉 Age and Attitudes on Trade

Vote Choice in 2012	Attitude on Trade and Security		
	Security	Trade	Row Total
〉= 25	46.9%	53.1%	10.1%
26-35	47.3%	52.7%	21.0%
36-45	50.9%	49.1%	28.0%
46-55	43.8%	56.2%	24.4%
〉= 56	50.6%	49.4%	16.5%
Column	48.0%	52.0%	100% (955)

lations with Mainland China; but 79.7 percent of those who would support the DPP candidate deems national security as more important than economic growth.

If we examine the relationship between attitude on trade and some of the demographic variables such as education and age, we find that respondents' attitudes on trade do not vary with age (see 〈Table 5b〉) and that those who are better educated actually are more likely to support trade with China than less educated re-

〈Table 5c〉 Education Level and Attitudes on Trade

Education Level	Attitude on Trade and Security		
	Security	Trade	Row Total
Elementary or Lower	52.9%	47.1%	5.3%
Junior/High School	54.2%	45.8%	43.7%
College or higher	42.0%	58.0%	50.9%
Column	47.9%	52.1%	100% (954)

spondents see 〈Table 5c〉.

IV. The Effects of China's Deterrence and Compellence Threats on Taiwan's 2012 Presidential Election

From the analysis presented in the previous sections, we learn that many respondents' positions on the issues of Taiwan independence and the cross-Strait trade are influenced by their perceptions of China's threat towards Taiwan. For example, a respondent might favor the status quo on the independence issue because she is afraid that the act of declaring independence would provoke China to attack Taiwan. On the cross-Strait trade issue, a respondent might not be in favor of expanding trade with China because she is worried that China might exploit Taiwan's economic dependence on China's economy for political purposes.

In this section, I develop a multinomial logit model to estimate more systematically the effects of these two types of China threat on respondents' vote choice in the forthcoming 2012 presidential election.

The dependent variable in the model is a ternary variable, where 0 indicates a vote for KMT candidate Ma Ying-jeou, 1 indicates a vote for the candidate nominated by the DPP, and 2 indicates neither of the above. The independent variables include a respondent's preferences on independence and unification issues, cross-Strait trade, perceptions of China's military threat, confidence in the US security commitment, as well as party identification, ethnic identity, age, and education as control variables. To represent a respondent's preferences on the cross-Strait trade issue, we code a dummy variable "Trade" for those who favor trade, versus those who favor security as the baseline category. We also code a dummy variable "Attack" for those who believe that China would attack Taiwan if Taiwan declared independence, and a dummy variable "Defend" for those who believe that the United States would defend Taiwan if attacked by China after declaring independence, versus those who do not believe China would attack and those who have no confidence in the US security commitment as the baseline category, respectively. To represent preferences on the independence issue, we code a dummy variable distinguishing the unconditional and the conditional independence supporters, with non-independence supporters as the baseline category. And to represent preferences on the unification issue, we code a dummy variable for the unconditional and conditional unification supporters with non-unification supporters as the baseline category.

The control variables include age, education, and a set of dummy variables representing a voter's party affiliation and ethnicity. We derive a measure of party identification from the question, "Among the main political parties in our country, including the KMT, DPP, NP, PFP, and TSU, do you think of yourself as leaning toward any particular party?" We code a dummy variable for KMT and DPP, with no party affiliation as the baseline category. To capture ethnicity, we define dummy variables for Mainlander and Hakka, based on the ethnic group of a respondent's father. The baseline category includes Min-nan and aboriginal groups. Coefficients for Ma Ying-jeou's supporters are normalized at zero. All other coefficients from the model are interpreted as the impact of that variable on the respondent's vote choice relative to that of Ma's supporters.

The multinomial logit regression results of the above model are shown in ⟨Table 6⟩. Several results are clear from the table. As for the supporters of the KMT candidate Ma Ying-jeou and the DPP candidate, party identification is, as we expect, statistically and substantively significant as a predictor of vote choice. DPP identifiers are more likely to vote for the DPP candidate, and KMT

〈Table 6〉 Multinomial Logit Model of Factors Explaining Intended Vote Choice in the 2012 Presidential Election in Taiwan

	DPP Candidate	Neither
Mainlander	-1.36** (.49)	-.15 (.28)
Hakka	-.42 (.36)	-.07 (.29)
Age	-.11 (.10)	.01 (.09)
Education	.02 (.22)	.05 (.19)
KMT	-3.92** (1.04)	-3.25** (.60)
DPP	3.77** (1.03)	.69 (1.17)
Unconditional Independence	1.67** (.35)	.21 (.29)
Conditional Independence	.42 (.33)	-.17 (.23)
Unconditional Unification	-.65* (.39)	-.57* (.31)
Conditional Unification	-.63** (.27)	-.43* (.22)
Attack	-0.61** (.24)	-.40* (.22)
Defend	.32 (.26)	.39* (.21)
Trade	-1.61** (.25)	-.99** (.21)
Constant	.70 (.77)	.62 (.66)
Percentage of Cases	30.%	26.3%
Number of Cases	821	

Entries are maximum likelihood coefficients with standard errors in parentheses.

* indicates $p < .10$, ** indicates $p < .05$, two-tailed

partisans are more likely to vote for KMT candidate Ma. Ethnicity is also an important predictor of vote choice, as respondents from Mainland China are more likely to vote for Ma.

As for the effects of the independence and the unification issues, only the unconditional independence supporters, but not the conditional supporters, are more likely to vote for the DPP candidate. And, both the conditional and unconditional unification supporters are more likely to vote for Ma Ying-jeou.

Controlling for ethnic identity, age, education, and preferences on the independence and unification issues, respondents who believe that China will attack Taiwan if Taiwan declares independence are more likely to vote for Ma. Respondents' preferences on the cross-Strait trade issue are also statistically and substantively significant as a predictor on vote choice. Those who would not trade national security for economic growth are more likely to vote for the DPP candidate.

Between those respondents who intend to vote for Ma Ying-jeou and those who did not express a vote choice, the following variables are significant: the KMT identifiers, the unification supporters, those who believe that China would attack and the United States would not help defend if Taiwan declared independence, and those who are willing to trade national security for economic growth. None of the other variables are statistically significant.

V. Conclusion

Much of the research on the relationship between public opinion and foreign policy study whether a nation's foreign policy reflects its public opinions. In this paper I study this relationship from a different perspective. The research question that I address is whether China's foreign policies toward Taiwan affect Taiwanese public opinions on the independence and trade issues, and in turn, affect Taiwan's domestic politics. The emergence of a democratic government on the island has made the Taiwan independence issue one of the most critical factors in relations between China and Taiwan. To prevent Taiwanese independence, Beijing refuses to renounce the use of force against Taiwan. Meanwhile, China continues to open its markets to Taiwanese businessmen and to promote other cross-Strait exchanges. The simultaneous presence of a perilous political rivalry and a healthy trade relationship between China and Taiwan must have profound impact on Taiwan's domestic politics. In this paper I focus upon and analyze the effects of China's deterrence and compellence threats on Taiwan's forthcoming 2012 presidential election.

Several interesting points become apparent from the analysis. First, in the complex overlay of politics, economics and military affairs, public opinions regarding charged topics of independence and unification require some unpacking. An interesting discovery here is the conditionality of preferences. Voters do not decide their stance on unification or independence in isolation from other factors. On the one hand, China's constant threats to use force restrain Taiwan from advancing toward independence. Many likely supporters of Taiwanese independence actually prefer the status quo to a declaration of independence. On the other hand, if China could persuade people in Taiwan that China has a promising prospect of becoming more prosperous, open, and democratic, then more of them might find unification an acceptable choice.

Second, perception matters when it comes to the intersection of politics and economics. Ma and the KMT, even while espousing a relatively pro-status-quo policy, are viewed with suspicion regarding their economic stance. Even the smallest increase in economic integration between Taiwan and the mainland is deemed favorable to the long-term interests of China. The DPP politicians, on the other hand, procure increased interdependence with fewer scruples from their supporters.

Third, identifying the "conditional" and "unconditional" supporters has discernible implications for the upcoming elections. Only the unconditional, not the conditional independence supporters are more likely to support the DPP presidential candidate in 2012, which might be because the conditional supporters are more worried that a pro-independence president could provoke China to use force. This result supports the claim that China's deterrence threat helps the KMT electorally.

Fourth, China could stand to gain considerably by gleaning lessons in leverage from the political landscape of Taiwan. A majority of the respondents are in favor of increasing trade with China and they are more likely to vote for Ma Ying-jeou in 2012. This implies that the compellence threat argument is not widely believed and the cross-Strait trade issue helps the KMT electorally. Thus, for the DPP, its strategies ought to try to lessen voters' fear of China's military threat and heighten the fear of Taiwan's economic dependence on China.

References

Author unknown. "Background Information on ECFA: Helping People Do Business to Improve Taiwan's Competitiveness." Mainland Affairs Council, Executive Yuan, March, 2010.

Chu, Yunhan, "The Political Economy of Taiwan's Mainland Policy," *Journal of Contemporary China* 6 (1997): 229-258.

Hickey, Dennis V, "America's Two-Point Policy and the Future of Taiwan," *Asian Survey* 28, no. 8 (1988): 881-896.

Taiwan Affairs Office of the State Council website, "The One-China Principle and the Taiwan Issue," Taiwan Affairs Office and the Information Office of the State Council, People's Republic of China, 21 February 2000.

Taiwan External Trade Development Council (TAITRA).

U.S. Department of State, http://www.state.gov/r/pa/ei/bgn/35855.htm.

Wu, Hsin-hsing. *Bridging the Strait: Taiwan, China, and the Prospects for Reunification* (Hong Kong: Oxford University Press, 1994), 171, quoted in Bolt, Paul J., "Economic Ties Across the Taiwan Strait: Buying Time for Compromise," *Issues and Studies* 37 (2001): 80-105.

Comparative Study of Identity Politics between Taiwan and South Korea

Nae-Young Lee (Professor, Korea University)

I. Introduction

The main purpose of this paper is to compare and examine the similarities and differences of identity politics in Taiwan and South Korea. National identity that gives a sense of unity or belonging to all members of a nation is not something static but is continually changing. The identity of a nation tends to be formed and re-constructed according to historical experiences and collective memories of a nation (Anderson 1983). There are contending theories about the origin and the meaning of a nation. There is an essentialism that insists ethnic community has existed historically, but there is also a contending constructivist view that a nation is an invented or imagined political community.[1]

One of the most important elements that constitute national identity is the issue of who to include in "the people" as members of a nation. In other words, national identity is clearly perceived through the establishment of boundaries.[2] Both Taiwan and South Korea seem to share meaningful similarities and differences in identity politics as divided countries. Both South Koreans and Taiwanese people tend to have twofold and divided perceptions towards North Korea and China, respectively. For Taiwan, Mainland China has been perceived as a brother sharing cultural heritage and historical bonds. At the same time, Mainland China has been considered a powerful villain who has threatened the survival of Taiwan. An imbalance in the population size and military power of Mainland China and Taiwan has created a sense of insecurity and anxiety in Taiwan people. The rapid rise of Mainland China since the early 1990s, especially in the realm of military power, has undermined Taiwan's sense of confidence . At the same time, the rising Chinese economy during the last twenty

---

1_Edward Shils and Anthony Smith are essentialists, whereas Ernest Gellner and Benedict Anderson represent the constructivist view. Smith, Anthony. *The Ethnic Origins of Nations* New York: Basil Blackwell, 1986; Gellner, Ernest Nations and Nationalism New York: Blackwell Publishing,1983; Anderson, Benedict Imagined Communities: Reflections on the Origin and Spread of Nationalism. New York: Verso, 1983.

2_Theiss-Morse, Elizabeth *Who Counts as an American?: The Boundaries of National Identity,* London: Cambridge University Press, 2009.

years has provided Taiwan an ample opportunity to benefit from it. Therefore, Taiwanese perceptions and attitudes toward China have been divided and at the same time have changed significantly in recent years (Sober 2010).

Meanwhile, the changing perception of South Koreans towards North Korea is in the core area where confusion regarding the national identity of Korean people occurs. During the prolonged period of Korea's division (1945 to the present), differences in the ideology, political system, and culture of the two Koreas have widened. Most Koreans maintain an ambivalent attitude towards North Korea. South Koreans have divided images of the North Korean regime and its people; they regard the latter as compatriots but at the same time regard the former as an enemy state. In other words, most Koreans feel ambivalent emotions of love and hate towards North Korea. Therefore, whether South Koreans include the North Korean regime or the people of North Korea inside or outside the boundary of who is Korean, remains an important indicator of the national identity of South Koreans (Lee 2007; Lee 2011).

This paper has two specific purposes. First, I will examine and compare how identity politics have changed both in Taiwan and South Korea. Cross-Strait relations and inter-Korean relations seem to show contrasting developments in recent years. While mainland China and Taiwan have managed to reduce tensions and improved economic cooperation, inter-Korean relations have deteriorated in recent years.

The relationship between Taiwan and the mainland has improved substantially during the first term of the Ma Ying-jeou government. The majority of Taiwanese people recognizes the economic benefits from cooperation with the mainland, given the rapid rise of Mainland China. In addition, the competing concepts of national identity –Taiwanese vs. Chinese– has been diluted as the number of people with multiple identities has increased. However, the division on unification versus independence has remained a salient issue which differentiates the position of the Kuomintang (KMT) from that of the Democratic Progressive Party (DPP).

In Korea, perception on North Korea has fluctuated over the years, depending on the nature of inter-Korean relations. The recent development of identity politics in South Korea has been quite different from thtat in Taiwan. After ten years of efforts to pursue reconciliation and cooperation, inter-Korean relations have returned to the period of mutual distrust and animosity during the last several years. In particular, the revelation of the nuclear weapons program of North Korea created a strong sense of betrayal vis-à-vis the North and the engagement policy, called the "Sunshine Policy," was criticized by many South Koreans as a naïve and improper policy.

Secondly, I will examine and compare how the issue of identity is related to party politics. In both South Korea and Taiwan, how to deal with North Korea and Mainland China has been a main source of political conflict. In Taiwan, the perception and policy towards Mainland China has been sharply divided by the major political parties. The identity issue has been the most salient one in Taiwanese politics over the last fifteen years. The victory of Chen Shui-bian, the Democratic Progressive Party candidate, in the 2000 presidential election was the crucial moment in which identity politics began a main cleavage of Taiwanese society. However, after the transfer of presidential power in 2008, KMT President Ma Ying-jeou pursued a new approach to cross-Strait relations and the nature of identity politics has changed profoundly (Chen 2013 Chu 2012).

Similarly, in South Korea, differing political parties have shown contrasting policy orientations and preferences toward North Korea. While progressive political parties including the Democratic United Party have supported the engagement policy toward North Korea, the conservative parties, especially the ruling Saenuri Party, have preferred the hard-line policy. In addition, among the Korean public there have been differing perceptions and policy stances towards North Korea according to party identification. Thus, inter-Korean relations have remained a contentious issue in Korean party politics (Lee 2011).

In carrying out this research, I rely on empirical analysis of various relevant survey data in both countries. Regarding South Korean data, I have been a principal researcher on various public surveys of Korean national identity and party politics as Director of the Center for Public Opinion in the East Asia Institute (EAI, 2010, 2005). Thus, I have utilized this data for this research. Regarding date from Taiwan, I rely on various surveys conducted by the Election Center of National Chengchi University, with which I have a cooperative relationship with. In addition, during my stay in Taiwan from August to December 2014, I conducted several interviews with prominent scholars and experts regarding changing national identity in Taiwan.

II. Fluctuation in Inter-Korean Relations and Identity Politics in South Korea

The attitude and perception of South Koreans towards North Korea is a core element in constituting the national identity of South Koreans. Most South Koreans have an ambivalent perception towards North Korea. The attitude and perception of South Koreans towards North Korea have fluctuated according to the political and economic changes in both North and South Korea, and the status of inter-Korean relations.[3] I will survey the fluctuations in inter-Korean relations from the Cold War era to the present, and then discuss the changing trend of public perception toward North Korea.

1. Changing Inter-Korean Relations and Public Perception toward North Korea from Confrontation to Dialogue and Reconciliation

During the Cold War era from the 1950s to the late 1980s, the two Koreas, which were founded on the contrasting ideologies and political systems, competed with each other as arch rivals. North Korea was considered a sworn enemy which could threaten the security of South Korea any time by military provocation. During this period, most South Koreans, while sharing a spirit of brotherhood with the people of North Korea, had a deep suspicion and fear of the North Korean regime and its belligerent stance towards the South.

Yet the demise of the Cold War international order, increasing power disparity between the two Koreas, and democratization of South Korea created profound change in Korean attitude towards North Korea. After the end of the Cold War era, South Korea established diplomatic relations with the Soviet Union and China

---

3_For historical analysis of changes in perception towards the North and reunification, refer to Lee, Nae-Young (2011).

during Roh Tae-woo's presidency (1988-1992). Losing communist allies and being more isolated from the international community, North Korea decided to engage in dialogue with South Korea, and the two Koreas finally joined the United Nations simultaneously in September 1991.

The failure of the North Korean regime and widening power disparity between the two Koreas also changed the South Korean attitude toward North Korea. Because of the revelation that the North suffered from severe famine and food shortage in the mid-1990s, South Koreans began to see Northerners as poor, starving brothers in need of help. The majority of the South Korean public perceived that the failed North Korean regime was on the verge of collapse and could not be a serious threat to South Korea due to power disparity between the two Koreas. According to Gallup Korea polls, most South Koreans had a view that North Korean military power was superior to South Korea until 1995. From the opinion poll of 1999 onwards, the South Korean public began to answer that South Korean military power was superior.

Moreover, the democratic transition in 1987 made peaceful coexistence with North Korea politically acceptable within South Korea for the first time. During Park Chung-hee and Chun Doo-hwan's presidencies from 1961 to 1987, economic growth and anti-communism were the two main pillars to justify their authoritarian rule. After the democratic transition, the successive governments commonly pursued an engagement policy with North Korea, though policy contents and intensities differed significantly from administration to administration. President Roh Tae-woo approached Pyongyang as a part of his "Nordpolitik" and signed a direct agreement between the two Koreas in 1992. The following President Kim Young-sam agreed to hold a summit with North Korean President Kim Il-sung, but it was cancelled due to the latter's sudden death.[4]

In 1998, President Kim Dae-jung abandoned South Korea's longstanding policy of hostility toward the North and pursued a new policy initiative, known as the Sunshine Policy. In June 2000, the Sunshine Policy achieved its greatest success when President Kim Dae-jung travelled to Pyongyang for an unprecedented summit with North Korean leader Kim Jong-il.[5] The two leaders issued a joint declaration, in which both sides pledged to work toward open dialogue between government officials, economic cooperation, reunions of family members, and cultural and athletic exchanges. Kim Jong-il also agreed to make a return visit to Seoul

---

4_Beck, Peter "Korea Backgrounder: How the South Views its Brother from Another Planet," *International Crisis Group Asia Report*. No. 89 (December 2004).

5_For the Sunshine Policy, see Son, Key-young *South Korean Engagement Policies and North Korea: Identities, Norms, and the Sunshine Policy*. London: Taylor & Francis, 2006; Lee, Dong Hyung "The Korean Sunshine Policy: Its Light and Shade," *Pacific Focus* 18:1 (Spring 2003).

at an appropriate time. The inter-Korean summit became a historical event that gave hope for peace and reconciliation on the Korean Peninsula. After the summit, the two Koreas developed official dialogue channels and various socio-cultural exchange programs flourished.

The Sunshine Policy and subsequent inter-Korean reconciliation mood initiated by Kim Dae-jung's government (1998-2002) significantly changed the South Korean attitude toward North Korea. In particular, the Korean summit held in June 2000 clearly had a deep emotional and psychological impact on views held by the Korean public towards North Korea. There was public euphoria over a thawing of the inter-Korean relationship after the summit.

The following Roh Moo-hyun government (2003-2007) continued to abide by the basic contours and tenets of the Sunshine Policy.[6] President Roh Moo-hyun and his key staff were ardent supporters of a policy of engagement and cooperation with North Korea. In October 2007, President Roh visited Pyongyang and

---

6_Due to the rapprochement between Seoul and Pyongyang, there has been a shift in the views of South Koreans, especially among the younger generation, toward the US, from that of 'patron of security' to 'impediment to rapprochement between Seoul and Pyongyang.' Refer to Lee, Nae-Young and Han Wool Jeong, "Fluctuating Anti-Americanism and the Korea-US Alliance," *International Studies Review* 5:2 (2004).

held the second Korean summit with Kim Jong-il. However, Republican US President, George W. Bush, who won the election in 2000 and took over from the Democratic President, Bill Clinton, held a different perception and pursued a hard-line policy toward North Korea. Thus Roh Moo-hyun's engagement policy toward North Korea created tension and discord with the hard-line approach of the Bush Administration, and the US-ROK alliance faced a difficult time.

Changing perceptions of the threat posed by the North combined with increasing national self-confidence in South Korea created a nationalistic and optimistic expectation about rapprochement and cooperation between the two Koreas. According to the Global Views 2004 survey, only 19 percent of the Korean public supported a harder line policy toward North Korea, while 52 percent wanted to maintain the current level of engagement with North Korea and 29 percent preferred to strengthen it (CCFR & EAI 2004).

In addition, the cumulative effect of these changes was to diminish substantially South Korean fear of North Korean threats. A majority of Koreans believed that North Korea no longer had the power to invade South Korea, even if it still had a desire to do so. ⟨Figure 1⟩ shows the changing attitude of South Koreans toward the North Korean threat during this period. To the question, "Do you think North Korea can force a war on South Korea?", 69 per-

〈Figure 1〉 South Korean views on the possibility of a North Korean invasion

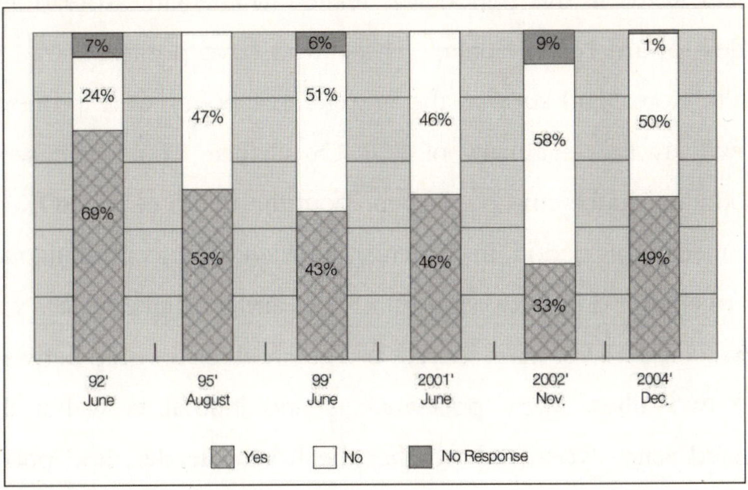

Data: Gallup Korea, Opinion Polls (various years)

cent of the Korean public answered "yes" in June 1992. Since then the percentage of "yes" answer declined steadily and reached its lowest point, 33 percent in November 2002. This result indicates that the threat perception of North Korea declined substantially in this period.

The changes in South Korea's perceptions of North Korea, however, intensified the debate about the future of the alliance with the United States, especially during the Roh Moo-Hyun government. The South Korean attitude toward North Korea was closely tied to the attitude toward the United States and the

ROK-US alliance. In this respect, the rise of anti-Americanism in South Korea in this period was related to changing Korean attitudes toward North Korea.[7] Those who have positive views of North Korea and support the engagement policy were prone to downplay the legitimacy of ROK-US alliance. Thus there were mounting doubts and pessimism about the future of the ROK-US alliance in this period. In particular, a widening perception gap toward North Korea between South Korea and the United States was considered one of main sources of a strained relationship between the two allies. Many policymakers and journalists within the United States wondered whether the Korean leaders and public still regarded North Korea as a common enemy.[8]

The Korean public's suspicion and fear of North Korea resurged after the mid-2000s. In October 2002, North Korean officials admitted their secret program of uranium enrichment. The revelation of the nuclear weapons program by North Korea created a sense of betrayal among the South Korean public. The July

---

7_On the historical development of anti-Americanism in South Korea, see Steinberg, David ed., *Korean Attitudes toward the United States: Changing Dynamics,* New York: M.E. Sharp, 2005.

8_Because of the improved relationship between the two Koreas and the deep involvement of Washington in the North Korean nuclear issue, a delicate "triangular relationship" has emerged among South Korea, the United States, and North Korea. Refer to Sung-han Kim, "Brothers versus Friends: Inter-Korean Reconciliation and Emerging Anti-Americanism in South Korea," in Steinberg (2005).

2004 EAI & CCFR joint survey result indicated that the Korean public had a high level of threat perception about the North Korean nuclear program. To the question "do you think North Korea has nuclear weapons?" 75 percent of the South Korean public answered "yes" and the remaining 25 percent answered "no." In addition, 88% of the Korean public would feel threatened if North Korea had nuclear weapons.

In addition, a skeptical view of the Sunshine Policy increased after the mid-2000s. Many Koreans became skeptical of the Sunshine Policy because there had not been much progress in inter-Korean relations in spite of economic and humanitarian aid to the North by both the Seoul government and NGOs. Critics believed that the North Korean leaders did not have a willingness and capability to pursue real change, and the Sunshine Policy only helped to prop up an evil regime. Another frequent criticism of the Sunshine Policy was that Pyongyang did not respond to Seoul's engagement policy with its own concession. Many Koreans called for greater reciprocity. Moreover, many Koreans felt vindicated by revelations late in Kim Dae-jung's presidency that North Korea received US$500 million shortly before the summit meeting.[9] Furthermore, in spite of a series of Six-Party Talks

9_There has been a heated debate on how to deal with North Korea. A so-called "South-South conflict" over the proper policy toward North Korea has emerged as a

which were established as a multilateral framework in order to resolve North Korea's nuclear program, North Korea conducted a first nuclear test in October 2006. Thus, North Korea's nuclear program emerged as a major threat to the Non Proliferation Treaty (NPT) and East Asian peace and stability.

2. Continuing Stalemate of Inter-Korean Relations and Increasing Public Skepticism of North Korea

Since the launch of the conservative Lee Myung-bak government (2008-2012), inter-Korean relations have cooled and the security threat from North Korea has also been heightened, which prompted negative perceptions towards the North among South Korean people. The main policy of President Lee toward North Korea was based on his campaign promise in the December 2007 presidential election, called "Vision 3000: Denuclearization and Openness", in which he proposed that if the North gave up its nuclear weapons program and opened its economy, the South would help the North improve its per capita income up to

---

major political division in South Korea. Fissures and cleavages are salient along generational and ideological lines. The older generation and conservatives tend to view North Korea with fear and suspicion and be skeptical of the Sunshine Policy. The younger generation and liberals, by contrast, are likely to view North Korea as a brother in need of help and be supportive of more engagement with North Korea.

US$3,000 within the next 10 years. Lee's policy was quite different from his predecessors' unconditional engagement approach. President Lee emphasized the denuclearization of North Korea as a prerequisite or pre-condition for continuing economic aid. Thus his policy can be called a conditional engagement policy. Lee's policy was rejected by Pyongyang. The Lee administration's North Korean policy linked large-scale economic assistance to denuclearization of the North, something which did not occur, causing South-North relations to become strained. As a result, official dialogue stopped and various socio-cultural exchanges were discontinued.

In addition, despite the efforts of the international community, including the United States, which tried to halt nuclear weapons development in North Korea through the Six Party Talks, Pyongyang went ahead with its program, testing nuclear weapons and expanding missile capabilities. Furthermore, military provocations such as the sinking of the Cheonan and the attack on Yeonpyeong Island in 2010 heightened the level of public anxiety about military threats from North Korea.[10]

10_The North's military attack on Yeonpyeong Island located in the Yellow Sea occurred on 23 Nov, 2010. Many South Korean soldiers and civilians died in the North Korean attack. It was the first military attack against civilians, which shocked the South Korean people. After this provocation, South Korean uncertainty about its own security reached its highest point. Refer to Lee, Nae-Young and Jeong Han-wool

The next president, Park Geun-hye, was elected in December 2012 as a candidate from the same conservative party. President Park's main policy toward North Korea is called the Trust-Building Process on the Korean Peninsula. This policy emerged mostly because of the assessment that distrust between the two Koreas had deepened during the Lee administration due to broken communication and breached agreements. The Trust-Building Process was pursued with three main goals: developing inter-Korean relations, estabishing peace and stability on the Korean Peninsula, and laying the groundwork for national unification.

The Trust-Building Process on the Korean Peninsula is a forward-looking North Korea policy based on the logic that humanitarian assistance and economic exchange may result in increased trust, and that such trust can lead to the denuclearization of North Korea.[11] However, President Park has made it clear that the Trust-Building Process on the Korean Peninsula is not a simple appeasement policy but a North Korea policy based on strong deterrence. In other words, it is a policy to reinforce deterrence of North Korean provocations and threats, which reached a zenith

---

(2010).

11_Park, In-hui "Candidate Park Geun-hye's foreign and security policy: The spread of the Trust-Building Process on the Korean Peninsula and Trust Diplomacy," *Hanbando Focus* [Korean Peninsula Focus]. (Nov-Dec, 2012).

with the third nuclear test, which occurred on February 12, 2013. In addition, the "Vision Korea" project was created by the Park administration to build an economic community between the two Koreas based on the inter-Korean trust-building process previously explained, as well as the denuclearization progress. The Vision Korea project is meant to achieve an economic community gradually by installing industrial infrastructure, such as railways, roads, power lines, and communications systems, in both South and North Korea.

Yet Park Geun-hye's North Korea policy has not produced meaningful progress in inter-Korean relations so far. Inter-Korean relations remain at a stalemate and official dialogue channels are deadlocked. In addition, North Korea's occasional military provocations, cyber terrorism, and human rights violations clearly indicate that the trust building process between the two Korea has not been successful. Furthermore, despite North Korea's progress in its nuclear weapons capability, the Six-Party Talks as a major multilateral framework for resolving North Korea's nuclear program have not convened for seven years.

3. Changing Public Perception toward North Korea and Party Politics

In this section, I will discuss the changes in perception in South Korea toward North Korea and reunification as they have been affected by the difficult inter-Korean relations for the last ten years. In order to examine recent changes in South Korean perception and attitude towards North Korea, I compare and discuss the key findings of two surveys which were conducted in 2005 and 2010, respectively.[12]

1) Ambivalent Perception of North Korea

〈Table 1〉 shows the findings of two surveys regarding the main images of North Korea among the South Korean public. Out of five images, respondents chose the ones they felt the most affinity with, resulting in the following order (from most to least) brother 〉 compatriot 〉 neighbor 〉 stranger 〉enemy. This finding indicates that there is still, among South Koreans, a sense of ethnic unity towards North Korea. However, alongside such a sense of unity, there was a significant number of people who said they regard the North as a "stranger" or "enemy". It shows that conflicting perceptions coexist in the mind of South Koreans towards North Korea; a neighbor and brother on the one hand, but an enemy or

12_The two surveys are as follows: East Asia Institute and Asiatic Research Institute. Korea University. *2010 Opinion Survey on Korean National Identity*. Seoul: EAI. 2010; East Asia Institute and Joong-Ang Ilbo. 2005. *Public Opinion Survey on Korean National Identity*. Seoul: EAI. 2005. *http://www.eai.or.kr*.

〈Table 1〉 South Korean Image of North Korea (%)

	Enemy	Stranger	Neighbor	Compatriot	Brother	No interest
2010(B)	14.9	15.9	17.7	20.6	25.0	5.6
2005(A)	8.0	10.0	21.0	30.5	25.2	4.5
(B)-(A)	6.9	5.9	-3.3	-9.9	-0.2	1.1

Data: EAI /Joong-Ang Ilbo(2005) & EAI /ARI(2010)

stranger on the other.

When I compare the survey results in 2010 and 2005 in order to examine how perceptions of North Korea have changed in the South, an interesting trend can be found. First of all, the tendency to regard the North as a stranger or enemy rather than brother/ compatriot/ neighbor increased during the intervening five years. That means more South Korean people regarded North Korea negatively. The perception of the North as a stranger increased to 15.9 percent in 2010 from 10.0 percent in 2005, and regarding it as an enemy increased to 14.9 percent from 8.0 percent. By contrast, seeing the North as a neighbor or compatriot considerably decreased in 2010 from 2005.

〈Table 2〉 shows the changes in perception of the North Korea according to age group, ideological orientation, and partisanship. First of all, the percentage of people regarding North Korea as a stranger or enemy rather than brother/ compatriot/ neighbor conspicuously increased in all age groups in 2010 compared to 2005. However, in both surveys, more older people regarded the North as an enemy, compared to the younger generation. On the other hand, the younger generation regarded the North as a stranger markedly more than the older generation. In other words, the negative attitude towards North Korea increased among the younger generation, and the main reason seems to be not because the North was an enemy who could threaten the South, but because they were a stranger, different from us. For the older generation, the North was an enemy that could repeat provocative military attacks at any time and could threaten the security of the South.

Meanwhile, the different perception toward the North according to respondents' ideological orientation appears to be more conspicuous than the difference shown in age groups. Those who evaluated themselves as being progressive were more prone to regard the North as brother/ compatriot/ neighbor, with a percentage of 68.8 percent, but only 56.4 percent of those who identified as conservative did so. The total percentage of people taking a moderate position on the North as such was 64.6%. Among respondents with a progressive orientation, the proportion regarding the North as an enemy was only 10.0 percent, but among conservatives, it reached 24.5 percent.

⟨Table 2⟩ also indicates that partisanship makes a difference in perceptions toward North Korea. Supporters of the Grand National Party (GNP) were more prone to have negative perceptions toward the North than supporters of the Democratic Party

〈Table 2〉 South Korean images of North Korea according to age, ideological orientation and partisanship (%)

	Enemy		Stranger		Neighbor		Compatriot		Brother	
	2005	2010	2005	2010	2005	2010	2005	2010	2005	2010
Total	8.0	14.9	10.0	15.9	21.0	17.7	30.5	20.6	25.2	25.0
Age Group 20s	7.9	12.4	11.0	20.7	19.7	15.1	37.1	14.9	20.3	25.3
30s	6.6	13.0	11.0	16.8	24.6	20.3	27.7	21.0	23.9	23.0
40s	5.7	18.1	8.9	14.3	19.4	17.4	32.9	19.0	27.6	24.2
50s	8.4	13.9	8.1	15.2	21.5	16.8	30.5	25.8	27.3	26.1
60s+	13.0	16.6	10.4	12.7	19.6	18.7	23.1	22.8	28.2	27.1
Ideological Orientation Progressive	4.2	10.0	10.1	15.4	22.0	14.9	35.9	22.1	24.9	31.8
Moderate	10.3	11.3	10.8	15.7	18.5	20.7	27.9	19.8	25.5	24.1
Conservative	9.4	24.5	8.8	16.7	23.5	16.1	27.9	20.2	25.1	20.1
Party Identity GNP	9.7	20.0	13.2	17.5	25.3	15.2	24.4	17.1	22.9	24.2
Democratic Party	6.8	19.2	8.2	12.5	24.8	16.2	33.7	25.5	23.5	24.1
Democratic Labor Party	9.0	7.9	5.8	22.4	19.2	10.0	38.8	25.5	23.8	31.7

Data: EAI /JoongAng Ilbo (2005) & EAI /ARI (2010)

(DP) or the Democratic Labor Party (DLP). Among the supporters of the GNP, the 20.0 percent of respondents regarded the North as an enemy, but among the Democratic Party or the DLP, those figures were 19.2 and 7.9 percent, respectively. Such wide gaps in perception toward North Korea among supporters of differing political parties indicate that North Korea or policy toward North Korea remain one of the most contentious issues in South Korean party politics. In fact, major political parties have competed with contrasting approaches and policy preference on North Korea over the years.

2) Changes in the attitude of South Koreans towards reunification: increasing skepticism

The attitude of South Koreans towards reunification is one of the core elements constituting the national identity of Koreans. That's because the attitude toward reunification is closely related to the issue of how to define the boundary of the Korenn nation. Reunification is a process of forming a new political community for South and North Korea, currently divided into two political entities. After the division of the Korean Peninsula for more than 65 years, the enthusiasm of Koreans for reunification has weakened. The ideological and cultural differences have widened during the prolonged division. The North Korean economy, backward and isolated, has almost completely broken down. Therefore, the worries of an economic burden and political chaos possibly suffered by the South have augmented the skeptical view of reunification.

⟨Figure 2⟩ shows how the attitude of Korean people towards reunification changed over the years. Support for a cautious execution of 'reunification at a controlled pace, taking the situation

〈Figure 2〉 Changes in attitude towards reunification (%)

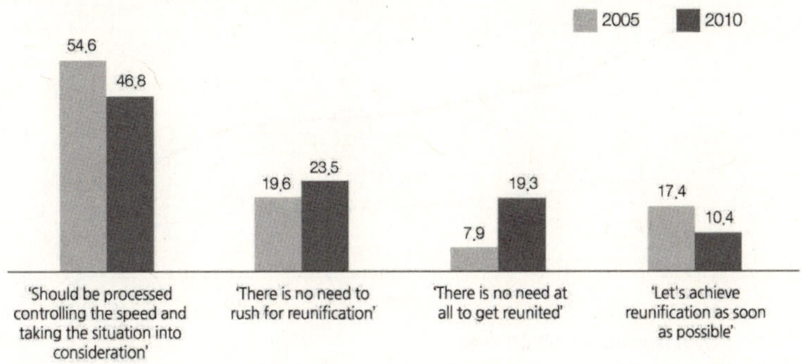

Data: EAI /Joong-Ang Ilbo(2005) & EAI /ARI(2010)

into consideration' still took the highest percentage at 46.8 percent in 2010, but this was greatly reduced compared to 2005. The opinion 'we don't really need to be reunited' increased from 8 percent in 2005 to 19 percent in 2010. The opinion 'we don't need to hasten unification' also increased from 19.6% to 23.5% in 2010. By contrast, the opinion 'we have to achieve reunification as soon as possible' was greatly reduced from 17.4 percent in 2005 to 10.4 percent in 2010. Such a result indicates that as the negative perception of North Korea has increased, more prudent and skeptical opinions towards reunification have spread.

When comparing the attitude towards reunification according to age group, people of the older generation regarded the issue of reunification more importantly, whereas those in their 20s and 30s

〈Figure 3〉 Percentage of anti-unification attitude according to age group (%)

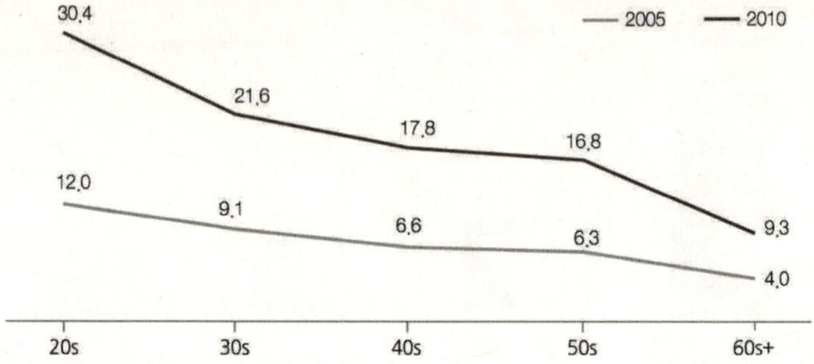

Data: EAI /Joong-Ang Ilbo(2005) & EAI /ARI(2010)

showed a higher rate of not recognizing the necessity of unification. 〈Figure 3〉 is the result of responses to the opinion 'no need for reunification,' according to the age group. In this figure, the anti-unification attitude was highest among the people in their 20s and 30s, and it is worth noting that, compared to 2005, the anti-unification attitude in each age group has conspicuously increased. This finding indicates that the younger generation has a weaker tendency to see reunification as a national task compared to the older generation, and the realistic concern that reunification could increase political chaos and an economic burden is stronger in the younger generation.

III. Changing Dynamics of Identity Politics in Taiwan

Disputes over the issue of national identity have been crucial features in Taiwan politics as well as cross-Taiwan Strait relations for the last two decades. The issue of national identity became the most salient cleavage when the Democratic Progressive Party (DPP) included the discourse of Taiwanese national identity and promotion of independent Taiwan in its party charter for the first time in 1991. The perception and policy towards China has been sharply divided among the major political parties.

Since President Lee Teng-hui, a native Taiwanese, supported full independence from China, the identity issue has been the salient political cleavage. During President Lee's term, the KMT gradually shifted from the one-China principle to the pursuit of de jure independence by launching a concerted diplomatic effort to join the United Nations and promoting the so-called "Republic of China on Taiwan". The shift in the KMT's mainland policies resulted in a split within the party and led to the establishment of the New Party, which endorsed a one-China policy.

After the year 2000, the so-called nativist faction under the leadership of Lee Teng-hui left the KMT and formed the new Taiwan Solidarity Party. Since then, two political camps have broadly emerged. The DPP and the Taiwan Solidarity Party have grouped together as the pan-Green camp, while the KMT and the

People First Party are usually called the pan-Blue camp.[13]

The formation of two political camps, each with different perspectives on national identity and cross-Strait relations, has increased political rivalry in the Taiwan politics. The victory of Chen Shui-bian, the candidate of the Democratic Progressive Party, in the 2000 presidential election was the crucial moment in which identity politics began to form a major cleavage of the Taiwan society. President Chen tried to search for Taiwanese identity in various ways. The Chen Shui-bian government pursued a full-scale "de-Sinification" campaign that was designed to erase the island's Chinese cultural heritage and suppress the Chinese identity.

In response to the Chen Shui-bian government's move, the KMT advocated a cross-Strait policy posture that was more moderate and less confrontational. The KMT advocated the normalization of cross-Strait economic exchange and a resumption of cross-Strait negotiations on the basis of the "1992 Consensus". Beijing was deeply worried about the pursuit of Taiwanese identity and independence from the mainland by the Chen Shui-bian

---

13_Rigger, Shelly "Is Taiwan Independence Passe?: Public Opinion, Party Platforms and National Identity in Taiwan," *Harvard Studies on Taiwan* Vol. 3 (2000); Hsieh, John Fuh-Sheng and Emerson M. S. Niou, "Salient Issues in Taiwan's Electoral Politics," *Electoral Studies* 15:2 (1996).

government. As a result, during Chen's presidency cross-Strait relations suffered.[14]

The relationship between Taiwan and Mainland China has improved substantially during the first term of the Ma Ying-jeou government from 2008 to 2012. After his inauguration, President Ma pledged to maintain the cross-Strait status quo by announcing the "Three-Noes" policy-no unification, no independence, and no war during his presidency. He successfully laid a solid foundation for cross-Strait peace by reducing military tensions, resuming the official dialogues and negotiations that had stalled during the previous DPP government, and concluding 16 bilateral pacts with Mainland China, covering a wide range of areas such as civil aviation, investment protection and food safety protection. In particular, the signing of the Economic Cooperation Framework Agreement (ECFA) in June 2010 was a milestone in cross-Strait relations. The ECFA made it possible for Taiwan to exploit growing business opportunities in Mainland China. In addition, the ECFA set in motion negotiations on a full-fledged cross-Strait free

---

14_Chu, Yun-han "Taiwan's National Identity Politics and the Prospect of Cross-Strait Relations," *Asian Survey* 44:1 (2004); Lee, W.C. "Taiwan's Cultural Reconstruction Movement: Identity Politics and Collective Action Since 2000," *Issues & Studies* 41:1(2005); Tan, Alexander C. "The 2008 Taiwan Elections: Forward to the Past?," *Electoral Studies* 28:3 (2009); Shubert, Gunter "Taiwan's Political Parties and National Identity: The Rise of Overarching Consensus," *Asian Survey* 44:1 (2004).

trade agreement. The ECFA also put Taiwan back in foreign capitals, which found new possibilities for incorporating Taiwan into their Greater China strategy. Another important agreement was the 2012 Memorandum of Understanding on Cross-Currency Settlement, which created the necessary mechanism for the two sides to settle their bilateral trade in Renminbi (RMB).[15]

As a consequence of improving cross-Strait relations, the competing concept of the national identity –Taiwanese vs. Chinese– has been diluted as people having Taiwanese identity have increased over the years. The commonly used measure to assess Taiwanese public opinion on the Chinese-Taiwanese identity is a 3-point scale. The respondents are usually given four choices: (1) exclusively Chinese; (2) both Chinese and Taiwanese; (3) exclusively Taiwanese; (4) no response. 〈Figure 4〉 shows the changes in Taiwanese/Chinese identities among the Taiwanese as tracked in surveys by the Election Study Center of National Chengchi University (NCCU).[16] According to 〈Figure 4〉, the percentage of those who identify as Taiwanese reached more than

15_Chu, Yun-han "The Political Implications of Taiwan-Mainland Economic Integration," *Global Asia* 7:1 (2012); Chen, Dean P. "The Strategic Implications of Ma Ying-jeou's "One ROC, Two Areas" Policy on Cross-Strait Relations," *American Journal of Chinese Studies* 20:1 (2013).

16_The graph is available at the homepage of the Election Study Center of National Chengchi University. See http://esc.nccu.edu.tw/news.

〈Figure 4〉 Changes in the Taiwanese/Chinese Identity of Taiwanese (1992-2014)

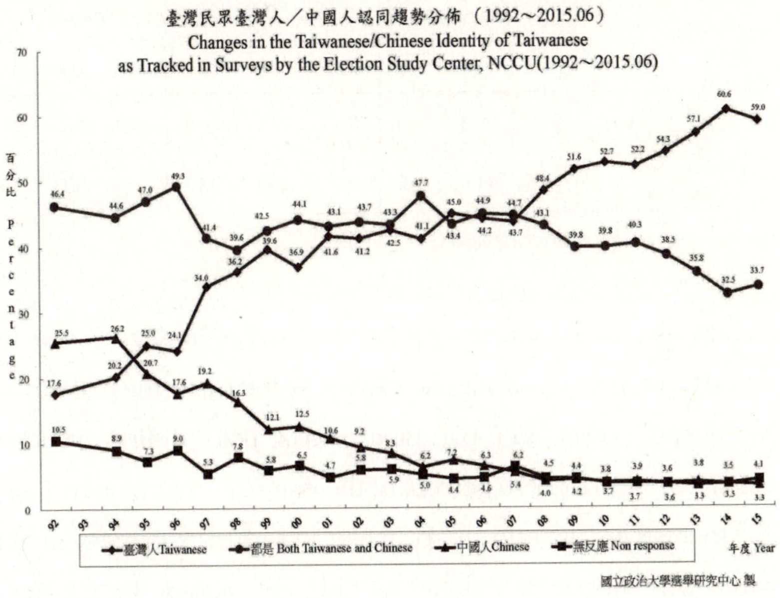

Sources: Election Study Center, N.C.C.U., important political attitude trend distriution, http://esc.nccu.edu.tw/news.

60.4 percent, while the percentage of those who identify as Chinese shrank to a mere 3.4 percent. The percentage of those who identify as both Taiwanese and Chinese fell to 32.7 percent. This trend indicates the increasing dominance of Taiwanese identity in terms of ethnic identity.

However, the increasing homogeneity of national identity does not necessarily reduce its significance. The saliency of national

〈Table 3〉 Changes in the Taiwanese/Chinese Identity (1996, 2004, 2012)

The Taiwanese / Chinese Identity

Year	Taiwanese			Both Taiwanese & Chinese			Chinese		
	1996	2004	2012	1996	2004	2012	1996	2004	2012
Pan-Blue Supporters	25.2	19.3	35.4	63.8	61.8	68.8	24.0	30.8	22
Pan-Green Supporters	70.6	71.7	84.3	24.1	25.8	14.5	5.3	2.5	1.1

*This table is cited from Chu, Yun-Han et. al(2014).

identity as a major source of political cleavage in Taiwan was reduced but remained strong. As 〈Table 3〉 indicates, the majority of pan-Green voters and pan-Blue voters hold distinct national identities. More than 70 percent of the pan-Green supporters identify themselves as Taiwanese, while less than 5 percent of the pan-Green supporters identify as Chinese. Among the pan-Blue supporters, by contrast, the percentage that identify as Chinese has been above 20 percent, while the percentage of those who identify as Taiwanese has been about 30 percent. This indicates that the issue of national identity remains a source of continuing confrontation in Taiwan politics.[17]

Moreover, Taiwanese people are sharply divided by their pref-

17_Balderas, Ulyses and Hans Stockton, "Whither Identity?: National Identity and Partisan Support in Presidential Elections on Taiwan 2004-2012," *American Journal of Chinese Studies* 20(1) (2013).

〈Figure 5〉 Changes in the Unification-Independence Stances of Taiwanese (1994-2014)

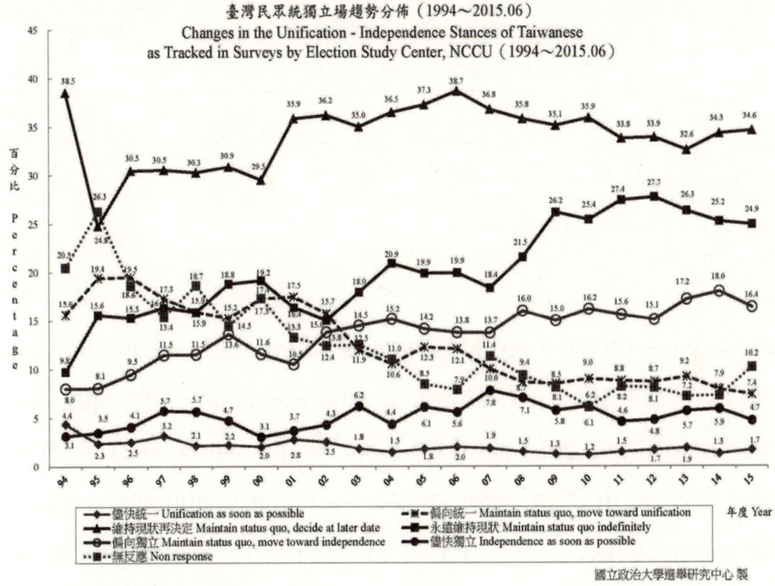

Sources: Election Study Center, N.C.C.U., important political attitude trend distriution, http://esc.nccu.edu.tw/news.

erence on Taiwan's relations with mainland China. The division over unification versus independence has remained a salient issue which differentiates the position of the KMT from the DPP. The most commonly used measure to assess Taiwanese public opinion on the unification-independence issue is a 6-point scale. The respondents are given six choices. 〈Figure 5〉 shows changes in the unification-independence stances of Taiwanese as tracked in sur-

〈Table 4〉 Changes in unification-independence stances by party identity (1996, 2004, 2012)

Year	Unification-Independence Stances								
	Independence			Status Quo			Unification		
	1996	2004	2012	1996	2004	2012	1996	2004	2012
Pan-Blue Supporters	12.3	7.4	9.2	63.8	61.8	68.8	24.0	30.8	22
Pan-Green Supporters	53.7	53.1	48.4	37.7	40.2	45.3	6.1	6.7	6.3

*This table is cited from Yun-Han Chu, et. al (2014).

veys by the Election Study Center of National Chengchi University (NCCU). According to 〈Figure 5〉, the percentage of respondents who held a "maintain status quo, decide at a later date" stance was 34.3 percent in 2014, while those with a "maintain status quo indefinitely" stance amounted to 25.2 percent. Combining the two categories, almost 60 percent of Taiwanese had a stance of "maintain status quo." Those that leadned towards independence were 13.8 percent of all respondents in 2014, while those who leaned towards unification shrank to a mere 9.2 percent in 2014. This trend indicates that the majority of Taiwanese has a clear preference for maintaining the status quo. In addition, it is noteworthy that the proportion supporting Taiwan independence steadily increased and yet the proportion preferring unification with China declined significantly over the years.

〈Table 4〉 shows that the supporters of the differing parties maintained contrasting preferences of cross-Strait relations. The proportion of the pan-Green supporters who preferred Taiwan independence decreased from 53.7 percent in 1996 to 48.4 percent in 2012. In addition, the proportion of pan-Green supporters who preferred to maintain the status quo increased from 37.7 percent in 1996 to 45.3 percent in 2012. By contrast, the proportion of the pan-Blue supporters who preferred to maintain the status quo increased from 63.8 percent in 1996 to 68.8 percent in 2012. This trend indicates that the attitude of Taiwanese in the unification-independence issue has moved toward the center and the degree of polarization has been substantially reduced.

The increasing preference of the status quo reflects the reality that the majority of Taiwanese people recognizes the economic benefits from cooperation with Mainland China, given its rapid rise. In this regard, the nature of identity politics in Taiwan has changed significantly during the last ten years. Some Taiwan scholars argue that the major paradigm of Taiwan politics has shifted from identity politics to economic issues or distributional politics.[18]

However, the great majority of pan-Green supporters maintain a strong sentiment that the rapid progress of cross-Strait economic cooperation, which has been accelerated during the Ma Ying-jeou

---

18_Wu, Yu-Shan "From Identity to Economy: Shifting Politics in Taiwan," *Global Asia* 8:1 (Spring 2013).

government, may undermine Taiwan's economic autonomy and sovereignty. Therefore, the DPP politicians have adopted various disruptive strategies in the legislature to block the Ma government's legislative initiatives on cross-Strait relations. Therefore, in recent years, the ECFA has been the most salient policy issue. The political debate regarding cross-Strait economic integration has revolved around the question of how the ECFA has affected the Taiwan economy and who has benefited from the ECFA. The KMT government has insisted that the ECFA provided Taiwan a new opportunity to exploit the rapid growth of the Chinese economy. Moreover, the KMT government justifies the ECFA, claiming that it has laid a solid foundation for cross-Strait peace and stability. The DPP, by contrast, has criticized the ECFA because its economic benefits went mainly to big business and export sectors.[19] As a result, the assessment of the impact of the ECFA on Taiwan's economy diverges significantly across different party identities. The supporters of the pan-Blue camp are optimistic about the impact of the ECFA on Taiwan's economy. As 〈Table 5〉 shows, about 70.6 percent of the pan-Blue supporters believe that Taiwan's economy

19_Qi, Dongtao "Divergent Popular Support for the DPP and the Taiwan Independence Movement, 2000-2012," *Journal of Contemporary China* 21:78 (2012); Wu, Yu-Shan "The Evolution of the KMT's Stance on the One-China Principle: National Identity in Flux," in Schubert, Gunter and J. Damm. eds. *Taiwanese Identity in the Twentiy-First Century: Domestic, Regional, and Global Perspectives.* New York: Routledge, 2011.

〈Table 5〉 Party Identification and Economic Conditions after the ECFA (2012)

	Party Identification			All
	None	Pan-Blue	Pan-Green	
Worse	15.46(60)	3.40(23)	25.72(131)	13.90(212)
The same	53.87(209)	26.04(176)	57.77(275)	42.86(643)
Better	30.67(119)	70.56(477)	14.71(70)	43.25(658)
All	100.00(388)	100.00(676)	100.00(461)	100.00(1513)

*This table is cited from Yun-Han Chu, et. al (2014).

improved after the ECFA, compared to 14.7 percent among the pan-Green supporters. By contrast, 25.7 percent of the pan-Green camp assesses that Taiwan's economy worsened, whereas only 3.4 percent of the pan-Blue camp thinks so.

1. Recent Increase of Anti-Chinese Sentiment in Taiwan

After the ECFA was enacted, economic integration between Taiwan and Mainland China substantially increased. As the process of economic integration negotiations moved to sensitive areas, worries have intensified within Taiwanese society. In this regard, the most crucial agreement would be the Cross-Strait Agreement on Trade in Services and Commodities, since this agreement may affect many small business and shops in Taiwan. Many Taiwanese, especially DPP supporters, have a negative view of the agreement. Therefore, the ratification in the legislature fomented serious tension and resistance. Increasing anti-Chinese sentiment was vividly expressed in the Sunflower Student Movement, which occurred between March 18 and April 10, 2014. This movement was a protest driven by a coalition of students and civic groups.[20] Occupying the Legislative Yuan and, later, also the Executive Yuan of Taiwan, the activists protested against the passing of the Cross-Strait Service Trade Agreement (CSSTA) by the ruling party KMT at the legislature without a clause-by-clause review. The protesters claimed further economic integration with Mainland China would hurt Taiwan's economy and leave Taiwan vulnerable to political pressure from Beijing. In contrast, advocates of the treaty argued that increased Chinese investment would provide a necessary boost to Taiwan's economy. The movement marked the first time that the legislature was occupied by citizens in the history of Taiwan. Taiwanese society was shocked by the Sunflower Movement, and consequently the passing of the Cross-Strait Service Trade Agreement was delayed. The movement indicated a rising public fear of rapid economic integration between Taiwan and the mainland. Despite increasing economic cooperation and declining tensions between Taiwan and Mainland China, since

20_Regarding the Sunflower Movement, see Cole, Michael J. "Sunflowers in Springtime: Taiwan's Crisis and the End of an Era in Cross-Strait Cooperation," *China Brief* 14:7 (April 9, 2014).

Beijing has maintained its "one-China principle" and Taiwan has been isolated from the international community, Taiwan's public worried that Taiwan may lose her sovereignty. Moreover, the Hong Kong Student Protests, which occurred from September to December 2014 intensified the Taiwanese public's fear. Hong Kong protesters demanded universal suffrage in the 2017 Chief Executive election. Yet the Chinese government rejected the protesters' demand and thus the protests ended without a tangible outcome. Observing closely the failed attempts of the Hong Kong protests, many Taiwanese had a fear that Hong Kong's current situation may be the future of Taiwan.[21]

The shocking defeat of the ruling KMT in the November 2014 local elections inevitably hinders the current government's policy toward China. While disappointment over the bad performance of the Ma Ying-jeou government, sluggish economy, high unemployment rate, and rising housing prices were the main causes for the defeat of the KMT, the public's negative assessment of Ma's policy pursuing economic integration with China also contributed to the KMT's crushing defeats.[22] The surprisingly lopsided victory of the

---

21_"Taiwan and Hong Kong in the same boat," Editorial, *The Liberty Times,* October 9, 2014.

22_"KMT trounced," *Taipei Times,* November 30, 2014; "Election outcome to slow China exchanges: experts," *Taipei Times,* December 1, 2014.

DPP in the 2014 local elections enhanced the possibility of power shift in the 2016 presidential election. If the KMT loses the 2016 presidential election, the next DPP government is likely to change the direction and pace of cross-Strait relations. Therefore, due to the uncertainty of Taiwan's electoral politics, it is very difficult to predict the future direction of cross-Strait relations.

IV. A Comparison of Identity Politics between South Korea and Taiwan

National identity has been one of the most contentious issues in both South Korea and Taiwan. South Korea and Taiwan share meaningful similarities and important differences in identity politics as divided countries. Both in South Korea and Taiwan, how to deal with North Korea and Mainland China has been a major source of political contention. Regarding the perception and policy towards North Korea, there have been differing views and policy preferences in the Korean public according to party identity, ideological orientation, and age group. In Taiwan, the identity issue has been the most salient issue in Taiwaneese politics over the last twenty years. The perception and policy towards Mainland China has been sharply divided by major political parties.

In spite of the significance of the identity issue, there are differences in the nature and saliency of identity politics between South Korea and Taiwan. They differ in the following three aspects: First, the issue of national identity and identity politics seems to have been more salient and intense in Taiwan than in South Korea. In Taiwan, the identity issue and cross-Strait relations have been the major determining factors in party politics since the late 1990s. The identity issue has become the most crucial determinant in major elections since 2000.

In South Korea, by contrast, the issue of North Korea has been one of the major issues and yet it was not a determining factor in party politics and electoral politics. In South Korea, regional cleavage has been the most salient factor for party politics since democratization. Generational cleavage has played an important role in recent elections as well. The North Korean issue has never been a determining issue in Korean electoral politics, unlike Taiwan.

There are two reasons for the differing saliency and intensity of identity politics between Taiwan and South Korea. First, since the sub-ethnic difference between Benshengren and Waishengren in Taiwan has created two differing national identities, namely Taiwanese and Chinese. In Taiwan, the issue of ethnic identity has been salient from the establishment of Republic of China in 1948. Identity politics emerged and became salient with the democratization of Taiwan. The increase of a Taiwanese national identity as opposed to a Chinese one, along with increasing support for Taiwanese independence, has been the most crucial raison d'être for the Democratic Progressive Party. The DPP tried hard to construct a Taiwanese identity and was able to take over the power from the KMT in 2000. Furthermore, the two different national identities have been related to two different visions regarding cross-Strait relations. In South Korea, by contrast, significant sub-ethnic differences within South Korea have not existed. Identity politics have revolved around divided perceptions and policies toward North Korea. In other words, the key issue of identity politics in South Korea has been whether North Korea or North Koreans should be regarded as "us" or "others."

In addition, the differing intensity and saliency of identity politics is related to the differing power balance of the two dyadic states. Mainland China is much larger and powerful than Taiwan. Moreover, because China has rapidly grown in economic and political power, Taiwan has to worry that a rising China can threaten the sovereignty of Taiwan. In fact, the PRC has never recognized Taiwan as a sovereign state, maintaining its "one-China principle." Thus, the identity issue is closely related to the survival or sovereignty of Taiwan. In South Korea, on the other hand, the population size and national capabilities of South Korea have been superior to North Korea. Power gaps between North and South have increased over the years. Many South Koreans perceived that a poor and isolated North Korea was no longer a real threat to the security of South Korea. Therefore, it is not conceivable that North Korea can threaten the sovereignty or survival of South Korea.[23]

The second difference of identity politics between Taiwan and South Korea is that South Korea and Taiwan have adopted different approaches and priorities in their efforts to improve inter-Korean relations and cross-Strait relations, respectively. Seoul and Pyongyang have tried to improve their relations through a top-down and government-directed approach, whereas Taiwan and China sought to build mutual trust through a bottom-up and society-oriented approach.[24]

The two Koreas primarily pursued political agreements, and

23_However, during the last several years, North Korea's nuclear weapons program and military provocation heightened the level of security concern among the South Korean public. While the rising power of Mainland China is a threat to Taiwan, the possible collapse of North Korea will be a threat to South Korea. The sudden death of Kim Jong-il fueled increased concern about the possibility of the collapse of North Korea. Many observers wonder if the country's new ruler, young and inexperienced Kim Jong-un, is able to consolidate power in Pyongyang. Kim Jong-un's failure to secure power would lead to a power struggle, an implosion, or the collapse of North Korea. Regime collapse in North Korea may bring instability and uncertainty on the Korean Peninsula as well as the East Asian region as a whole.

24_For the different approaches adopted by South Korea and Taiwan, see Im, Hyug-Baeg and Choi, Yu-Jeong "Inter-Korean and Cross-Strait Relations through the Window of Regional Integration Theories," *Asian Survey* 51:5 (2011); Chang Liao, Nien-Chung "Comparing Inter-Korean and Cross-Taiwan Strait Trust Building," *Asian Survey* 54:4 (2014).

economic cooperation and non-governmental exchanges followed. The leaders of the two Koreas held two historical summits in Pyongyang in 2000 and 2007. In addition, there have been numerous official contacts at ministerial and sub-ministerial levels between the two Koreas. The two Koreas established formal communication channels while their social interactions were restrained. Due to extreme societal control in North Korea, approaching North Korean citizens individually was very difficult, if not impossible.

In addition, trade volume between the two Koreas has been very limited. Taiwan and Mainland China, by contrast, sought to increase economic cooperation and socio-cultural exchanges as a basis for further political negotiations. Official contacts at the government level between Taiwan and China have been restrained. In February 2014, Beijing and Taipei held a formal ministerial meeting for the first time in more than six decades. However, non-governmental level contacts and interactions have become widespread. Cross-Strait business activities have increased rapidly. The total amount of trade and mutual investment across the Strait has rapidly increased. As a result, Taiwan's trade dependence on China was about 23 percent in 2013. In the socio-cultural realm, exchange and cooperation has been enhanced. The number of mainland Chinese tourists increased from below 300,000 in 2008 to 2.3 million in 2013.[25]

Finally, cross-Strait relations and inter-Korean relations seem to show contrasting developments in recent years. While China and Taiwan have managed to reduce tensions and improved economic cooperation, inter-Korean relations have deteriorated in recent years. During the first term of the Ma Ying-jeou government, relations between Taiwan and China have improved substantially. Signing the economic cooperation framework agreement (ECFA) in 2010 was a significant turning point for cross-Strait relations. In addition, the competing concept of national identity –Taiwanese vs. Chinese– has been diluted as the number of people having multiple identities has increased.

Regarding the future of cross-Strait relations, the majority of people in Taiwan supports the status quo rather than independence or unification. The political debate regarding cross-Strait relations revolves around the question of who benefits from the ECFA. In other words, identity politics increasingly overlaps with distributive politics in Taiwan. In this regard, the nature of identity politics has changed significantly during the last five years. Relations with Mainland China have become an economic issue as well as identity issue.

The recent development of identity politics in South Korea has

25_Government of the ROC, Mainland Affairs Council, *Cross-Strait Economic Statistics Monthly* (August 2014).

been quite different from Taiwan. Unlike in Taiwan, inter-Korean relations under the four years of the Lee Myung-bak presidency and two years of the following Park Geun-hye government have remained stagnant, if not deteriorated. The sense of mutual distrust has increased and inter-Korean dialogue has been almost stopped. Occasional military provocations by North Korea have raised the security concerns of South Koreans and hindered the possibility of resuming inter-Korean dialogue. Due to the increasing provocation by North Korea, South Korean perceptions of North Korea have worsened. Nonetheless, major political parties prefer different policies toward North Korea and thus ideological conflict and political battle over North Korea policy are very likely to continue in South Korea.

V. Concluding Remarks

The main purpose of this paper is to compare and examine the similarities and differences of identity politics in Taiwan and South Korea. Since both South Korea and Taiwan are divided countries, North Korea and China have been a major source of contention or confusion in national identity. In addition, the national identity issue has been closely related to party politics in both countries. While the identity issue has been significant in both countries, the nature and saliency of identity politics in Taiwan and South Korea have been significantly different. Thus, important policy implications or lessons can be drawn from the two countries' experiences.

First, both countries commonly face divided public opinion regarding cross-Strait relations and inter-Korean relations. In South Korea, perception toward North Korea and policy preference diverges significantly with ideological orientation, age group, and party identity. Thus, divided public opinion is a daunting hindrance for South Korean government's policy toward North Korea. For example, even though the current Park government pursues reunification as a main policy goal, it is very difficult to mobilize public support for reunification. In the similar vein, Taiwan's public remains divided in terms of their competing national identities. The majority of pan-Green supporters and pan-Blue supporters possess distinct national identities. In addition, Taiwanese people are sharply divided by their preference on relations with Mainland China. The division over unification versus independence has remained a salient issue which differentiates the position of the KMT from that of the DPP. The majority of the pan-Green supporters maintain a strong sentiment that the rapid progress of cross-Strait economic cooperation, which was accelerated during the Ma Ying-jeou government, may undermine Taiwan's economic autonomy and sovereignty. Therefore, in both Taiwan and South

Korea, overcoming divided public opinion and building a policy consensus is the most crucial yet daunting task.

Second, differing policy stances between the major political parties have been a crucial impediment for policy consistency and effectiveness in both South Korea and Taiwan. Whenever a power shift has occurred, South Korea's policy toward North Korea has moved between an engagement policy and a hard-line policy. Thus power transition has often resulted in stalemated inter-Korean relations. In Taiwan, since the KMT and the DPP have contrasting policy preferences on cross-Straits relations, power transition between the two parties is likely to affect significantly cross-Straits relations. While the KMT government has pursued dialogue and cooperation, the DPP government's policy priority has been enhancing Taiwan's sovereignty and autonomy vis-à-vis China. Recent Taiwanese political developments indicate that power transition from the KMT to the DPP is likely in the 2016 presidential election. Due to a continued economic recession and rising unemployment, the approval rating of the Ma Ying-jeou government has fallen below 10 percent. As a result, the ruling KMT suffered a major defeat in the November 2014 local elections. If the DPP takes presidential power in 2016, it may change policy direction on cross-Straits relations. In any case, in both Taiwan and South Korea, alleviating policy inconsistency and uncertainty derived from power transition is another crucial task for improving cross-Strait relations and inter-Korean relations.

Finally, in dealing with North Korea and mainland China, South Korea and Taiwan have adopted contrasting approaches: South Korea's top-down approach and Taiwan's bottom-up approach. Yet the two approaches have both advantages and limitations. The top-down approach adopted by the two Koreas contributes to the rapid progress of cooperation and rapprochement. However, due to the low level of non-governmental dialogue and economic cooperation, when official dialogue is halted, inter-Korean relations are completely stagnant. In this regard, South Korea needs to adopt Taiwan's bottom-up approach. Since the current North Korean regime rejects official dialogue and maintains a hard-line policy, non-governmental organizations can be alternative channels for resuming official dialogue. In addition, in order to pursue reunification as a long-term goal, South Korea needs to deliver a good image and benign message to the North Korean people. Therefore, South Korea needs to pursue a two-track policy toward North Korea. Regardless of the fluctuation of government-level inter-Korean relations, various types of economic cooperation and socio-cultural exchanges at the non-government level should be pursued and maintained.

Meanwhile, Taiwan needs to adopt the South Korean top-down approach as a complementary policy. Despite the rapid progress of economic integration and widespread human exchange, the level of cooperation and trust has been very low in the area of politics and security. In particular, Taiwan public's fear and distrust of a rising China remain a major hurdle for improving cross-Strait relations. Therefore, if official dialogue between Taiwan and China can produce a significant compromise and formula regarding the future of cross-Straits relations, mutual distrust and fear can be substantially reduced. In particular, Beijing needs to go beyond its "one-China principle" and find a new formula which can alleviate Taiwanese people's fear and anxiety regarding Taiwan's future status.

References

Anderson, Benedict. *Imagined communities: reflections on the origin and spread of nationalism.* New York: Verso, 1983.

Balderas, Ulyses Balderas and Hans Stockton. "Whither Identity?: National Identity and Partisan Support in Presidential Elections on Taiwan 2004-2012." *American Journal of Chinese Studies* 20:1, 2013.

Beck, Peter. "Korea Backgrounder: How the South Views its Brother from Another Planet." *International Crisis Group Asia Report.* No. 89, 2004.

Chang, Eric. "Vote Shifting and Democratic Consolidation in East Asian Democracies: Evidence from Taiwan and South Korea," *Taiwan Journal of Democracy* 6:2, 2010.

Chang Liao, Nien-Chung "Comparing Inter-Korean and Cross-Taiwan Strait Trust Building," *Asian Survey.* 54:4, 2014.

Chen, Dean P. "The Strategic Implications of Ma Ying-jeou's "One ROC, Two Areas" Policy on Cross-Strait Relations." *American Journal of Chinese Studies* 20:1, 2013.

Chu, Yunhan. "Navigating in between China and America: Taiwan's Politics of Identity," in Byung-Kook Kim. ed. *Power and Security in Northeast Asia: Shifting Strategies.* New York: Lynne Rienner Publisher, 2007.

-------. "Taiwan's National Identity Politics and the Prospect of Cross-Strait Relations," *Asian Survey* 44:1, 2004.

-------. "The Political Implications of Taiwan-Mainland Economic Integration," *Global Asia* 7:1, 2012

Chu, Yunhan. et. al. "The Blue-Green Divide and the Function of Democracy in Taiwan." A paper presented at Asian Barometer Workshop on Democracy in a Divided Society: East Asia in Comparative Perspective, Taipei, Taiwan, August 11, 2014.

Chicago Council of Foreign Relations(CCFR) and East Asia Institute. *Global View 2004: Comparing South Korean and American Public Opinion and Foreign Policy.* Chicago: Chicago Council on Foreign Relations, 2004.

Cole, Michael J. "Sunflowers in Springtime: Taiwan's Crisis and the End of an Era in Cross-Strait Cooperation." *China Brief* 14:7 (April 9), 2014.

East Asia Institute and Asiatic Research Institute, Korea University. *2010 Opinion*

Survey on Korean National Identity. http://www.eai.or.kr. 2010.

East Asia Institute and JoongAng Ilbo. *Public Opinion Survey on Korean National Identity*. http://www.eai.or.kr. 2005.

Gellner, Ernest. *Nations and nationalism*. New York: Blackwell Publishing, 1983.

Hsieh, John Fuh-Sheng and Emerson M. S. Niou. "Salient Issues in Taiwan's Electoral Politics." *Electoral Studies* 15:2, 1996.

Kim, Sung-han. "Brothers versus Friends: Inter-Korean Reconciliation and Emerging Anti-Americanism in South Korea." In David Steinberg, ed. *Korean Attitudes toward the United States: Changing Dynamics*. New York: M.E. Sharp, 2005.

Lee, Dong Hyung. "The Korean Sunshine Policy: Its Light and Shade." *Pacific Focus* 18:1, 2003.

Lee, Nae-Young. "Changing Korean Perceptions on North Korea and the Question of National Identity," In Wontaek, Kang. ed. *Korean National Identity and Korean Politics*. Seoul: EAI, 2007.

-------. "Evolving Korean Attitude Toward North Korea." paper prepared for the Conference on "The Changing Korean Peninsula and the Future of East Asia" co-hosted by the Seoul Forum for International Affairs, The Brooking Institution, and JoongAng Ilbo, Seoul, December 1, 2005.

-------. "Korean National Identity and Changing Perception on North Korea and Unification." In Wontaek Kang and Lee Nae-Young. eds. *Koreans, Who are We: Exploring Korean Identity by Public Opinion Survey*. Seoul: East Asia Institute, 2011.

-------. "Vision and Policy Direction of the Park Geun-hye Administration and its East Asia Diplomacy." *The Gakushuin Journal of International studies*. Vol. 1, 2014.

Lee, Nae-Young and Han-Wool Jeong. "How does Attack on Yeonpyong Island change Public Opinion?." *EAI Opinion Briefing*. No. 91, 2010.

-------. "Fluctuating Anti-Americanism and the Korea-US Alliance." *International Studies Review* 5:2, 2004.

Lee, W. C. "Taiwan's Cultural Reconstruction Movement: Identity Politics and Collective Action Since 2000." *Issues & Studies* 41:1, 2005.

Lim, Hyug-Baeg and Yu-Jeong Choi. "Inter-Korean and Cross-Strait Relations through the Window of Regional Integration Theories." *Asian Survey* 51:5, 2011.

Lin, Jih-Wen. "How are the Taiwanese Divided: National Identity or Generation Gap?", A paper presented at Asian Barometer Workshop on Democracy in a Divided Society: East Asia in Comparative Perspective, August 11, 2014, Taipei,

Taiwan, 2014.

Park, In-hui. "Candidate Park Geun-hye's foreign and security policy: The spread of the Korean Peninsula Trust Process and Trust Diplomacy." *Hanbando Focus* [The Korean Peninsula Focus] Nov/Dec 2012.

Qi, Dongtao. "Divergent Popular Support for the DPP and the Taiwan Independence Movement, 2000-2012." *Journal of Contemporary China* 21:78, 2012.

Rigger, Shelly. "Is Taiwan Independence Passe?: Public Opinion, Party Platforms and National Identity in Taiwan." *Harvard Studies on Taiwan*. Vol. 3, 2000.

-------. "Strawberry Jam: National Identity, Cross-Strait Relations, and Taiwan's Youth," in C. Clark. ed. *The Changing Dynamics of Relations Among China, Taiwan, and the United States*. Cambridge: Cambridge Scholars Publishing, 2011.

Shubert, Gunter. "Taiwan's Political Parties and National Identity: The Rise of Overarching Consensus." *Asian Survey* 44:1, 2004.

Smith, Anthony. *The Ethnic Origins of Nations*. New York: Basil Blackwell, 1986.

Steinberg, David. ed. *Korean Attitudes toward the United States: Changing Dynamics*. New York: M.E. Sharp, 2005.

Sobel, Richard, William-Arthur Haynes, and Yu Zheng. "Taiwan Public Opinion Trends, 1992-2008: Exploring Attitudes on Cross-Strait Issues." *Public Opinion Quarterly* 74: 4, 2010.

Son, Key-young. S*outh Korean Engagement Policies and North Korea: Identities, Norms, and the Sunshine Policy*. London: Taylor & Francis, 2006.

Tan, Alexander C. "The 2008 Taiwan Elections: Forward to the Past?." *Electoral Studies* 28:3, 2009.

Theiss-Morse, Elizabeth. *Who Counts as an American?: The Boundaries of National Identity*. London: Cambridge University Press, 2009.

Wu, Yu-Shan. "From Identity to Economy: Shifting Politics in Taiwan." *Global Asia* 8:1, 2013.

-------. "The Evolution of the KMT's Stance on the One-China Principle: National Identity in Flux." In Gunter Schubert and J. Damm. eds. *Taiwanese Identity in the Twentiy-First Century: Domestic, Regional, and Global Perspectives*. New York: Routledge, 2011..

Identity and Economic Interests in the 2008 Taiwanese Presidential Election

Eunju Chi
(Research Professor at the Peace & Democracy Institute at Korea University)

Ⅰ. Introduction

In every election since the 1990s, national identity has been the most important variable for the Taiwanese people in selecting parties and candidates. Taiwanese identity has started to grow since the late 1970s, when the Republic of China (hereafter Taiwan) was defeated by the People's Republic of China (hereafter China) in diplomatic competition. Economic development and successful democratic transition have also nurtured the Taiwanese identity. Yet, the moment when national identity be-

* This chapter was published on the *Journal of Korean Political Science Review* Vol. 46, no.1.

came salient in the elections was formulated by the Democratic Progressive Party (DPP). The DPP carefully observed the increase in the Taiwanese identity and adopted such an identity as its stance. The DPP mobilized voters with national identity in competing against the Kuomintang (Nationalist Party, or KMT).[1]

The mobilization of national identity was successful. The DPP won the 2000 and 2004 presidential elections, and even the 2001 and 2004 Legislative Yuan elections. Most of the analysis of the electoral results showed that national identity was the most critical variable for voters. China issued warnings concerning the DPP's identity mobilization, threatening that they would take military action if the party declared Taiwanese independence. Yet, the threat

1_吳乃德. 1993. "國家認同和政黨支持: 臺灣政黨競爭的社會基礎."『中央硏究院民族學硏究所集刊』 74, 33-61; 王甫昌. 1994. "族群同化與動員: 臺灣民衆政黨支持之分析."『中央硏究院民族學硏究所集刊』 77, 1-34.; Lin, Chia-lung. 1999. *Paths to Democracy: Taiwan in Comparative Perspective*. Yale University Ph. D. Dissertation. Department of Political Science; Corcuff, Stephane ed. 2002. *Memories of the Future: National Identity Issues and the Search for a New Taiwan*. New York: M.E. Sharpe; Chu, Yun-han. 2004. "Taiwan's National Identity Politics and The Prospect of Cross - Strait Relations." *Asian Survey* 44(4), 484-512; Kim, Bum Suk Kim. 2005. "Taiwan's Democratization and the Changes of the Cross-Strait Relations: Applying Democratic Peace Theory," *Korean Journal of International Relations* 45(2), 57-80 [in Korean]; Chi, Eunju. 2009. Independence Issues and Party Realignment in Taiwan after Democratic Transition," *Korean Political Science Review* 43(1), 203-28 [in Korean]; Kang, Qwi Young. 2010. "Research and Analysis into Taiwan's Political Leadership and National Identity." Ph. D. dissertation submitted to the Department of Chinese Studies, GSIS, Hanyang University. [in Korean].

from China could not prevent the spread of Taiwanese identity on the island. On the contrary, it made the Taiwanese doubt the likelihood of a military threat from China, which served to a further growth in Taiwanese identity. As a result, Taiwanese identity increased from 17.3 percent in 1993 to 34 percent in 2000, when the DPP candidate, Chen Shui-bian, was elected president; it further increased to 43 percent in 2004 when President Chen was re-elected (see 〈Figure 1〉).

However, in the 2008 presidential election, the KMT candidate, Ma Ying-jeou, who did not represent Taiwanese identity, was elected as president with 58.5 percent of the votes. In the 2008 Legislative Yuan election on December, the KMT had won 81 out of 113 seats and became the majority party. During Chen's two terms, Taiwan suffered from economic recession, and the KMT made economic issues its main agenda during the campaign. Thus, the KMT's consecutive victories in 2008 could be explained by its economic stance. Before the 2004 presidential election, economic growth had slowed and the unemployment rate had grown.

Yet the DPP won the election by mobilizing Taiwanese identity. Rawnsley analyzed that if the KMT candidate, Lien Chan, had not taken the identity issues seriously, and if he had focused more on economic issues, the KMT could have had a chance of winning the election.[2] Compared to the 2004 election campaign, the KMT did focus more on economic issues in 2008. Ma

Ying-jeou selected Xiao Wan-chang, an economy expert, as his vice-presidential candidate, and emphasized the importance of the economy during the campaign.

The change in the KMT's strategies in the 2008 election campaign raises the following questions. Were voters' concerns about the economic situation the deciding factor? Furthermore, was the 2008 election the moment when national identities were replaced by economic factors as salient issues? Specifically, did the role of national identity in the party competition decrease? This paper attempts to answer these questions. This paper is organized as follows. The following section reviews the existing literature regarding the deciding factor in the elections, and then proposes two hypotheses for analysis. The third section examines the socio-economic circumstances and cross-Strait exchanges under Chen's two terms. It also explains party competition between the KMT and the DPP in preparing for the 2008 presidential election. The fourth section tests the two hypotheses by analyzing the 2008 election survey data. Most significantly, this section tests whether national identity was replaced by economic factors in Taiwanese party politics. The concluding section summarizes the findings

2_Rawnsley, Gary. "Sean Connery Has Left the Building? : Thoughts on the 2004 Presidential Election in Taiwan. " Paper presented at the 27th East Asia Colloquium, Korea University, 2004.

and suggests some implications.

II. Related Literature

Rational choice theorists commonly divide voting behavior into rational and irrational votes. Butler and Stokes suggest two different motivations of voters, which are 'instrumental' and 'expressive' motivations. They explain that 'instrumental' motivation leads to a rational vote and 'expressive' motivation leads to an irrational vote.[3] Downs says that voting is purely instrumental, thus, voters will not vote if any costs are associated with it.[4] Yet, in reality, many people do not follow the rationalist theory. Some people vote irrationally sometimes out of nationalism or specific identities. Rational choice theorists identify this kind of irrational voting as "citizens' duty"[5] or "political identity."[6] Among them, identity voters cast their votes depending on the opinion or choice

---

3_Butler, David, and Donald Stokes. 1969. *Political Change in Britain*. New York: St. Martin's.

4_Downs, Anthony. 1957. *An Economic of Democracy*. NewYork: Harper & Row, pp. 260-76.

5_Riker, William H. and Peter C. Ordeshook. 1968. "A Theory of the Calculus of Voting," *American Political Science Review* 62: 25-42.

6_Schuessler, Alexander A. 2000. "Expressive Voting," *Rationality and Society* 12: 87-119.

of the group that they think they belong to.

The Michigan school, which has researched voting behavior, suggests three main factors in voting: issues, party identification, and the images of the political party or the candidate.[7] Among them, voting on issues is rational voting, and voting on image is also rational voting to the extent that the voters decide their votes by considering the policies suggested by the party or the candidate. On the other hand, party identification [8] is irrational voting because it is close to group identity. In Taiwan, the main factors in elections have been national identity, party identification, and issues.[9] In advanced democracies, the role of party identification has been replaced by issue voting due to the emergence of a new social cleavage, diverse campaign strategies, and the fact that voters have come to calculate rationally.[10] Yet party

7_Niemi, Richard G. and Herbert F. Weisberg. 1993. "What Determines the Vote?" in Richard G. Niemi and Herbert F. Weisberg eds. *Classics in Voting Behavior*. Washington D.C.: Congressional Quarterly Press, pp. 93-4.

8_Party identification can be defined as a consistent affective orientation to a specific political party, and it forms part of a voter's self-identity for party identification. See Campbell, Angus, Philip E. Converse, Warren E. Miller, and Donald E. Stokes. 1976. *The American Voter*. Chicago: University of Chicago Press, p. 121.

9_鄭夙芬. 2009. "族群, 認同與總統選舉投票抉擇."『選舉研究』16(2), 23-49; 陳陸輝, 耿曙, 王德育. 2009. "兩岸關係與 2008年台灣總統大選: 認同, 利益, 威脅與選民投票取向."『選舉研究』16(2), 1-22.

10_Farrell, D. M. 1996. "Campaign Strategies and Tactics." in Lawrence Le Duc, Richard G. Niemi, Pippa Norris eds. *Comparing Democracies: Elections and Voting in Global*

identification remains one of the main factors in electing parties and candidates in Taiwan.[11]

In Taiwan, the nation consists of Taiwanese identity, Chinese identity, and dual identity, which includes both identities. Before the democratic transition, there was no conflict in terms of identity. Most people regarded themselves as Chinese. They identified themselves as being the people of the Republic of China covering alll of Mainland China. However, after being defeated in the diplomatic competition with China, the people of the island came to realize that the Republic of China could not represent the whole of China. In addition, economic development and a successful democratic transition nurtured Taiwanese national pride, which led to an increase in Taiwanese identity. Taiwanese identity increased during the 1990s, with about 40% of the population identifying themselves as Taiwanese rather than Chinese. As the DPP adopted Taiwan's independence issues as its electoral agenda, they came to represent the interests of those who have Taiwanese identity.

Therefore, most studies on Taiwanese elections focused on identity politics; moreover, the party system was rearranged in line

---

Perspective. Thousand Oaks : Sage Publications. P. 160; Fiorina, Morris P. 1981. *Retrospective Voting in American National Elections*. Yale University Press.

11_鄭夙芬. 2009; 陳陸輝 et al. 2009.

with national identity. However, party competition and the result of the 2008 presidential election imply several changes. First, the 2008 presidential election implies a possible change to issue-based voting. As time passed, issues became an important factor for voters in selecting parties and candidates in the advanced democracies with the decrease of party identification. Democratized Taiwan could be following this track. As a result of the economic recession during the first half of the 2000s, people ascribed utmost importance to economic issues. People who had experienced the rapid economic development under the KMT administration came to be dissatisfied with the low and stable economic performance of Chen Shui-bian. Thus, many pundits suggested the prospect that the political party that endorsed economic issues would win the election.[12] Second, the concept and the composition of identity among the Taiwanese are changing. As Taiwanese identity increases, dual identity also increases. Approximately 34 percent of the people on the island responded as having dual identity in 2000; this rate increased to 46 percent in the first half of 2008 (see 〈Figure 1〉). These changes imply that the role of dual identity became important in the election if voters still vote depending on their identity. Thus, the preference and

12_Chu, Yun-han. 2008. "Taiwan in 2007: The Waiting Game." *Asian Survey* 48(1), 124-132.

political attitude of dual identity needed to be searched.

When voters cast their votes depending on the issues, they vote for the party and for the candidate providing better utilities.[13] In Taiwan, issue-based voting increased during the early 1990s. Issues, such as economic, environmental, gender, and welfare issues, were paid more attention by the voting public and the political parties.[14] Yet the results of the elections demonstrated that voters initially cast their votes depending on their identities rather than on their issues. National identity was still the main voting factor in the 2000 and 2004 presidential elections. Thus, not only the DPP, but also the KMT attempted to represent Taiwanese identit y.[15] However, by the time of the 2008 presidential election, the KMT put economic issues on the centerpiece of the campaign agenda, and the result of the election was Ma's victory. Considering this election result, the following two hypotheses can be raised.

13_Downs. 1957; Key, V. O. 1966. *Responsible Electorate: Rationality in Presidential Voting, 1936-1960*. Cambridge: Belknap Press; Fiorina, Morris P. 1981. *Retrospective Voting in American National Elections*. Yale University Press.

14_Lin, Tse-min, Yun-han Chu and Melvin J. Hinich. 1996. "Conflict, Displacement and Regime Transition in Taiwan: A Spatial Analysis." *World Politics* 48(4).

15_Fell, Dafydd. 2004. "Measurement of Party Position and Party Competition in Taiwan," *Issues and Studies*. 40(3/4), p. 16; Wu, Yu-shan. 1999. "Moving toward the Center: Taiwan," www.taiwansecurity.org/TS-Wu.htm (accessed August 7, 2011).

Hypothesis 1: The economy became a new important factor in the Taiwanese presidential elections. Taiwanese voters chose the candidate based on their economic preferences. Ma Ying-jeou's victory is a good example.

As cross-Strait exchanges increased, the Taiwanese economy came to rely heavily on China. Furthermore, economic growth was also influenced by the political relationship between the two sides. The increasing dependency of the Taiwanese economy on China gave rise to new problems. As for the DPP, the pro-independence party had difficulty in negotiating with China. Meanwhile, the pro-China KMT had a channel through which it could talk with China. In a situation where the KMT has superior status over the DPP on economic issues, rational voters would give their votes to the KMT.

Hypothesis 2: Identity is still an important factor for choosing a candidate in the Taiwanese presidential elections. Since national identity has been an important factor in the elections, it has never been replaced by any other factors. Therefore, national identity was an important factor in the 2008 presidential election.

National identity, an irrational factor, has been an important factor for the electorate in Taiwan. Despite the fact that Taiwan experienced an economic recession in the early 2000s, the Taiwanese voted mainly along national identity lines in the 2004 election. As for the electorate, economic growth through cross-Strait exchanges implied political risks regarding national integrity. Most of all, the group identifying themselves as Taiwanese worried about the long-term political effects of cross-Strait economic exchanges and thus, supported the DPP candidate. Yet, the increase of those with a dual identity and the change in their voting behavior could have led to new changes in identity voting in 2008. In this regard, it can be stated that identity voting is still effective, even though there may be changes on the inside.

During the campaign in the 2008 presidential election, Ma Ying-jeou promised that he would lead economic growth by expanding cross-Strait economic exchanges. Hence, voters chose him as president. Does this result then mean that identity has been replaced by economic issues (Hypothesis 1)? Or can the increase in dual identity contribute to explaining the result of the 2008 election? (Hypothesis 2)? The following section explains economic performance and identity changes under Chen Shui-bian's administration in order to understand the background before conducting an analysis.

Ⅲ. Economic Performance and Identity Change under Chen Shui-bian's Administration

1. Economic Performance

For eight years from 2000 to 2008, under the Chen Shui-bian administration, the Taiwanese economy was in a recession. Even though Taiwan was not affected by the East Asian economic crisis of the late 1990s, they could not escape its influence. The economic growth rate in 2001 was -2.2 percent, which was the first negative growth rate ever for Taiwan. In 2004, when Chen was re-elected, the economic growth rate had recovered to 6.2 percent; yet, the unemployment rate did not recover from the peak of 5 percent in 2002. People began to worry about a possible long-term recession. Most of all, per capita GNP decreased in 2001 and 2002.

In addition, Taiwan's economic dependency on China had become wider and deeper. Taiwan's exports to China have almost doubled its imports. This imbalance between exports and imports was caused not by market principles but by the political purpose of the Chinese. China treated Taiwanese companies as domestic companies, and provided benefits, such as tax credits. The Chinese intention was motivated by political purposes, attempting to make Taiwan more economically dependent on China.[16]

〈Table 1〉 Main Economic Indices under the Chen Shui-bian Administration

Year	Economic Growth Rate (%)	Per Capita GNP (US $)	Unemployment Rate (%)
2000	5.8	13,090	2.99
2001	-2.2	11,692	4.57
2002	4.6	11,914	5.17
2003	3.5	12,242	4.99
2004	6.2	13,252	4.44
2005	4.2	14,075	4.13
2006	4.8	14,455	3.91
2007	5.7	15,122	3.91

Source: Executive Yuan, ROC(Taiwan), Council for Economic Planning and Development, Taiwan Statistical Data Book (2009).

Taiwan was aware of China's intention; yet it sustained and extended economic exchanges with China. The primary reason is that Taiwan can take advantage of China's political purposes in order to increase its own economic benefit. Regardless of the wide gap between the economic developments, each side has its comparative advantage and as a result, Taiwan made a huge profit.

Chen Shui-bian attempted to make political reconciliation with China when he was elected president in 2000. During the campaign, his election agenda was Taiwanese independence. However, when he took power, he drew back from his original

16_Naughton, Barry. 1997. "Economic Policy Reform in the PRC and Taiwan." in Barry Naughton, ed., T*he China Circle: Economic and Electronics in the PRC, Taiwan, and Hong Kong*. Washington, DC: Brookings Institution Press, 84.

stance and declared the "Five Nos," which meant that there would be no attempt to cause any change in the cross-Strait relationship. In August 2001, Chen adopted the "aggressive liberalization, effective management" policy. By allowing market openings toward China, his administration promoted more open exchanges than that of the KMT. By adopting his new policy, direct economic exchanges were allowed and restrictions on investing in China were lifted. Investments in China of less than 20 million dollars were automatically allowed, and areas of semiconductors, civil aircraft, law service, and real estate were liberalized.[17]

Yet there was a turning point in August 2002. As Chen declared "one country on each side," which meant Taiwan and China are different countries, the relationship between the two sides turned sour. Before long, a change in cross-Strait economic policies followed. After Chen succeeded in reelection, he declared "effective liberalization, aggressive management," tightening the regulations. The change in cross-Strait policies mainly came from his independence policies. However, Taiwan's attempts to approach China were limited due to the fact that China's responses did not meet expectations.

China had a principle of not talking with any group or person

---

17_Kastner, Scott L. 2009. *Political Conflict and Economic Interdependence Across the Taiwan Strait and Beyond*. Stanford: Stanford University Press.

〈Table 2〉 Cross-Strait Economic Exchanges during Chen' s Two Terms (US$million)

Year	Export	Import	Total
2000	25,009.9	6,229.3	31,239.2
2001	25,607.4	5,903.0	31,510.4
2002	31,528.8	7,968.6	39,497.4
2003	38,292.7	11,017.9	49,310.6
2004	48,930.4	16,792.3	65,722.7
2005	56,271.5	20,093.7	76,365.3
2006	63,332.4	24,783.1	88,115.5
2007	74,245.9	28,015.0	102,260.9

Source: http://www.mac.gov.tw/public/Attachment/9111817342527.pdf (Table 6 Estimated Total Trade between Taiwan and Mainland China).

representing Taiwanese independence. Chen Shui-bian attempted to talk with the CCP by offering open relationships with China. However, China refused his offer and kept its pro-KMT attitude. Just after the 2000 presidential election, Wu Po-hsiung, the vice president of the KMT, had a meeting with Qian Qichen in order to discuss cross-Strait economic exchanges. During Chen's second term, this situation continued. Lien Chan, a former presidential candidate for the KMT, had a meeting with the Chinese leader, Hu Jintao on May 2004. Meetings with the Chinese top leader were not allowed to the DPP.[18]

18_Goldstein, Steven M. 2008. "Chen Shui-bian and the Political Transition in Taiwan." in Goldstein, Steven M. and Julian Chang eds. *Presidential Politics in Taiwan: the Administration of Chen Shui-bian*. Norwalk: Eastbridge, p. 303; Kastner, 2009, 60-75.

Even though "effective liberalization, aggressive management" had been adopted, economic exchanges with China had increased. According to ⟨Table 2⟩, the total sum of cross-Strait exchanges increased from US$32.2 billion in 2000 to US$102.2 billion in 2007. In addition, direct investment in China also increased from 32.2 percent in 2001 to 64.4 percent in 2006. These increases imply that cross-Strait economic exchanges became critical for the economic growth of Taiwan. As a result, questions of how to handle and who can handle the cross-Strait relationship became the most critical issues.

2. Identity Changes

After the democratic transition, one of the important changes in political society was the growth of a Taiwanese identity. In the first stage, a Taiwanese identity had spread among the Hokkien and the Hakka people. They are descendants of those who moved to Taiwan from China in the sixteenth and seventeenth centuries. Even though they have the same racial and cultural backgrounds as the Chinese, they were differentiated from the people who came to the island in 1948 with Chang Kai-shek's army. The earlier settlers' period of living separately had created their own culture and the experience of Japanese colonialism deepened it. In addition, they have their own dialects, which are incomprehensible to those who speak Mandarin. Yet, the Hokkien and the Hakka people make up about 85% of the total population, which is a significant percentage for the politicians in Taiwan.[19]

The DPP grew with strong support from the people who have Taiwanese identity. As has been noted, the DPP's emphasis on Taiwanese identity was the main factor in their electoral victories. Thus, one of Chen Shui-bian's main political activities was to mobilize that identity. In every important address he made, he did not neglect to mention Taiwanese identity or independence.[20] When Chen declared "one country on each side [of the Strait]," China felt uncomfortable; nevertheless, it gained him support from the Taiwanese identity groups. During the 2004 presidential campaign, the DPP suggested a revision of the Constitution in order to promote Taiwanese independence and submitted a bill for a referendum.

Mobilizing Taiwanese identity led to the "pursuit of name changes." This movement aimed to change the names of public buildings or roads that imply Chinese legacy into names that represent Taiwanese identity. Chen Shui-bian changed the name of

---

19_吳乃德. 1993; 王甫昌. 1994.

20_Chang, Hui-ching and Rich Holt. 2009. Taiwan and ROC: A Critical Analysis of President Chen Shui-bien's Construction of Taiwan Identity in National Speeches. *National Identities* 11(3), 301-330.

"Taipei" to "Taipei City," so that it can be seen as the capital of a nation; he also added the English name "Taiwan" to newly issued passports. He changed the "Office of the President, Republic of China" into "Office of the President, Republic of China (Taiwan)" and changed the "Chiang Kai-shek International Airport" to "Taiwan Taoyuan International Airport."Also, the name of "Chiang Kai-shek Memorial Hall" was converted to "National Taiwan Democracy Memorial Hall."[21]

However, Taiwanese identity started to wane from Chen's second term. According to 〈Figure 1〉, there was a clear difference between Chen's first and second term. During the first term, a sense of Taiwanese identity was stronger than that of a dual identity by about 10 percentage points on average; yet during the second term, Taiwanese identity waned and the dual identity was stronger at times. In particular, from May 2005 to July 2007, dual identity was clearly stronger than a Taiwanese one. During this period, by coincidence, the DPP also went through a difficult time. Soong Chu-yu, the PFP party leader, originally from the KMT, visited China in order to negotiate on cross-Strait issues. The visit worked to reveal the DPP's limitation on cross-Strait issues once

---

21_Park, Byoung Seok. 2010. "Taiwan's De-sinicization Movement Viewed from the Perspective of Post-colonialism." *Political Thought of East Asia*. 9(1), 111-139. [in Korean]

〈Figure 1〉 National identities during Chen Shui-bian' s Two Terms (1999-2008) (%)

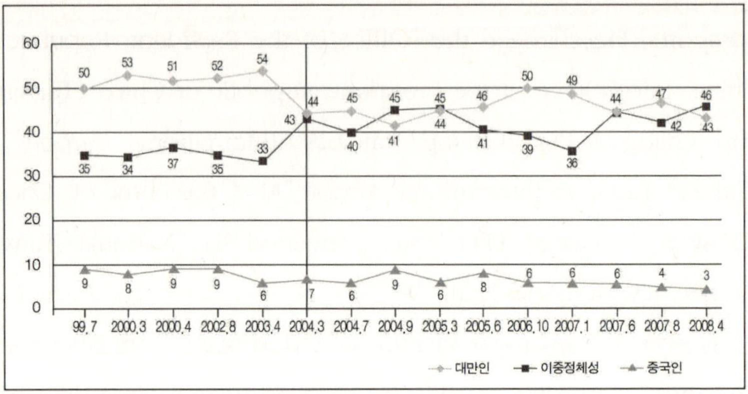

again. In addition, KMT legislators began to criticize President Chen Shui-bian over corruption scandals involving his family.

The dual identity group describes themselves as both Taiwanese and Chinese. If identity means self-identification toward a nation, this definition would be paradoxical. However, dual identity in Taiwan is understood as "politically Taiwanese, while culturally Chinese".[22] More specifically, the members of the dual

22_Shen, Shiau-chi. 2005. "Explaining Dual Identity in Taiwan: A Two-Dimensional Perspective on National Identity." APSA Annual Meeting.Washington, D.C. U.S.A. September; Lin, Chia-lung. 2002. "The Political Formation of Taiwanese Nationalism." in Stephane Corcuff, ed. *Memories of the Future*, Armonk: M.E. Sharpe. 220.

identity group define themselves as the people of the Republic of China and descendants of Chinese culture. These people comprised about 40 percent of the population in the early 1990s. This percentage has remained relatively stable, yet, it increased during Chen's second term.

IV. Party Competition during the 2008 Presidential Campaign

The increase in dual identity along with the increasing significance of economic issues was not a good sign for the DPP. Its main support had come from the Taiwanese identity group; thus, they could not take the initiative in cross-Strait issues. In addition, the corruption scandal involving Chen's family broke out before the 2008 presidential campaign. Under these conditions, the KMT candidate, Ma Ying-jeou, and the DPP candidate, Hsieh Chang-ting, commenced their quest for the presidency.

1. Economic Issues

The KMT candidate, Ma Ying-jeou, asserted that Taiwan had suffered due to low economic development and high unemployment during Chen's two terms. For economic recovery and growth, he proposed the 633 Plan, which meant a 6 percent economic growth rate, a GDP of US$30,000 per capita, and a 3 percent unemployment rate. He also promised to deregulate unnecessary restrictions. In addition, Ma promised that he would promote direct economic exchanges, direct flights, tourism in Taiwan for Chinese people, the expansion of Taiwanese direct investment in China, permission for Chinese currency exchanges in Taiwan, and recognition of Chinese education qualifications. The vice presidential candidate, Xiao Wan-chang, was an economy expert who had been involved in the creation of the cross-Strait common market by expanding cross-Strait economic exchanges.

Meanwhile, the DPP candidate, Hsieh Chang-ting, suggested that the real income increasing strategy was to renovate the tax system and manage inflation. Hsieh criticized Ma's economic plan, arguing that the cross-Strait common market was essentially the same as a "One China Market." He raised the concern that this would harm farmers and laborers in small and medium-sized industries. In addition, he criticized Ma's economic plan on the basis that it would deepen Taiwanese dependence on China, which would finally threaten the sovereignty of the former. He also raised questions as to the consequences of exporting Taiwanese agricultural products without equivalent imports from China, and Taiwanese migration to China without corresponding Chinese migration to Taiwan.

2. Identity

In 2007, the DPP raised a Constitutional revision issue with the idea of making Taiwan a normal state. This revision issue was initiated by Chen Shui-bian; however, this was later changed to "Applying for United Nations membership in the name of Taiwan," due to strong opposition from the United States and the short period of President Chen's term that remained. This was a strategy to mobilize the Taiwanese identity group in preparing for the 2008 presidential election. As the DPP mobilized its identity as an electoral agenda item, the KMT also made a similar suggestion in response. The KMT revived their old version of "Re-entering the United Nations in the name of the Republic of China." Entering or re-entering the United Nations is not that simple a matter, and the DPP, the KMT, and even the voting public knew that Taiwan could not be a member. Nevertheless, the issue of competition to enter the United Nations became salient due to the fact that each party's position on national identity was now revealed.

In addition, Chen Shui-bian intentionally asserted the pursuit of name changes as Election Day drew close. This issue was a difficult challenge to the KMT, in that Taiwanization means superficially "de-Sinicization;" yet, it actually means a "de-KMT movement." Thus, the KMT, which had a majority of seats in the Legislative Yuan, cut the revenues of state-owned companies who attempted to change their names at the request of Chen Shui-bian. Further, they also criticized the name change, as it aimed "to remold the thoughts and to distort the roots of national culture and development." Regardless of their efforts, the KMT had to consider that about 40 percent of the people in Taiwan had a Taiwanese identity, implying that they could not ignore this even though they opposed the extreme movements for name changes. In this vein, Ma Ying-jeou used to call himself a "new Taiwanese," and in 2007, he published a book titled Yuanxiangjuingshen, which described the importance of "Taiwanese Consciousness."[23]

During the election campaign, the DPP revealed and criticized that Ma Ying-jeou and his family had received US Green Cards in the 1970s, when the ROC-US diplomatic relation were broken off. The DPP criticized Ma for an alleged intention to move to the United States if Taiwan had trouble with China. The DPP further insisted that Ma's family's Green Cards were still valid, implying that they still have intentions to emigrate. Controversies regarding the Green Cards meant that, as far as the DPP was concerned, Ma Ying-jeou was not a suitable candidate for the leader of Taiwan.

23_Goldstein, 2008, p. 305.

3. Converging Competition around Economic Issues and Identity

Competing issues among the parties used to converge in previous elections in Taiwan. In particular, the KMT and the DPP moved to the center, deviating from the parties' original stances on cross-Strait relationship issues and identity issues.[24] In the 2008 presidential election, the KMT and the DPP showed similar converging patterns on identity issues and economic issues. Converging competition made no difference in the parties' positions on the issues. Both candidates, Ma and Hsieh, suggested that they were going to ease tensions between Taiwan and China and revitalize the economy by expanding cross-Strait economic exchanges.

On economic issues, the KMT and DPP agreed that Taiwanese economic growth heavily relied on the cross-Strait relationship. The KMT suggested creating a cross-Strait common market and more aggressive solutions, but the DPP also promised to expand cross-Strait economic exchanges within a boundary that retained Taiwanese sovereignty. On identity issues, "Applying to the

---

24_Fell, Dafydd. 2008. "Inter-Party Competition in Taiwan: Toward a New Party System." in Goldstein, Steven M. and Julian Chang, eds. *Presidential Politics in Taiwan: the Administration of Chen Shui-bian*. Norwalk: Eastbridge; Fell, 2004; Wu, 1999.

United Nations in the name of Taiwan" and "Re-entering the United Nations in the name of the Republic of China" have almost the same substance, but expressed in different words. Meanwhile, Ma said that the ROC is an independent country with its own sovereignty, and Hsieh said that Taiwan is an independent country with its own sovereignty.[25] By speaking to the political center, Hsieh even warned that the DPP should not provoke China by mobilizing Taiwanese identity.[26] Just before the election, he stated the following:

> I think it is essential to improve the atmosphere between the two sides [of the Strait]. We should stop policies or languages that provoke one another. My administration should be consistent and predictable, to move toward reconciliation and cooperation … I don't think it is necessary to provoke mainland China, verbally or through our behavior.[27]

Ma Ying-jeou endorsed the 1992 Consensus on One China (hereafter the 92 Consensus), which was a compromise between the KMT and the Chinese Communist Party (hereafter the CCP) re-

---

25_Romberg, D. Alan. 2007. "Election 2008 and the Future of Cross-Strait Relations." *China Leadership Monitor* 21. http://media.hoover.org/sites/default/files/documents/CLM21AR.pdf, 1.

26_Chu, Yun-han. 2008. "Taiwan in 2007: The Waiting Game." *Asian Survey* 48(1), 129.

27 _Romberg, 2007, 9.

garding cross-Strait relations. The 92 Consensus means that the KMT and the CCP acknowledge the "One China" principle, however, their interpretations can differ from those of the ROC and the People's Republic of China. The reason why Xiao Wan-chang was elected as vice president candidate to the KMT was not only owing to the fact that he was an economist but also because he was born in Taiwan and was from the southern province where the DPP's main supporters lived.[28] Ma could not ignore the 40 percent of people claiming to have a Taiwanese identity. However, he said that the most important thing for Taiwan was to first solve its urgent problems:

> There is no chance that we can solve the sovereignty issue in our lifetime, but instead we can manage the issue … so that we can shift our emphasis, our energy onto other more urgent issues, such as the economy, security, education, and cultural issues.[29]

Just before the 2008 presidential election, there was a movement for independence in Tibet, and China oppressed it forcefully. Regarding this incident, Hsieh raised concerns that it could be the future of Taiwan. He further said that Ma's "One

28_Chu, 2008, 127.

29_Romberg, 2007, 3.

China market" idea would push Taiwan into the same situation as Tibet. On the other hand, Ma stated that China should guarantee freedom of religion in Tibet and that any forceful oppression could not be accepted. He also stated that he would not send athletes to the 2008 Beijing Olympics unless China stopped oppressing Tibetans.

During the election campaign, the KMT and the DPP converged on economic issues and identity issues. Meanwhile, the voters' perceptions of the candidates were different from their expectations. The voters simply perceived that the KMT candidate could revitalize the economy through cross-Strait economic exchanges, whereas the DPP candidate would attempt to retain the independent status of Taiwan. The pro-KMT attitude of China gave an advantage to Ma Ying-jeou on economic issues due to the fact that the Taiwanese economy relied heavily on China. On the other hand, even though the KMT and the DPP both moved to endorse Taiwanese identity, the DPP was seen as being closer to Taiwanese identity. Thus, the 2008 presidential election became a competition between economic issues and identity issues. Moreover, Ma Ying-jeou, who gave priority to economic issues, won the election.

V. Determinants of the Voters' Choice in the 2008 Presidential Election

This election result indicated that voters' choices were made based on their consideration of economic interests. However, is this correct? In order to find the main factors influencing voters' choices, we conducted a logistic regression by using data from the 2008 Presidential Election Telephone Survey.[30] As a dependent variable, we chose the question "If there were a presidential election tomorrow, for whom are you going to vote?" From the answers, we coded Ma Ying-jeou as 1 and Hsieh Chang-ting as 0. As independent variables, we chose economic issues, identity, party identification, security, satisfaction with Chen's administration, and secio-economic status (SES).

As for economic issues, two questions were selected: "What do you think about the effects of the expanded cross-Strait economic exchanges on Taiwan's economy?" (National EI) and "What do you think about the effects of expanded cross-Strait exchanges on your (personal) economy?" (Personal EI).The variable was coded as follows: 1. Worst, 2. Worse, 3. Same, 4. Better, 5. Best. The reason as

30_This survey was conducted three times during the period from March 7 to March 21, 2008. It covers the entire island, except Jinmen and Majou. The respondents were 1,919 men and women over 20 years of age. http://srda.sinica.edu.tw.

to why the two questions were chosen is that there was a difference between votes from considering the national economy and those considering personal economy. Generally, the voters considered national economy more than their personal economy.[31]

The second independent variable was identity. There were two related questions for identity, which are identity itself and the attitude toward unification and independence. Identity was coded as follows: 1. Taiwanese identity, and 2. Dual identity. Chinese identity was excluded because Chinese identity was too small to be tested. The attitude toward unification and independence (Position on U-I) has been regarded as closely related with identity in Taiwan.[32] Answers regarding the attitude toward unification and independence were coded as follows: 1. Independence at once, 2. Independence later, 3. Status quo for now, independence later, 4. Status quo indefinitely, 5. Status quo, unification later, or 6. Unification at once.

Party identification (Party ID) has been an important factor in the party competition in Taiwan. For this reason, it was included as an independent variable. Except for the KMT and the DPP,

---

31_Kiewit, D. Roderick, and Donald R. Kinder. 1981. "Sociotropic Politics." *British Journal of Political Science* 11, 129-161.; Lee, 1999. Lee, Hyeon-Woo. 1999. "Re-examination of Private Economic Voting in the United States." *Korean Political Science Review* 33(2), 241-257. [in Korean]

32_Shen, 2005, 5.

there are small parties, such as the People First Party (PFP), the New Party (NP), and the Taiwan Solidarity Union (TSU). These parties are divided into two groups, the pan-Blue and the pan-Green, by their ideological stance on unification and their stance on the independence spectrum. The KMT leads the pan-Blue alliance (including the PFP and NP), which pursues unification in the long run. The DPP leads the pan-Green alliance (including the TSU), which pursues Taiwan independence. Since the 2008 presidential election was a contest between the two candidates, Ma and Hsieh, party identification was coded as a dummy variable: 0. pan-Green and 1. pan-Blue.

As for security, the attitude of China toward Taiwan (China's Hostility) was chosen as a dependent variable. In the past, China has threatened Taiwan militarily, and the cross-Strait crisis in 1996 drove the voters to become conservative. However, these threats have never been realized, and, if anything, they have taught the Taiwanese that China only threatens and does not attack. Yet, China's verbal hostility and desire for unification still continue. Thus, it was included as an independent variable. Regarding the question about China's hostility, answers were coded as follows: 1. Very hostile, 2. Not hostile, 3. A little favorable, or 4. Very favorable.

In addition, satisfaction with the incumbent Chen administration (Satisfaction with Chen) was added as a dependent variable. Satisfaction with the incumbent covers large areas. However, the Chen family corruption scandals were revealed just before the election, which could have led to apparent dissatisfaction with the Chen administration's performance and support for Ma. This variable was coded as follows: 1. Very satisfied 2. Satisfied, 3. Dissatisfied, or 4. Very dissatisfied.

However, candidate factors, regarded as significant by the Michigan school, were excluded. As mentioned, image voting used to be decided by policies, not by the candidates' personal images. The 2008 survey includes questions on the candidates' factors, such as attractiveness, reliability, and ability; however, most of the respondents did not answer the questions or chose the answer "I do not know."

The result of the analysis is shown in ⟨Table 3⟩. It shows that economic interest (National EI and Personal EI) and identity (Identity and Position on U-I) were significant in deciding the president in the 2008 election. This result satisfies the existing explanation that economic issues were the main determinants in the 2008 election (H1). It also shows that identity factors are still effective (H2).

As for economic interest, respondents who considered that expanding cross-Strait economic exchanges would benefit national and personal economies supported Ma Ying-jeou. Generally, voters used to vote more depending on their national economic inter-

〈Table 3〉 Economic Interests and Identity in the 2008 Presidential Election

Variables		B	S.E.	P-value
Economic Interest	National EI	.886	.111	.000
	Personal EI	.491	.139	.000
Identity	Identity	1.692	.259	.000
	Position on U-I	.592	.111	.000
Party Identification	Party ID	.875	.475	.066
Security	China' s Hostility	-.026	.163	.872
Satisfaction	Satisfaction with Chen	.147	.169	.387
Socio-economic status (SES)	Gender	.438	.247	.076
	Age	-.017	.112	.877
	Education	-.020	.116	.861

Model Chi-Square: 515.304, n =1,919.

ests than on personal economic interest; thus, two independent variables were tested here. The results show that the economic motivation of the voters influenced both national and personal levels. Thus, focusing on economic issues proved to be effective for Ma's campaign.

On the other hand, identity is still an important variable. Most of the Taiwanese identity group chose the DPP candidate Hsieh, whereas most of the dual identity group chose the KMT candidate Ma. Further, the more the respondents supported unification, the more they supported Ma, and the more the respondents supported Taiwan independence, the more they supported Hsieh. In this regard, this analysis has further implications. That is, the role of the Taiwanese identity group was still important in 2008; yet, the role of the dual identity group was receiving greater importance. The size of the dual identity group has been on the increase since 2004, and sometimes, its percentage was higher than that of the Taiwanese identity group. According to the analysis, most of the dual identity group prefers Ma Ying-jeou.

VI. Electoral and Political Effects of Economic Interest and Identity in the 2008 Presidential Election

Comparing the voters' choices in the 2000 and 2004 presidential elections, whether the voting behavior in the 2008 election has changed from an identity vote to an economic one can be examined. ⟨Table 4⟩ shows a cross-tabulation analysis between economic interests and voters' choices. The question of economic interest is represented as National EI. In ⟨Table 4⟩, the respondents who selected "Best," supporting the KMT, were 28.1 percent in the year 2000. However, this percentage increased to 63.6 percent in 2004 and to 85.5 percent in 2008. On the other hand, the respondents who selected "Worst," supporting the DPP, were 62.7 percent in 2000, and the same percentage supported the DPP in 2008. This result shows that the people who think that expanding economic exchanges would be beneficial to the national economy have dramatically increased in number, lending greatly

<table>
<caption>〈Table 4〉 Economic Interests and Voters' Choices in Presidential Elections (2000, 2004, 2008)</caption>
<tr><th rowspan="3"></th><th colspan="3">2000</th><th colspan="2">2004</th><th colspan="2">2008</th></tr>
<tr><th colspan="2">pan-Blue</th><th rowspan="2">Chen (DPP)</th><th rowspan="2">Lien (KMT)</th><th rowspan="2">Chen (DPP)</th><th rowspan="2">Ma (KMT)</th><th rowspan="2">Hsieh (DPP)</th></tr>
<tr><th>Lien (KMT)</th><th>Soong (PFP)</th></tr>
<tr><td rowspan="2">Best (100%)</td><td colspan="2">56.8</td><td rowspan="2">19.8</td><td rowspan="2">63.6</td><td rowspan="2">16.3</td><td rowspan="2">85.5</td><td rowspan="2">3.6</td></tr>
<tr><td>28.1</td><td>28.7</td></tr>
<tr><td rowspan="2">Better (100%)</td><td colspan="2">51.3</td><td rowspan="2">19.1</td><td rowspan="2">52.5</td><td rowspan="2">19.5</td><td rowspan="2">73.4</td><td rowspan="2">7.5</td></tr>
<tr><td>26.8</td><td>24.5</td></tr>
<tr><td rowspan="2">No Change Same (100%)</td><td colspan="2">28.6</td><td rowspan="2">32.7</td><td rowspan="2">28.4</td><td rowspan="2">34.8</td><td rowspan="2">41.8</td><td rowspan="2">24.9</td></tr>
<tr><td>14.6</td><td>14.0</td></tr>
<tr><td rowspan="2">Worse (100%)</td><td colspan="2">24.0</td><td rowspan="2">44.8</td><td rowspan="2">11.5</td><td rowspan="2">62.5</td><td rowspan="2">13.5</td><td rowspan="2">49.0</td></tr>
<tr><td>12.5</td><td>11.5</td></tr>
<tr><td rowspan="2">Worst (100%)</td><td colspan="2">16.9</td><td rowspan="2">62.7</td><td rowspan="2">12.5</td><td rowspan="2">69.4</td><td rowspan="2">8.5</td><td rowspan="2">62.7</td></tr>
<tr><td>9.2</td><td>7.7</td></tr>
</table>

Note. 2008 Presidential Election Telephone Survey, cross-tabulation analysis (n=1,919).

increased support to the KMT.

Meanwhile, 〈Table 3〉 demonstrates that identity is still an important determinant in the 2008 election. In particular, the fact that the dual identity group supporting Ma Ying-jeou was a major factor in his victory. As indicated by 〈Table 1〉, the percentage of dual identity increased by 10 percent during Chen's second term, whereas the percentage of Taiwanese identity decreased marginally. Therefore, analyzing the voting behavior of the dual identity would be necessary in order to explain the 2008 election result.

〈Table 5〉 presents the changes in the dual identity group's

〈Table 5〉 Identity and Their Choices in Presidential Elections (2000, 2004, 2008)

<table>
<tr><th rowspan="3"></th><th colspan="3">2000</th><th colspan="2">2004</th><th colspan="2">2008</th></tr>
<tr><th colspan="2">pan-Blue</th><th rowspan="2">Chen (DPP)</th><th rowspan="2">Lien (KMT)</th><th rowspan="2">Chen (DPP)</th><th rowspan="2">Ma (KMT)</th><th rowspan="2">Hsieh (DPP)</th></tr>
<tr><th>Lien (KMT)</th><th>Soong (PFP)</th></tr>
<tr><td rowspan="2">Dual identity (100%)</td><td colspan="2">47.5</td><td rowspan="2">18.9</td><td rowspan="2">50.2</td><td rowspan="2">19.5</td><td rowspan="2">66.4</td><td rowspan="2">6.9</td></tr>
<tr><td>25.5</td><td>22.0</td></tr>
<tr><td rowspan="2">The Taiwanese (100%)</td><td colspan="2">25.2</td><td rowspan="2">45.7</td><td rowspan="2">23.6</td><td rowspan="2">49.0</td><td rowspan="2">30.2</td><td rowspan="2">40.4</td></tr>
<tr><td>11.9</td><td>13.3</td></tr>
</table>

Note. 2008 Presidential Election Telephone Survey, cross-tabulation analysis (n=1,919).

voting behavior. More than half of them supported the KMT in the presidential election, and this support has also been increasing. Moreover, 47.5 percent of the dual identity group (2008) voted pan-Blue in 2000, which increased to 50.4 percent in 2004 and 66.4 percent in 2008. Support from the Taiwanese identity group for the DPP is somewhat stable, but the dual identity groups' support for the presidential candidate from the KMT and pan-Blue has increased by over 10 percent.

Considering the electoral and political effects regarding economic interests and identity, the changes of both variables brought about victory to the KMT. Of the respondents who thought that enlarging cross-Strait economic exchanges would have a positive effect on Taiwan's economy, a greater number supported the KMT's candidate in 2008 than in 2000 or 2004. Meanwhile, the support for the KMT amongst the dual identity group has steadily been increasing.

〈Table 6〉 Stance on Unification: Independence of the Dual Identity and the Taiwanese

	Dual Identity (100%)	The Taiwanese (100%)
Unification at once	0.8	0.5
Status quo now, unification later	13.1	4.7
Status quo now, decide later	46.0	27.9
Status quo indefinitely	23.9	19.3
Status quo now, independence later	7.8	24.6
Independence at once	0.7	12.5
No answer	7.7	10.6

Note. 2008 Presidential Election Telephone Survey, cross-tabulation analysis (n=1,919).

Then, what and who are the dual identity group? As was defined earlier, the dual identity group consists of people who are politically Taiwanese while culturally Chinese. Most of them want a stable a cross-Strait relationship, not leaning toward either unification or independence. According to 〈Table 6〉, about 46 percent of the respondents who answered that they have dual identity selected "status quo for now, decide later," and 23.9 percent selected "status quo indefinitely." Thus, about 70 percent of the dual identity group wants to retain the status quo. This opinion of the dual identity respondents is quite different from that of the Taiwanese identity group, of whom 27.9 percent selected "status quo for now, decide later," and 24.6 percent selected "status-quo for now, independence later."

Rigger (2006) divided the respondents by generation and analyzed their identities and features. She found that the younger the respondents, the more dual identity they have. These generational differences come from different experiences they had in their late teens. Different experiences create a generational cohort effect. She found that the generations who were born between 1954 and 1968 have a more balanced and positive attitude toward China. Moreover, the generations who were born after 1969 and those who grew up after democracy was established never experienced a conflict between loving Taiwan and pursuing economic interests through cross-Strait exchanges. Specifically, the younger generation is used to having a dual identity, resulting in a more rational and flexible attitude toward China.[33]

VII. Conclusion

The analysis of the 2008 election survey shows that economic issues and identity were determinants in choosing the president. This result satisfies Hypothesis 1, in that economic issues were salient in the 2008 presidential election. The voters voted for Ma because economic interests were their priorities. However, the analysis shows more than that. It shows that identity, in addition to eco-

33_Rigger, Shelly. 2006. *Taiwan's Rising Rationalism: Generations, Politics, and "Taiwanese Nationalism."* Washington, D.C: East-West Center Washington.

nomic interests, is also an important determinant for the voters. The voters' positions on unification and independence still affect their choices. This result also satisfies Hypothesis 2 that identity was still an important variable in the 2008 presidential election.

This paper defines the votes by economic interests as being rational, and the votes by identity as being irrational. Although the existing explanations only use a rational vote hypothesis, this paper also tested an irrational vote hypothesis simultaneously. In 2008, voters' choices relied on economic interests on the one hand and identity on the other hand. The voters who cared more about economic interests chose Ma Ying-jeou, and some other groups who cared more about identity chose Hsieh Chang-ting. Meanwhile, the dual identity group, who are rather rational, chose Ma Ying-jeou.

Regarding dual identity, the increase of dual identity during the second term of Chen Shui-bian implied that there would be a change in the majority vote. The dual identity group generally wanted the status quo in the relationship with China, and had come to support the KMT candidate gradually over time since 2000. In the mid-2000s, Rigger found that younger voters were more likely to have a dual identity. Therefore, further research about the role of this dual identity group is required. Hence, research questions for future studies should deal with the followin g:[34] whether the dual identity group came to be rational because they are originally a rational group, or due to their belief that Taiwan's independent status would be sustained for the time being.

34_Current researches mostly deal with Taiwanese identity. Dual identity compromises of some parts of identities research in Taiwan such as Rigger, 2006, Niou, 2004. Shen's works are the only research analyzing the dual identity. See Shen, 2005.

References

吳乃德. 1993. "國家認同和政黨支持:臺灣政黨競爭的社會基礎."『中央研究院民族學研究所集刊』74, 33-61.

鄭夙芬. 2009. "族群, 認同與總統選舉投票抉擇."『選舉研究』16(2), 23-49.

陳陸輝, 耿曙, 王德育. 2009. "兩岸關係與 2008年台灣總統大選: 認同, 利益, 威脅與選民投票取向."『選舉研究』16(2), 1-22.

陳陸輝. 2000. "臺灣選民政黨認同的特續與變遷."『選舉研究』7(2), 109-141.

彭懷恩. 2005.『臺灣政黨論』臺北: 米羅文化.

王甫昌. 1994. "族群同化與動員: 臺灣民衆政黨支持之分析."『中央研究院民族學研究所集刊』77, 1-34.

黃紀. "2008年總統選舉電訪." https://srda.sinica.edu.tw (2010. 12. 25)

Brass, Paul R. *Ethnicity and Nationalism: Theory and Comparison*. Newbury Park, CA: Sage, 1991.

Butler, David, and Donald Stokes. *Political Change in Britain*. New York: St. Martin's. Campbell, Angus, Philip E. Converse, Warren E. Miller, and Donald E. Stokes. 1976. *The American Voter*. Chicago: University of Chicago Press, 1969.

Chang, Hui-ching and Rich Holt. Taiwan and ROC: A Critical Analysis of President Chen Shui-bien's Construction of Taiwan Identity in National Speeches. *National Identities* 11(3), 2009.

Chi, Eunju. "Independence Issues and Party Realignment in Taiwan after Democratic Transition," *Korean Political Science Review* 43(1), 2009. [in Korean]

Chu, Yun-han. "Taiwan in 2007: The Waiting Game." *Asian Survey* 48(1), 2008.

-------. "Taiwan's National Identity Politics and The Prospect of Cross-Strait Relations." *Asian Survey* 44(4), 2004.

Corcuff, Stephane, ed. *Memories of the Future: National Identity Issues and the Search for a New Taiwan*. New York: M.E. Sharpe, 2002.

Downs, Anthony. *An Economic of Democracy*. New York: Harper & Row, 1957.

Farrell, D. M. "Campaign Strategies and Tactics." in Lawrence Le Duc, Richard G. Niemi, and Pippa Norris, eds. *Comparing Democracies: Elections and Voting in Global Perspective*. Thousand Oaks: Sage Publications, 1996.

Fell, Dafydd. "Inter-Party Competition in Taiwan: Toward a New Party System." in Goldstein, Steven M. and Julian Chang, eds. *Presidential Politics in Taiwan: the*

Administration of Chen Shui-bian. Norwalk: Eastbridge, 2008.

-------. "Measurement of Party Position and Party Competition in Taiwan." *Issues and Studies* 40(3/4), 2004.

-------. "Party Platform Change in Taiwan's 1990s Election." *Issues and Studies* 38(2), 2002.

Fiorina, Morris P. *Retrospective Voting in American National Elections*. Yale University Press, 1981.

Goldstein, Steven M. "Chen Shui-bian and the Political Transition in Taiwan." in Goldstein, Steven M. and Julian Chang eds. *Presidential Politics in Taiwan: the Administration of Chen Shui-bian*. Norwalk: Eastbridge, 2008.

Hsieh, John Fuh-sheng, Dean Lacy and Emerson M.S. Niou. "Retrospective and Prospective Voting in a One-Party-Dominant Democracy: Taiwan's 1996 Presidential Election." *Public Choice* 97(3), 1998.

Kang, Qwi Young. "Research and Analysis into Taiwan's Political Leadership and National Identity." Ph.D. dissertation to Department of Chinese Studies, GSIS, Hanyang University, 2010. [in Korean]

Kastner, Scott L. *Political Conflict and Economic Interdependence Across the Taiwan Strait and Beyond*. Stanford: Stanford University Press, 2009.

Key, V. O. *Responsible Electorate: Rationality in Presidential Voting, 1936-1960*. Cambridge: Belknap Press, 1966.

Kiewit, D. Roderick, and Donald R. Kinder. "Sociotropic Politics." *British Journal of Political Science* 11, 1981.

Kim, Bum Suk. "Taiwan's Democratization and the Changes of the Cross-Strait Relations: Applying Democratic Peace Theory," *Korea Journal of International Relations* 45(2), 2005. [in Korean]

Lee, Hyeon-Woo. "Re-examination of Private Economic Voting in the United States." *Korean Political Science Review* 33(2), 1999. [in Korean]

Lin, Chia-lung. *Paths to Democracy: Taiwan in Comparative Perspective*. Ph. D Dissertation of Yale University. Department of Political Science, 1999.

-------. "The Political Formation of Taiwanese Nationalism." in Stephane Corcuff, ed. *Memories of the Future*, Armonk: M.E. Sharpe, 2002.

Lin, Tse-min, Yun-han Chu and Melvin J. Hinich. "Conflict, Displacement, and Regime Transition in Taiwan: A Spatial Analysis." *World Politics* 48(4), 1996.

Moon, Heung-ho. "KMT's Return to Power and the Prospects of Policy Variation in Taiwan." *New Asia* 15(2), 2008. [in Korean]

Naughton, Barry. "Economic Policy Reform in the PRC and Taiwan." in Barry Naughton, ed., *The China Circle: Economic and Electronics in the PRC, Taiwan, and Hong Kong*. Washington, DC: Brookings Institution Press, 1997.

Niemi, Richard G. and Herbert F. Weisberg, eds. *Classics in Voting Behavior*. Washington D. C.: Congressional Quarterly Press, 1993.

Niou, Emerson M.S. "Understanding Taiwan Independence and Its Policy Implications." *Asian Survey* 44(4), 2004.

Park, Byoung Seok. "Taiwan's De-sinicization Movement Viewed from the Perspective of Post-colonialism." *Political Thought of East Asia*. 9(1), 2010. [in Korean]

Rawnsley, Gary. "Sean Connery Has Left the Building?: Thoughts on the 2004 Presidential Election in Taiwan." Paper presented at Korea University, East Asian New Governance Education Team, 2004.

Rigger, Shelly. *Taiwan's Rising Rationalism: Generations, Politics, and "Taiwanese Nationalism.*" Washington, D.C: East-West Center Washington, 2006.

Riker, William H. and Peter C. Ordeshook. "A Theory of the Calculus of Voting." *American Political Science Review* 62, 1968.

Romberg, D. Alan. "Election 2008 and the Future of Cross-Strait Relations." *China Leadership Monitor* 21. http://media.hoover.org/sites/default/files/documents/CLM21AR.pdf, 2007.

Schuessler, Alexander A. "Expressive Voting." *Rationality and Society* 12, 2000.

Shen, Shiau-chi. "Explaining Dual Identity in Taiwan: A Two-Dimensional Perspective on National Identity." APSA Annual Meeting. Washington, D.C. U.S.A. September 2005.

Tsai, George, Woei and Peter Yu Kien-hong. *Taiwanization: Its Origin and Politics*. EAI Contemporary China Series, 31, 2001.

TVBS 民意調查中心. 2011. 總統大選與統獨國族認同民調 http://www1.tvbs.com.tw/FILE_DB/PCH/201108/mcq69ajqc7.pdf (2011. 9. 7)

Wu, Yu-shan. "Moving toward the Center:Taiwan." www.taiwansecurity.org/TS-Wu.htm, 1999.

Taiwan's Response to China's Peaceful Reunification during the Lee Teng-hui Administration, 1988-2000

Chi-Hsiung Chang
(Research Fellow, Institute of Modern History, Academia Sinica)

I. Introduction

The Republic of China (ROC) ruled China before the People's Republic of China (PRC) did. This shift from ROC to PRC fits into the big picture of Chinese history - an ongoing replacement of one dynasty by another. A fundamental principle driving this succession of dynasties is a concept that the "Great Empire of the Chinese World" (中華世界帝國) can be ruled by any ethnic group that is a member of the Empire. This constant change of dynasties invigorates China or the Great Empire of the Chinese World, and it is a key feature of the Twenty-Five Histories of China.

When looking at this succession of dynasties from the perspective of a fight for the throne, we can find that the ROC overthrew the Qing Dynasty and became the legitimate ruler of China. But before too long, it was defeated by the PRC in the Chinese Civil War, lost the mainland, and retreated to Taiwan. A major similarity between the two governments across the Strait is that the ROC had once ruled Mainland China while the PRC, its successor, is the one that is currently ruling the mainland. Another similarity between the two is that they both once established their central government in Nanjing first, followed by Beijing. In other words, both of these two "dynasties" are not only founded on the historical and cultural values that they share, but they are also prompted by the theory of a Chinese world order as well as the great unification theory to quest for the throne and the unification of China.

Historically speaking, the Wuchang Uprising in the third year of the Xuantong Emperor (1911) brought down the Qing Dynasty, and after this revolution, the ROC replaced Qing and formed the government of China. This transition is what is commonly referred to as dynastic succession. In Year 38 of the ROC (1949), the Chinese Civil War brought China a new fate: the ROC government, losing the war, retreated from China, fled to Taiwan, seeking opportunities to launch counterattacks against the mainland. The Communist Party, the winner of the Civil War, established the central government in Beijing and formed the PRC. Unfortunately, neither the PRC government in Beijing was capable of liberating Taiwan, nor was the ROC government in Taipei ready to recover

China. This situation has created a stand-off across the Taiwan Strait, resulting not only in two governments ruling China separately, but also opening an era of incomplete government succession due to incomplete dynastic transition. This split territory governed by two different governments can be represented by the following formula: China = ROC+PRC, whereas the reunification trend for the future can be represented by ROC+PRC = China. The former suggests a split from great unification, whereas the latter suggests the opposite direction: moving from separation toward grand unification.

From a perspective of historical and cultural values as well the so-called "one country, two governments," which is the political reality of cross-Strait relations, both governments concurrently declare that there is only one China and they are the only legitimate and true China. Under the one China principle, Beijing proposes the concept of peaceful reunification, which promotes the historical and cultural values of national unification and is basically rooted on the "great unification theory." (大一統論) According to the "orthodox theory," (正統論) both governments must claim themselves to be the only legitimate government and that their own party is the true and orthodox administrator of China. This matter affects the international participation of the two governments; Simply speaking, it is about practicing the "status-and-order theory" (名分秩序論) as well as the"five cardinal relationships in international relations theory" (五倫國際關係論) in determining the hierarchical order according to ethics, i.e. principal vs. subordinate or superiority vs. inferiority. Another derived issue is about the calendar systems used in dating archives and documents exchanged between the two governments. According to the "theory of calendar-based legitimacy," (奉正朔論) the calendar year printed on these documents for both parties across the Strait, actually conceals a contest for central vs. local government, which is especially significant for the strategy of "one country, two systems." Last but not least, the "fight for the throne theory" (爭天下論) has been clearly demonstrated in Chinese history to be a critical factor for dynastic succession and national unification achieved either through peaceful means or by force. They are not only the historical and cultural values of the "theories of Chinese world order" (中華世界秩序原理) but also the theoretical framework for analyzing cross-Strait relations. How to transform this theoretical framework into an effective tool for analyzing cross-Strait relations is the central question of this paper.

Taken together, the cultural values of the movement starting from the great unification theory to the orthodox theory, followed by the theory of calendar-based legitimacy, the order-and-status theory, the five cardinal relationships in international relations theory, the fight for the throne theory, and then returning to the great unification theory, have generated not only a set of inference mechanisms with tightly intertwined theories but also a comprehensive theoretical framework that can be used for analyzing cross-Strait relations. The analytical and explanatory ability of this theoretical framework can be further expanded to analyze the split and unification of nations possessing Eastern historical and cultural values based on shared Confucian culture. Due to a limited number of words, theoretical discourses were eliminated in this paper. The focus of this paper is placed on the more practical aspects of cross-Strait relations according to the great unification theory. The author will first present the strategic deployment of Beijing's peaceful reunification, corresponding responses from Lee Teng-hui of Taiwan, and other relevant practices adopted by the two parties. Then the author will give an in-depth analysis and discussion on these topics. Therefore, the above is the major direction of this paper.

1. Peaceful reunification vs. unifying China with the Three Principles of the People

In October 1971, the PRC, replacing the ROC and becoming the only legitimate China, obtained the seat as well as the status as the permanent member in the United Nations. The ROC government, in contrast, was expelled from the United Nations. In September 1972, the PRC and Japan normalized diplomatic relations, and while these diplomatic ties between Japan and the PRC were established, those between Japan and the ROC were broken. In December 1978, the PRC and United States concurrently released the Joint Communiqué on the Establishment of Diplomatic Relations between the People's Republic of China and the United States of America, and the US government willingly accepted the three conditions for establishing diplomatic relations with China, which are to break diplomatic ties with the ROC, to withdraw troops and relevant facilities from Taiwan, and to abolish the Sino-American Mutual Defense Treaty. Later, on January 1, 1979, the PRC and United States official established diplomatic relations. Japan and the United States were once the two major nations diplomatically allied with the ROC, but not only did they turn to the PRC eventually in return for diplomatic relations, but they also cut off their official links with the ROC. This is the point when the international posotions of the PRC and the ROC began to reverse.

Taking advantage of such good timing, the PRC released its Message to Compatriots in Taiwan at the National People's Congress on January 1, 1979. It is the very first time that the PRC proposed peaceful reunification and peace talks between the two sides of the Strait. The PRC government also stressed that Mainland China was the only legitimate representation of China. On September 1981, Ye Jianying formally announced The General Policies and Measures Regarding to the Peaceful Reunification with Taiwan. He stressed that Taiwan can be set up as a special administrative region possessing a high level of autonomy and keeping its troops, and the central government will not intervene in local Taiwanese affairs.[1]

In January 1982, Deng Xiaoping announced the notion of one country, two systems for the first time. According to this policy, Mainland China will practice socialism, while Taiwan can practice capitalism under the premise of national reunification.[2]

In December 1979, the ruling Kuomintang (KMT) convened the fourth plenary session of its 11th Central Committee (第十一屆四中全會) and decided that "Reunifying China with the Three Principles of the People" would be the propaganda slogan in response to Mainland China's peaceful reunification overture. In March 1981, the scheme of the implementation of unifying China with the Three Principles of the People was formally passed in the twelfth National People's Congress convened by the KMT. The party also stated that unifying China with the Three Principles of the People was its goal.[3] That is how the contest between the two

1_Chinese Communist Party Literature Research Center. ed. "The principles and policies on Taiwan's return to the motherland and the realization of peaceful reunification." *Selective Important Literature on One-nation with Two-systems* Beijing: Xinhua Press. 1997. pp. 1-7.

2_Taiwan Affairs Office of State Council PRC. 1993. *The Taiwan issue and China's reunification*. Beijing: State Council Information Office. pp. 13-14.

sides of the Taiwan Strait to become the only legitimate government of China began.

2. Lee Teng-hui carrying on the policy of unifying China with the Three Principles of the People

Chiang Ching-kuo died in January 1988, and Lee Teng-hui succeeded him, becoming the president of Taiwan. Initially, Lee kept the policies from Chiang's era with little or no modification. In February 1988, Lee, as the chairperson of the KMT, which was the ruling party, as well as the president of the ROC, stated in his first press conference after becoming president that "There is only one China, and the two-China policy does not exist at all. Because there is only one China, we have to reunify China with the Three Principles of the Peoples."[4] Lee clearly claimed that he would continue the counteracting policy of Chiang, which is unifying China with the Three Principles of the People, and with this behavior Lee disappointed the PRC government.

3_Lee, FC. "The Three Principles for China's unification." *Encyclopedia of Taiwan*. (Viewed on January 28, 2012). http://taiwanpedia.culture.tw/web/fprint?ID=3904

4_"Lee Teng-hui." *Wikipedia*. (Viewed on January 28, 2012). http://zh.wikipedia.org/wiki/%E6%9D%8E%E7%99%BB%E8%BC%9D

3. Responses from Jiang Zemin

At the 40th anniversary of the funding of the PRC (September 1989), Jiang Zemin stated that the Taiwanese government is still insisting on its anti-communism standpoint and refusing peaceful reunification. He considered that the Three-Noes policy of Taiwan will hinder the development of friendly cross-Strait relations. He also pointed out that the so-called flexible diplomacy or any effort for creating two Chinas or one China, one Taiwan or prolonging this split encourages the independence of Taiwan. He said at the end that "Our hope for a unified motherland lies in the people of Taiwan as well as the government of Taiwan."[5]

In general, the great unification theory has to be founded upon the status-and-order theory, while for the status-and-order theory, it is important to consider the hierarchical order of the two parties, i.e. inferiority vs. superiority, in order to determine which one is the principal and which one is the subordinate (or the order of priority) before negotiations. Under the great unification theory, since the PRC adopted peaceful reunification as its propaganda slogan and was likely to have considered the fact that the ROC is

5_Jiang, ZM. "Peaceful reunification and one-nation with two systems are the principle policies for the goal of reunification." *Selective Important Literature on One-nation with Two-systems*. pp. 111-112.

more familiar with international laws and relations of the Western world (thus significantly influenced by Western concepts of leader status and national sovereignty), the PRC had no choice but to hold on to a relationship based on status and order of the status-and-order theory as well as the vertical-horizontal relations in order to attain its goal in cross-Strait negotiations.

4. The transition of Lee Teng-hui's thoughts on cross-Strait relations

Before the end of 1989, Lee Teng-hui announced the one-country, two-government strategy at the National Conference in an attempt to rebuild the relationship between the ROC and PRC. He mentioned that the ROC is willing to carry out cross-Strait dialogue with the PRC at a govern-to-government level, yet the dialogues have to be founded on the basis of one-China, government-to-government, and equal status between the two parties across the Strait. Lee also stated that the ROC is willing to negotiate, but this negotiation shall not be conducted by two political parties across the Strait, because national unification involves not only two political organizations but also the fact that the same nation is currently ruled by two governments. Furthermore, Lee raised four premises for normalizing cross-Strait relations, which are 1) the PRC must implement systems of political democracy and free economy, 2) the PRC shall abandon the use of military force on Taiwan, 3) the PRC should stop excluding Taipei from international communities, and 4) the PRC should promote cross-Strait exchanges based on the principle of one China and the two governments should have equal status.[6] In short, while Lee was willing to participate in official negotiations under the conditions that the negotiations are held at a government-to-government level, under the one China principle, and that both sides of the Strait have equal status, he refused the traditional faction-to-faction (party-to-party) type of cross-Strait communication.

In June 1989, Jiang Zemin was appointed General Secretary of the Chinese Communist Party and became Mainland China's new leader. In June 1990, he showed his approval for what Lee Teng-hui had recently mentioned, including "Taiwan and mainland China are inseparable territory," "All Chinese are compatriots share the same bloodline," "A united, strong, and prosperous China is a hope shared by all Chinese," "(The ROC is) willing to establish cross-Strait communication channels," and "(The ROC is) willing to discuss matters related to national reunification." Yet Jiang also criticized some "highly inappropriate" words of Lee

---

6_"Monograph: Review of the attitude on cross-Strait exchange and communication." *China Review News*. (Viewed on February 3, 2012). http://www.chinareviewnews.com/doc/1017/4/4/2/101744253_2.html?coluid=137&kindid=4930&docid=101744253&mdate=0627003740

Teng-hui, even though they were still better than the Three-Noes policy (no contact, no compromise and no negotiation). For Jiang, aside from continuing Deng Xiaoping's one-country, two-systems policy in order to realize the idea of cross-Strait reunification, he also pointed out that according to international law, a nation can only be represented by one legitimate government; it is impossible to have two governments of equal-status represent the same nation. According to Jiang, the term "one-country, two-governments" implies nothing but two-Chinas or one-China, one-Taiwan, which means separation instead of reunification. Jiang reaffirmed that there is space for negotiating and communicating China's reunification as long as the two parties truly follow the one-China principle rather than producing anything like two-Chinas, or one-China, one-Taiwan, or one-country, two-governments. Furthermore, Jiang stated that prior to formal negotiations, three links across the two sides of the Strait should be implemented as soon as possible to broaden bi-directional exchanges across the Strait. As for those more explicit issues regarding cross-Strait exchanges, they can be resolved via appropriate negotiation channels. Lastly, Jiang expected Mr. Lee to be realistic, to make the country as well as the great Chinese ethnicity his priority, to respect the people, to be responsible for history, and make contribution to the reunification of the motherland as well as the revival of the Chinese people.[7]

It can be seen here that the PRC is absolutely against the notion of one-country, two-governments, and its attitude toward the ROC is as the central to the local: The central government is the only one that is legitimate, or otherwise the nation is split in two. Yet in this case, the PRC did permit the policy of one-country, two-factions and treated both factions as equals; after all, political factions are not the equivalent of governments. Therefore, the term "equal status of both sides" means that the Communist Party of China and the KMT are equal in status, but this equal status is not applicable between the PRC and the ROC. Again, it is because admitting two central governments as equals suggests a split nation, namely two Chinas. This kind of thought that there will be only one central government after the peaceful reunification and that the central government will be in Beijing is refused by the ROC government in Taipei. From the perspective of the PRC, insisting on the one China principle can realize the great reunification of China, and the policy of one-country, two-systems is an effective strategy for achieving the great unification goal of China.

7_Jiang, ZM. "One-nation with two-system is the best approach for realizing the reunification of China." *Selective Important Literature on One-nation with Two-systems*. pp. 160-162. Jiang, ZM. "Working on developing the most extensive patriotic reunification front." People. (Viewed on February 3, 2012). http://www.people.com.cn/BIG5/shizheng/8198/37736/37760/2788853.html

As a result, the PRC failed to fully grasp the idea of what Lee had proposed at the end of 1989, namely to hold official negotiations under a government-to-government level under equal status conditions. That is, the negotiation that Lee expected is not simply a faction-to-faction negotiation.

5. Systemized cross-Strait exchanges

In 1990, Lee Teng-hui was elected the President of the ROC at the National Assembly. Afterward, Lee instituted the National Unification Council, the Mainland Affairs Council, and the Straits Exchange Foundation to cope with Beijing's peaceful reunification strategies. Although interactions across the Strait had become more and more frequent, the relations between the two sides remained undefined. Accordingly, Lee expressed in October 1990 that there is only one China, and it should be unified using the Three Principles of the Peoples. It is every Chinese citizen's responsibility to unify China with the Three Principles of the Peoples, and every Chinese citizen should make efforts to realize that goal.[8]

It is clear that at this stage, Lee was still following what was left

8_"Li, Deng-hui." *Wikipedia*. (Viewed on January 28, 2012). http://zh.wikipedia.org/wiki/%E6%9D%8E%E7%99%BB%E8%BC%9D

to him by Chiang: using the policy of unifying China with the Three Principles of the People to respond to Beijing's peaceful reunification.

6. The Guidelines for National Unification foreshadow a ROC-PRC split

To cope with a volatile cross-Strait situation, Guidelines for National Unification were passed in the third convention of the National Unification Council under Lee's instructions in February 1991. In April 1991, Lee announced the official end of the period of "communist rebellion" and terminated the Temporary Provisions Effective during the Period of Communist Rebellion. From then, Chinese communists are no longer regarded as rebels, and the government of the ROC acknowledges the fact that it is the PRC that governs China, while the territory governed by the ROC is limited to Taiwan, Penghu, Kinmen, and Matsu. This one-sided recognition of the PRC by the ROC during Lee's era means that at least the latter is no longer fighting with the PRC internationally for the status of the true China. From then on, there was only one China, which is the PRC. It is the time when the international communiy started to recognize that there was only one China, which is the PRC, and Taiwan (or the ROC) is not China. This new cross-Strait condition foreshadowed a possibility that the two sides of the Strait could be two distinct countries.

The willingness of Taiwan to fight for legitimacy or priority through historical and cultural values indicates that it still identifies itself with China and is oriented toward this direction. Yet when it fights no more, it is a sign that it has lost interest and is walking away from China.

7. 1992 Consensus: One-China vs. one-China, with respective interpretations

In 1992, the frequent private cross-Strait exchanges increased the need for document certification and a joint fight against crime. Consequently, the Strait Exchange Foundation (SEF) delegated some representatives to Beijing to hold the first negotiation with the Association for Relations across the Taiwan Straits (ARATS) in March. After frequent communication via letters and telegrams, these two organizations finally arranged a meeting in Hong Kong on October 28, 1992 to make an agreement on cross-Strait document certification. Mainland China raised the issue that the one China principle has to be the premise for cross-Strait negotiations and requested relevant phrases to be recorded in the agreement. For Taiwan, even though it disapproved of this proposal, it also understood that the only way to resolve this deadlock is to deal with the one-China principle. As a result, the National Unification Council was consulted to define the term "one-China" prior to the negotiation, so there would be a definition that could be used by the ROC as a basis.[9]

From October 28 to 30, SEF and ARATS held a work-related negotiation on the application of cross-Strait notarial certification (document verification). Once again, ARATS stressed that the negotiation should be based on the one-China principle, and for business-type negotiations, political connotations of one-China can be put aside, as long as both parties insist on the principle. The SEF, in turn, suggested that under the premise of mutual understanding, the two parties can verbally declare the one-China principle. On October 30, the SEF further presented its verbal declaration in an attachment, stating that during the process where both sides of the Taiwan Strait are jointly pursuing national reunification, both sides shall insist on the one-China principle, even though their definition for one-China is different. At the end of the convention, the SEF formally notified ARATS on November 3 that it had acquired approval from relevant parties to verbally deliver the one-China policy. ARATS, in turn, stated that it fully respects and accepts the SEF 's suggestion. Meanwhile, ARATS also mentioned that it would notify the SEF via correspondence on key

---

9_The National Security Group of National Policy Foundation. 2001. "What is the 1992 Consensus?" *National Policy Analysis*. September 6, (Viewed on February 4, 2012). http://old.npf.org.tw/PUBLICATION/NS/090/NS-B-090-001.htm

points to be delivered by ARATS, which is that the two sides across the Strait should insist on the one-China principle and work on national reunification, yet defining the term "one-China" is unnecessary for business-type cross-Strait negotiations.[10] Taken together, ARATS only proposed the one-China principle, while the SEF proposed one-China, with respective interpretations. In 2000, Su Chi repackaged the idea of one-China, with respective interpretations, into what is referred to as the 1992 Consensus, to blur the perception gap on one-China between the two sides of the Taiwan Strait.

According to correspondence between the two parties during the negotiation process, the 1992 Consensus is indeed a contest between the one-China policy and the policy of one-China, with respective interpretations. Mathematically speaking, the greatest common factor between the two parties is one-China. It is true that what made Beijing interested in interacting with Taipei was the one-China principle of the 1992 Consensus, and yet it is the proposition of "respective interpretations" that made Taipei willing to come to play. "One-china" and "respective interpretations" can be regarded as the foundation for practical negotiations between

---

10_Su, C. and Cheng, AK. ed. "Letters from ARATS to SEF." *History and facts of the consensus on one-China, with respective interpretation.* Taipei: National Policy Foundation. 2002. pp. 43-46.

Taipei and Beijing. According to the orthodox theory, the notion of one-China, with respective interpretations, for Beijing, even though it does not fully match, but it is in the long-term goal of Beijing's reunification, i.e. peaceful reunification with one-country, two-systems. Nevertheless, to avoid generating more problems, such as two Chinas, one China and one Taiwan, or the independence of Taiwan, Beijing chose this creative but fuzzy strategy. Although Beijing insistently denied that the two parties across the Taiwan Strait are allowed to have separate interpretations, its attitude is low-key, demur, or even friendly. Therefore, finally, the two parties established a channel for practical negotiations and found a focal point for exchanges.

Considering the perception gap on the 1992 Consensus across the Taiwan Strait, the government of the ROC specifically clarified its stance by having the National Unification Council define one-China in "Regarding the Definition of One-China" in August 1992. First of all, it stated that both parties have insisted on the one-China principle, but their definitions for the principle are somewhat different. Mainland China, when it considers one-China, means the PRC, and after unification, Taiwan will become a special administrative region governed by the PRC. Taiwan, on the other had, considers one China to mean the ROC, which was founded in 1912. As for the ROC's sovereignty, though currently its effectively control region covers only Taiwan,

Penghu, Kinmen, and Matsu, it should comprise the whole of China. It is true that Taiwan is a part of China, but so is Mainland China.[11] As for the concept of one-China, regardless of the perception gap across the Strait, both parties agreed to build a base for practical negotiations under the one-China principle.

What is noteworthy is that the viewpoint on sovereignty and the right to govern differs between the two parties. Mainland China claims that one China is the PRC, while Taiwan is only a special region under the PRC's governance. In contrast, Taiwan considers that the ROC's sovereignty covers China while the right to govern comprises Taiwan, Penghu, Kinmen, and Matsu only. Briefly, both sides of the Taiwan Strait consider that though the right to govern is limited to the land they rule respectively, sovereignty covers the territory governed by the other party as well. As a result, in Taiwan, there is a proposition of one country with two regions of the ROC.

With the one-China principle, ARATS expressed their wish for holding a Wang-Koo summit as soon as possible in correspondence on November 16, 1992. ARATS also recommended that

11_Su, C. and Cheng, AK. ed. 2002. p. 32. "Recognizing the concept of one country with two-body, hoping the government of mainland China to compromise; The definition of one-China formulated by the National Unification Council." *United Daily News*, August 2, 1992, First edition.

both parties prepare for negotiations in early December, so that the meeting could be held at the end of December.[12] After numerous preparatory negotiations, both parties determined that the formal negotiations should be private, business-oriented, economy-oriented, and functional. Mediated by Lee Kuan Yew, the Senior Minister of Singapore, SEF and ARATS held the first Koo-Wang summit in Singapore on April 27, 1993, and on April 29, four business-related agreements were signed. This cross-Strait government-authorized negotiation system finally delivered the intended purposes. The long lasting tension between the ROC and PRC began to relax, and the door to practical negotiations via the third party (or the so-called "white-gloves" in Chinese) was at last opened for both sides of the Strait.

8. Viewing governmental document exchanges based on the calendar-based legitimacy theory

When analyzing the two official letters from ARATS to SEF based on the calendar-based legitimacy theory, the dates inscribed

12_Su, C. and Cheng, AK. ed. 2002. pp. 48-49. "Recognizing the concept of one country with two-bodies, hoping the government of Mainland China to compromise; The definition of one-China formulated by the National Unification Council." *United Daily News*. August 2, 1992, p. 1.

on both letters are "November 16, 1992" and "November 30, 1992," whereas the date inscribed on the letter from SEF to ARATS is "December 3" without the year that the letter was sent. According to the calendar-based legitimacy theory, it is a convention to use the calendar year to indicate the head of the nation (用其曆卽歸其統屬). It is therefore understandable that in order to preserve its national dignity, the way for the ROC to escape from treating Beijing as the legitimate government is to eliminate the calendar year, even though the ROC had definitely got the message hidden behind ARATS' inscription.

In fact, if the SEF had used the year of the ROC on the letter, Mainland China would certainly reject the letter, because the calendar-based legitimacy theory is a cultural value of China that the Mainland government is familiar with, too. The PRC's intentional manipulation of the calendar-based legitimacy theory is significant. Since the SEF, which regards itself as part of the true China, already knew that the PRC adopts the western calendar, it had definitely already thought about the possibility that Mainland China would take advantage of this calendar-based legitimacy theory to proclaim its legitimacy. As a result, the SEF purposively put only the month and date without the year on the official letter to save itself from the trap of the calendar-based legitimacy theory.

In December 1992, the KMT passed the one China policy in which it defined and explained the term one-China.[13] In the first article, it is stated that the ROC is the only true and legitimate China and rejected the idea of one country, two systems. The second article stressed the fact that there is a gap between the two sides of the Taiwan Strait and there are insufficient conditions for reunification. In this case, Taiwan should be prioritized in terms of national existence and development (台灣優先) and the two sides of the Taiwan Strait should be treated as equal. At this stage, it can be found that Lee Teng-hui had planned a split from Mainland China and its one-China policy. The third article stressed that for national security, the KMT definitely prohibits the independence of Taiwan or the one-China, one-Taiwan proposition. The fourth article is about the ROC claiming itself as the orthodoxy of Chinese culture and is against communism. Within the same article, it also mentions that Taiwan will participate in international affairs as a sovereign country. According to the KMT's one-China policy, though KMT still stressed that ROC is the true China, its passion to be the true China was nevertheless fading.

9. Moving toward a sovereign and independent cross-Strait relationship

Considering the wide gap between the systems of the two

13_Su, C. and Cheng, AK. ed. 2002. pp. 50-51.

sides of the Taiwan Strait, as well as different perspectives and living standards, Lee Teng-hui began using the term "new Taiwanese" to stresses the subjectivity of Taiwan and to promote Taiwanese localization. While visiting his alma mater, Cornell University, in the United States, Lee mentioned the ROC and the idea of sovereignty of the people frequently in his speech "Always in My Heart." This shift away from the one-China principle made China furious and wrecked cross-Strait relations. Meanwhile, Mainland China's Taiwan policy also shifted from active promotion of reunification toward a passive anti-independence.

In 1996, Lee was presidential candidate in the ROC's ninth democratic presidential election. Beijing at this point purposively held military exercises at the Taiwan Strait, using missile testing to threaten Taiwan. To protect the common interests of Taiwan and the United States, the US government sent two aircraft carriers to defend the Taiwan Strait. In this Taiwan Strait crisis, the KMT in full force advertised the importance of securing the core of the leadership, which helped Lee win the presidential election with more than half of the votes. After the election, Lee used the "no haste and be patient" strategy to restrict cross-Strait policies while promoting interactions with South-east Asia as an alternative. Lee also worked on constitutional amendment, congressional reform, incorporation of referenda into the constitution, and the abolition of the National Assembly. His plan was to comprehensively reelect the congressmen and to switch the presidential election from an indirect election by the National Assembly to a direct election by the citizens (in a referendum).

Regarding Lee's movement toward de facto independence of Taiwan, Qiao Shi, chairperson of the mainland's National People's Congress, indicated that reunification cannot be achieved in one shot because, after all, the two sides of the Taiwan Strait have been separated for nearly 50 years. It takes time, and the PRC will be patient enough. Qiao also pointed out that what is important is that both parties have to move toward reunification. He stated that the PRC will be dedicated militarily to anti-secession and anti-Taiwanese independence, to demonstrate to the world, as well as those on the island promoting secession and independence, that the PRC is more than determined and capable of protecting the sovereignty of the nation and forbids anyone to separate Taiwan from China. Qiao finally stated that "Our basic guideline for resolving this Taiwan problem is peaceful reunification with the one-country, two-systems policy. Taiwanese authority must stop creating any situation like two-Chinas or one-China and one-Taiwan in the international community because it not only violates the one-China principle but also corrupts the foundation for peaceful reunification.[14]

Beijing stressed again and again that Taiwan is part of China's territory and resolving the Taiwan problem is part of China's domestic affairs, so as a result, solving the Taiwan issue is nothing but a matter of domestic affairs for China. Yet at the same time, Qiao also recognized that this Taiwan issue affects United States' national interests and international deployment. Therefore, Qiao mentioned that the US government will strictly follow the three joint communiques, instead of using Taiwan issue to hinder healthy development of the relations between China and the United Srares, which will be good for China as well as the fundamental interests of the United States. Qiao stated that "It is true that the US government has repeatedly expressed that it will work in accordance with the one-China policy and will not support Taiwan in joining the United Nations or to be independent. We hope that the US government can keep on with this attitude as always." [15]

10. National identity of the two-state theory

On July 1, 1997, the sovereignty of Hong Kong was returned to the PRC, while the PRC's propaganda of peaceful reunification

---

14_Qiao, S. 1997. "The basic guidelines for resolving the Taiwan problem are peaceful reunification and one-nation with two-system." *Selective Important Literature on One-nation with Two-systems*. pp. 294-295.

15_Ibid.

and one-country, two-systems created much pressure on Taiwan. At this stage, US cross-Strait experts kept pushing for an interim agreement between the two sides of the Strait. Consequently, Lee instructed the institution of Strengthening ROC's Sovereignty and Identity Team to develop corresponding strategies. In May 1999, the team redefined cross-Strait relations using the concept of "special state-to-state relations."

To gradually promote the identity of Taiwan as a sovereign country, Lee, when interviewed by Deutsche Welle (July 9, 1999), interpreted cross-Strait relations. He pointed out that "after several constitutional amendments since 1991, the ROC has redefined its territory to include Taiwan, Penghu, Kinmen, and Matsu only, had a president, vice president, as well as congressmen, elected by citizens in this territory, and recognized the legitimacy of the PRC. Consequently, relations between Taiwan and China have already become state-to-state or at least a special type of state-to-state relations, instead of domestic relations under the one-China policy, such as a legitimate government vs. a rebel government, or a central government vs. a local government." Further, regarding the choice between announcing the independence of Taiwan and one-country, two systems, Li stated that "Since its founding in 1912, the ROC has always been a sovereign and independent country. After the amendment of the constitution in 1991, relations across the Strait have been defined as special state-to-state relations. Therefore, there is no need to reclaim the independence of Taiwan." [16] This is the so-called two-state theory, a policy of the later era of Lee Teng-hui that identifies Taiwan as a sovereign nation, thereby altering the one-China relation between the mainland and island. This interview not only shocked the two sides of the Strait but also disturb the international community.

11. China's fierce reaction to the transition from Taiwan's rejection of unification as the ROC to making Taiwan a sovereign nation

Furious about Lee showing a stronger and stronger inclination toward Taiwanese independence, Mainland China found its patience had run out, and used military intimidation against Taiwan. Between June and July of 1995, mainland China conducted its first missile test while Lee was visiting Cornell University. Prior to Taiwan's first democratic presidential election, mainland China conducted a second missile test in March 1996. For the US, these provocative measures were against democracy, and therefore, they sent two aircraft carriers to the open sea near Taiwan. In July 1999, after Lee announced his two-state theory, Mainland China not only carried out military exercises directed toward Taiwan, but

---

16_"Special Two-state Theory." *Wikipedia*. (Viewed on February 5, 2012). http://zh.wikipedia.org/wiki/%E7%89%B9%E6%AE%8A%E5%85%A9%E5%9C%8B%E8%AB%96

also broke the rules by having its fighter planes entering the Taiwan Strait and crossing the midline. This is known as the Third Taiwan Strait Crisis.[17]

Lee Teng-hui definition of cross-Strait relations as special state-to-state relations elicited not only military intimidation from the PRC government in Beijing, but also criticism from the Taiwan Affairs Office of the Central Committee of the Communist Party of China and the Taiwan Affairs Office of the State Council of the PRC. They stated that "his openly twisting cross-Strait relations into state-to-state relations has revealed a constant intention and a political nature of splitting the territory as well as the sovereignty of China." Once recognizing that Lee had shifted from Taiwan's rejection of unification as the ROC, to maintain the status quo of Taiwan (獨台), to making Taiwan a sovereign nation (台獨),[18] Tang Shubei, the executive vice president of ARATS, attacked Lee by saying that the two-state theory had wrecked the foundation for Koo-Wang summits and prevented Wang Daohan's visit to Taiwan from taking place. Tang restated that the PRC will not give up the possibility of using military force on Taiwan.[19] Eventually, Jiang

17_Su, C. (2011). "The key is no unification, no independence, and no military force." *United Daily News*. December 27, 2011, p. A17

18_"Special Two-state Theory." *Wikipedia*. (Viewed on February 5, 2012). http://zh.wikipedia.org/wiki/%E7%89%B9%E6%AE%8A%E5%85%A9%E5%9C%8B%E8%AB%96

19_"Tang Shubei criticized the Two-state Theory in US." *United Daily News*. September

Zemin cancelled the plan for Wang Daohan, the president of ARATS, to visit Taiwan. Jiang further suspended the dialogues between SEF and ARATS as well as ARATS officials' visiting Taiwan prior to the presidential election of Taiwan in March 2000.[20] Cross-Strait relation were seriously cast into shadow.

In March 2000, ROC held another presidential election (held every four years). In this election, Chen Shui-bian, a presidential candidate of the pro-independence Democratic Progressive Party (DPP), won the election and became the tenth president of the ROC. Chen not only continued Lee's Taiwan independence stance but also elaborated it further by proposing the one side, one country theory for Taiwan and China on August 2, 2001. Chen stressed that Taiwan is a political entity generated from democratic elections by its citizens, and, therefore, it is a sovereign and independent country.[21] This action of Chen destroyed all of Beijing's efforts since the release of the Message to the Compatriots in Taiwan on January 1, 1979. In response to that, the PRC drew up the Anti-Secession Law on March 14, 2005, which stipulates that to defend the integrity of the country's sovereignty

21, 1999. (Viewed on February 5, 2012). http://issue.udn.com/FOCUSNEWS/TWOSTATES/Official_Statement/C_official_statement/09_21_030.htm

20_Ibid.

21_"One Side One Country Theory." *Wikipedia*. (Viewed on February 6, 2012). http://zh.wikipedia.org/wiki/%E4%B8%80%E9%82%8A%E4%B8%80%E5%9C%8B

and territory, any future Independence Day of Taiwan would be the Reunification Day of China through military force. The objective of the law is to establish a legal basis for the PRC to confront the issue of Taiwanese independence, to halt the same, and to promote peaceful reunification.[22] For the great national unification, Mainland China has no choice but to opt for reunification through military force.

II. Conclusion

In the contest between the ROC and PRC for the throne, the loser, the ROC, retreated to Taiwan, while the winner, the PRC, obtained the mainland and started developing its military force. The two parties across the Taiwan Strait, although they differ in size significantly, each rule their territory respectively. After 1949's cross-Strait hostilities, there was a period of time when Mainland China deliberately and forcefully broadcast propaganda about liberating Taiwan, while Taiwan, in turn, was waiting to make its comeback. Both parties at this point shared a common goal: termi-

22_"Anti-secession Law." 2005. *Xinhua Net.* (Viewed on February 6, 2012). http://big5.xinhuanet.com/gate/big5/news.xinhuanet.com/tai_gang_ao/2005-03/14/content_2694168.htm

nating the opposite party to unite China.

Since the bombing stopped in 1979, the attitude of Mainland China has begun to switch from reunification through force to peaceful reunification. Later, it adopted the one-country, two-systems policy in an attempt to attract Taiwan to accept the Hong Kong and Macao model, namely becoming a highly autonomous administrative region. Practically, the PRC opened the three cross-Strait channels (post, trading, and transportation), using them as a focal point for cross-Strait exchanges. Taiwan, on the other hand, adopted the Three-Noes policies, i.e. no contact, no compromise and no negotiation, in response to China's strategies. Later on, Taiwan also called for unifying China with the Three Principles of the People. Soon after, Chiang abolished martial law and allowed the Taiwanese to visit their relatives in Mainland China. The two parties across the Strait drew closer and their interaction became less restricted. In 1991, the abolishment of the Temporary Provisions Effective during the Period of Communist Rebellion helped trading across the Strait to flourish. To resolve issues derived from cross-Strait exchanges, both sides of the Strait recognized a need for document certification. Therefore, in 1992, the two parties met in Hong Kong for negotiations, which generated the one-China principle and the 1992 Consensus of one-China, with respective interpretation, which became the foundation for cross-Strait exchanges. The end of this stage was marked by the Goo-Wang summit in 1993 at Singapore.

In 1995, Lee Teng-hui delivered a speech at Cornell University that irritated Mainland China. In 1996, the ROC held its first presidential election directly voted by the people. In 1999, Lee announced his two-state theory i.e., a special state-to-state relationship. Mainland China considered that his behavior had violated the one China principle and showed an inclination towards Taiwanese independence, and therefore it used missile testing to alert Lee, which worsened cross-Strait relations. In 2002, Chen Shui-bian proposed the one-side, one-country theory for relations between Taiwan and China, causing China to counteract with the Anti-secession Law. The tensions between the two parties across the Strait was heightened at that point, and lasted until Ma Ying-jeou, advocating no unification, no independence, no force but eventual reunification, was elected the president of Taiwan in 2008. Ma restored the 1992 Consensus and the one-China, with respective interpretation, policy and restarted cross-Strait exchanges. The two sides of the Taiwan Strait have gradually recovered their close interaction and returned to the peaceful reunification policy with a belief that the pen, after all, is mightier than the sword.

When we examine the circular inference mechanism of theories on cross-Strait relations and considering the fact that the two parties across the Strait rule separately, i.e., China = ROC+PRC, then if it is de facto and de jure (求實求名) that are pursued by either party, the dominant party will regard itself as the true one and treat the other party as the non-legitimate one (閏統), based on the principle that the great unification theory is the equivalent of the one China principle. Consequently, according to the calendar-based legitimacy theory, the non-legitimate, or local, government has to adopt the calendar and the name of years given by the true, or central, government in the exchanges of governmental correspondence. The minor party will rely on the policy of one-China, with respective interpretations, for its survival and prosperity and apply the de facto and de jure theory (名實論) to fortify itself and to try to reverse the condition. The dominant party, under the status-and-order theory, will incorporate the minor party into the international order directed by the dominant party according to the hierarchical system. The dominant party will also apply the cardinal guides (人倫綱常) and constant values of human relationships onto the Chinese world order to form five cardinal oriented international relations, such as central vs. local or superior vs. inferior. Then the dominant party will call for the one-country, two-systems policy (central vs. special administrative region) to achieve the goal of reunification and win the throne, either through peaceful means or by military force, and either overtly or covertly. At the end, everything will return to the great unification theory, either a peaceful reunification or reunification by force, and have the great reunification theory deliver its functions that are rendered by the traditional cultural values for completing the reunification mission, i.e. ROC+PRC=China. This is the circular inference system of the great unification theory for cross-Strait national unification.

References

Author unknown. "Anti-secession Law." *Xinhua Net.* (〈反分裂國家法〉, 《新華網》). 14 March, 2005.

-------. "Monograph: Review of the attitude on cross-Strait exchange and communication." *China Review News.* (〈專論: 兩岸交流溝通態度之評議〉, 《中國評論新聞》). 27 June, 2011.

-------. "Recognizing the concept of one country with two-body, hoping the government of mainland China to compromise; The definition of one-China formulated by the National Unification Council." *United Daily News.* (〈承認一國兩體分治概念深盼大陸當局捐棄成見　國統會確立「一個中國」涵義〉, 《聯合報》, August 2, 1992.

-------. "Tang Shubei criticized the Two-state Theory in US." *United Daily News.* (〈唐樹備在美抨擊兩國論〉, 《聯合報》) 21 September, 1999.

Chinese Communist Party Literature Research Center. ed., "The principles and policies on Taiwan's return to the motherland and the realization of peaceful reunification." *Selective Important Literature on One-nation with Two-systems.* Beijing: Xin-hua Press.(中共中央文獻研究室, 〈關於台灣回歸祖國實現和平統一的方針政策〉, 《一國兩制重要文獻選編》 北京: 新華書店). 1997.

Jiang, ZM. "One-nation with two-system is the best approach for realizing the reunification of China." *Selective Important Literature on One-nation with Two-systems.* (江澤民, 〈"一國兩制"是實現中國統一的最好辦法〉, 《一國兩制重要文獻選編》, 北京: 新華書店). 1997.

-------. "Peaceful reunification and one-nation with two systems are the principle policies for the goal of reunification." *Selective Important Literature on One-nation with Two-systems.* (江澤民, 〈"和平統一,一國兩制"是我們完成統一大業的基本政策〉, 《一國兩制重要文獻選編》, 北京: 新華書店). 1997.

-------. "Working on developing the most extensive patriotic reunification front." *People.* (江澤民, 〈努力發展最廣泛的愛國統一戰線〉, 《人民網》). No date.

Lee, FC. "The Three Principles for China's unification." *Encyclopedia of Taiwan.* (李福鐘, 〈三民主義統一中國〉, 《台灣大百科全書》). No date

National Security Group of National Policy Foundation. 2001. "What is 1992 Consensus." National Policy Analysis. (財團法人國家政策研究基金會國家安全組, 〈何謂「九二共識」〉, 《國政分析》). 6 September, 2001.

Qiao, S. "The basic guidelines for resolving the Taiwan problem are peaceful reunification and one-nation with two-system." Chinese Communist Party Literature Research Center. ed., *Selective Important Literature on One-nation with Two-systems.* (喬石, 〈解決台灣問題的基本方針是"和平統一,一國兩制"〉 (1996年 12月 28日), 《一國兩制重要文獻選編》 北京: 新華書店). 1997.

Su, C. 2011. "The key is no unification, no independence, and no military force." *United Daily News.* (蘇起,〈「不統,不獨,不武」才是關鍵〉,《聯合報》 27 December, 2011.

Su, C., and Cheng, AK. ed., "Letters from ARATS to SEF." *History and facts of the consensus on one-China, with respective interpretation.* National Policy Foundation, Taipei. (蘇起, 鄭安國編, 〈海峽兩岸關係協會函海峽交流基金會〉, 《「一個中國,各自表述」共識的史實》, 台北: 國家政策研究基金會), 2002.

Taiwan Affairs Office of State Council PRC. *The Taiwan issue and China's reunification.* Beijing: State Council Information Office. (中華人民共和國國務院台灣事務辦公室, 《台灣問題與中國的統一》, 北京: 國務院新聞辦公室), 1993.

Wikpedia. "Lee Teng-hui." (〈李登輝〉, 《維基百科,自由的百科全書》). No date.

-------. "One Side One Country Theory." (〈一邊一國〉, 《維基百科,自由的百科全書》). No date.

-------. "Special Two-state Theory." (〈特殊兩國論〉, 《維基百科,自由的百科全書》). No date.

Cross-Strait and Inter-Korean Relations from a Comparative Perspective

Edward I-hsin Chen
(Professor, Graduate Institute of the Americas at Tamkang University)

I. Introduction

The main purpose of this article is to explore cross-Strait and inter-Korean relations from a comparative perspective. After this introduction, the second part will analyze cross-Strait relations during the periods from 1982 to 1992, from 1992 to 2000, from 2000 to 2008, and from 2008 on. The third part will scrutinize inter-Korean relations during the periods 1988 to 1998, 1998 to 2003, 2003 to 2008, and from 2008 on. The fourth part will compare cross-Strait and inter-Korean relations on their nature and the substance, the US factor, and the prospect of national reunification. The fifth part will provide concluding remarks, demonstrating that comparison is fruitful and worthy. It is argued that the substance of cross-Strait relations seems more important than the formality of inter-Korean relations, whereas a bottom-up cross-Strait relationship seems more crucial than a top-down inter-Korean relationship. Therefore, cross-Strait relations are characterized by frequent and substantial people and business exchanges, whereas inter-Korean relations are by and large a rhetoric of national cooperation without face-to-face contacts among people and business circles on a daily basis.

II. Cross-Strait Relations

1. Cross-Strait Relations from 1982 to 1992

Taiwan was particularly afraid of cross-Strait negotiations under political pressure from the United States. When he was still alive, the late president Chiang Chin-kuo proposed the "Three-Noes policy" (namely no contact, no compromise and no negotiation), worrying that Taiwanese society would collapse once Taipei was forced to sit down with Beijing for negotiations.

It was in this context that then President Ronald Reagan decided to grant Taipei the so-called "six assurances" prior to his decision to conclude the Joint Communiqué of August 17, 1982 with Beijing. On July 14, weeks before the inking of the communiqué, the Reagan administration transferred the "six assurances" to the Chiang administration through an appropriate channel.[1]

Despite US promises not to play any mediation role across the Taiwan Strait, it was surprising that Taipei and Beijing themselves engaged in important negotiations when a Boeing 747 cargo jet from Taiwan's China Airlines (CAL) was hijacked by a Taiwanese pilot Wang Xijue and landed in Guangzhou (Canton), a large city in southern China, on May 3, 1986.[2] The political significance of the cross-Strait negotiations between the CAL and its counterpart, the state-run Civil Aviation Administration of China (CAAC), lied in a delicate manner that the handover problem of the CAL cargo plane and its crewmen was handled. Although it was the first time for both Taiwan and China to tackle such a hijacking incident,

---

1_In the "Six Assurances," the United States assure Taiwan that it (1) has not set a date for ending arms sales to Taiwan; (2) has not agreed to consult with China on arms sales to Taiwan; (3) will not play any mediation role between Taipei and Beijing; (4) has not agreed to revise the Taiwan Relations Act (TRA); (5) has not altered its position regarding sovereignty over Taiwan; and (6) will not exert pressure on Taiwan to enter into negotiations with China. See Harding, Harry. *A Fragile Relationship: U.S. and China Since 1972.* Washington, D.C.: The Brookings Institution, 1992, 389-390; and Romberg, Alan D. *Rein In at the Brink of the Precipice.* Washington, D.C.: The Henry L. Stimson Center, 2003, 134-35.

2_Chen, Edward I-hsin "Chinese Negotiating Styles: A Case Study of CAL-CAAC Talks," paper presented at the International Conference on Cross-Cultural Negotiations and Communication, sponsored by Soochow University at the Grand Hotel in Taipei on September 29-30, 1987.

both parties decided to deal with the problem through a process of negotiations with dedication, treating the negotiations as a sort of routinized business.

In such business-style negotiations, both sides of the Taiwan Strait benefited from a learning process of their first face-to-face contacts.[3] Beijing began to understand that Taipei could be more flexible than expected if necessary, and that some sort of sincerity could persuade Taipei to sit down for negotiations. On the other hand, Taipei had more confidence in adopting a policy of greater flexibility in dealing with Beijing after 1986. Taipei also learned that it might make some gains in the process of negotiations as long as it could make good use of its bargaining chips. Hence, there seemed to be less reason for being afraid of negotiating with China. Obviously, the somewhat pleasant experience of the process of cross-Strait negotiations between the CAL and the CAAC made Washington believe that there might be more and more cross-Strait negotiations as long as a favorable contextual environment could be created.

While this incident might have led Beijing to discount Taipei's Three-Noes policy, with some important political implications for the future, it might also have led Washington to think of the

3_Ibid.

unthinkable. Secretary of State George Shultz made a surprising remark when he paid a visit to China in 1987. On March 5, 1987, in a banquet toast in Shanghai, he pointed out: "We support a continuing evolutionary process toward a peaceful resolution of the Taiwan issue. The pace, however, will be determined by the Chinese on either side of the Taiwan Strait, free of outside pressure." He even added: "For our part, we have welcomed developments, including indirect trade and increasing human interchange, which have contributed to a relaxation of the tensions in the Taiwan Strait. Our steadfast policy seeks to foster an environment in which such developments can continue to take place."[4]

The political implication of his remarks was clear enough. While honoring its promise of not playing any mediating role between Taipei and Beijing, Washington would be willing to support a continuing evolutionary process toward a peaceful resolution of the Taiwan issue and even foster an environment in which cross-Strait exchanges could continue to take place in relaxed circumstances.

4_For full text of George Shultz's remarks, see *Department of State Bulletin*, May 1987, 11; Harding (1992) 159-61; and Romberg (2003) 148-49.

2. Cross-Strait Relations from 1992 to 2000

Cross-Strait negotiations were conducted between the Strait Exchanges Foundation (SEF) on behalf of Taiwan's Kuomintang government and the Association for Relations Across the Taiwan Strait (ARATS) on behalf of the Chinese Communist government during the period 1992 to 1998.[5] At that time, the SEF and ARATS undertook numerous cross-Strait talks on cracking down smuggling and piracy, verifying the notarization of official documents, tracing and compensating for lost registered post, and so forth. However, these talks always turned out to be a virtual standstill whenever the issue of how to express "the principle of one-China" was touched. Therefore, both ARATS and SEF had to make mutual concessions on the issue, so that the deadlock could be resolved.

It was in this context that, on May 20, 1992, when Tang Shubei, standing deputy chairman of ARATS, visited New York, he proposed that while all negotiations between ARATS and SEF should be conducted under One-China principle, there was no need to discuss in depth the meaning of "one-China" because do-

5_Chiu, Hungdah "The Koo-Wang Talks and the Prospects for Building Constructive and Stable Relations across the Taiwan Strait," in Gong, Gerrit W. and Bih-jaw Lin (eds.) *Sino-American Relations at a Time of Change*, Washington, D.C.: Center for Strategic and International Studies (CSIS), 1994, 6-12.

ing so would only lead to displeasure for both sides. In response to China's newly flexible position, Taipei's National Unification Council (NUC) adopted a resolution on the meaning of "one-China" at its August 1, 1992 meeting, indicating "that both sides of the Taiwan Strait have been adhering to the principle of one-China but that the positions of the two sides are somewhat different." According to the resolution, China contends that one-China means the People's Republic of China (PRC) founded in 1949, whereas Taiwan contends that it means the Republic of China (ROC) founded in 1912 and that its sovereignty covers all of China. Later on, through prolonged exchanges of ideas, both sides agreed in November 1992 that the different version of the one-China principle could be presented verbally but would not be included in the written agreement. This was the so-called "one China, with respective interpretation." [6] On August 4, 1992, Wang Daohan, then chairman of ARATS, sent a personal letter to Koo Chen-fu, then chairman of SEF, inviting Koo to meet him to discuss cross-Strait exchanges. Koo accepted the invitation and suggested that they meet in Singapore. After two preparatory meetings in March and April 1993, the first round of Koo-Wang talks was conducted in Singapore on April 27 and 28, 1993.[7] Given the

6_Romberg (2003) 105-117.

7_Chiu (1994) 13-14.

cross-Strait consensus of "one China, with respective interpretation," the first Koo-Wang summit was followed by a series of cross-Strait working-level negotiations, as well as the second round of Koo-Wang talks in Shanghai in 1998.

It is interesting to note that, during the period 1992 to 2000, the United States emitted signals to Taiwan in support of the improvement of cross-Strait relations. For example, President George H.W. Bush approved the provision of sophisticated weapon systems such as 150 F-16 jet fighters and 4 E-2T AWAC planes to Taiwan in September 1992. The goodwill of the first Bush administration helped Taiwan to strengthen its confidence in dealing with China, in turn contributing to the formation of a tacit agreement of "one China, with respective interpretation" in late December 1992. Under such a tacit agreement, both sides of the Taiwan Strait agreed with the concept of "one China," but "each could interpret China in their own terms." Actually, it was a gentleman's agreement based on mutual trust between Taipei and Beijing without being expressed directly or written clearly in black-and-white. Both sides of the Taiwan Strait understood the existence of such a tacit mutual agreement. The cross-Strait unwritten consensus of "one China, with respective interpretation" in turn contributed to the subsequent Koo-Wang talks in 1993.

President Bill Clinton further provided Taiwan with a diplomatic boost by making some adjustments in his policy toward

Taiwan, i.e. the so-called "Taiwan Policy Review" on September 7, 1994. The Clinton administration upgraded its substantial relations with Taiwan, ranging from refining the name of Taiwan's representative office, to allowing officials from Taipei to deal with their counterparts in the offices with the exception of the State Department, and to lending its assistance to Taiwan to let its voice be heard in international organizations. Moreover, Washington even agreed to grant better status to Taiwan's high-level leaders in their transit visits in the United States.[8]

The goodwill of the Clinton administration made former President Lee Teng-hui demand more from the United States - by paying a visit to Cornell University and delivering a speech there as an alumnus – so that he could make a diplomatic breakthrough to win the support of his compatriots and secure his nomination as presidential candidate for the ruling KMT. Nevertheless, Lee's successful visit to Cornell resulted in a series of repercussions for Taiwan. On the one hand, Chinese leader Jiang Zemin thought that he lost face because he did not pay a "state visit" to the United

8_According to Taiwan Policy Review, Taiwan's representative office in the United States has been allowed to change its name from the Coordination Council for North American Affairs (CCNAA) to the Taipei Economic and Cultural Representative Office (TECRO) since September 7, 1994. For full text of the Taiwan Policy Review, see 'Adjustment to U.S. Policy toward Taiwan Explained,' Transcript: Background Briefing at the State Department in Washington, D.C. on September 9, 1994, 1-17

States prior to Lee's "private visit." On the other, when Lee had mentioned "the Republic of China on Taiwan" seventeen times in his speech at Cornell, Chinese leaders thought that he was determined to separate Taiwan from China. As a result, China aimed criticism and military threats against Taiwan. And the People Liberation Army (PLA) started its missile drills targeting Taiwan.

In the wake of the 1996 Taiwan Strait crisis, President Clinton decided to take action to improve relations with China. He ordered National Security Adviser Anthony Lake to start the work of engaging the United States in a strategic dialogue with China in late 1996. In 1998, he further surprised Taiwan with two important announcements. He announced America's own "3 Noes" policy in Shanghai on June 30, 1998. His 3 Noes policy includes (1) not supporting Taiwanese Independence, (2) not supporting "One China, One Taiwan" or "Two Chinas," and (3) not supporting Taiwan's participation in the international organizations requiring statehood.[9] And then he declared that the United States and China were moving in the direction of a strategic partnership in 1998.

9_For full text of President Clinton's China policy declared in Shanghai on June 30, 1998, see White House Office of the Press Secretary, Remarks by the President and the First Lady in Discussion on Shaping China for the 21st Century, June 30, 1998, http://clinton6.nara.gov/1998/06/1998-06-30-remarks-by-president-and-first-lady-at-shanghai-library.html〉. For the evolution of the '3 Noes' Policy, see Romberg (2003) 180-85.

While the pro-Taiwan messages of the first-term Clinton administration encouraged Lee to pursue a bold policy toward China, the pro-China messages of the second-term Clinton administration only helped Lee to easily find a pretext for not proceeding with the third round of Koo-Wang talks that was scheduled in Taipei in October 1999. Anyway, Lee decided to sabotage the talks as the presidential election was approaching. On July 9, 1999, he proposed the so-called "Two States Theory" (special relationship between state and state) as a provocative gesture towards China. Cross-Strait relations were deadlocked.

3. Cross-Strait Relations from 2000 to 2008

When Chen Shui-bian was surprisingly elected the president of the ROC in 2000, the Democratic Progressive Party (DPP) became the ruling party. The newly elected President Chen was very cautious in taking positions on his mainland policy when he was in office for the first year. During a very short period from March 18 to 20, 2000, he was forced to swallow the so-called "5 Noes" according to the suggestions of the Clinton administration.

When he was inaugurated on May 20, 2000, he first made the pledge to promise (1) not to declare independence; (2) not to change the official title of the ROC; (3) not to put the "Two States Theory" into the Constitution; (4) not to hold a referendum to change the status quo across the Taiwan Strait; and (5) not to abolish the National Unification Council (NUC) and National Unification Guidelines.[10] He even tried at least once to go back to the era of Lee Teng-hui when he met with American visitors in the presidential hall on June 27, 2000. On that occasion, he proposed the resumption of NUC meetings and the cross-Strait dialogues under the tacit agreement of "one China, with respective interpretation," a formula seriously violating the DPP's traditional position. It was not until Ms. Tsai Ing-Wen, then chairperson of the Mainland Affairs Council (MAC), contradicted his goodwill and friendly gesture on the next day that he changed his mind. People would not be surprised at her political position if they understood her role in the process of proposing the Two States Theory. At that time, she was the chief in charge of writing the report of the "ROC Sovereignty Team" to conduct a secret mission of "de-Sinicization" under the leadership of former President Lee during the period 1998 to 2000.

Given the likely standstill across the Strait, Dr. Chi Su, former MAC Chairman in the KMT government, intended to develop a

10_The so-called '5 Noes,' a gentleman's agreement between the Clinton and Chen administrations, was reached between March 18, and May 20, 2000. For English text of Chen Shui-bian's inaugural speech, see "Taiwan Stands Up: Toward the Dawn of A Rising Era," May 20, 2000, http://www.taipei.org/chen0520.htm.

new formula that not only the Chinese Communist Party (CCP) and KMT could agree on, but also the ruling DPP. He was fully aware that the DPP leaders were hostile to the "one-China principle" and reluctant to mention the wording "one-China." In his opinion, the DPP government would be unlikely to send its representatives to sit down for negotiations with its Chinese counterparts under the KMT formula of "one China, with respective interpretation." However, a new formula that avoided mentioning the wording "one-China" would be acceptable to the DPP government without much difficulty. Therefore, he proposed a new formula, the "1992 Consensus" for the basis of the resumption of cross-Strait negotiations at an academic conference at Tamkang University on April 28, 2000. There are three implications in the "1992 Consensus." First, it could help remind China of its ambiguous gentleman's agreement to "one China, with respective interpretation." Second, it could help the DPP government to find it not that difficult to skip the wording of "one-China." Third, it could remind both sides of the Taiwan Strait of the good old days during the period from 1992 to 1995. In a word, such a consensus was designed to break the deadlocked cross-Strait negotiations, in particular for the new DPP government.

Indeed, President Chen once took the resumption of cross-Strait negotiations into consideration. At a meeting with American visitors in the presidential hall on June 27, 2000, he proposed that his administration would be willing to accept "one China, with respective interpretation" of the Kuomintang (KMT) era to resume the cross-Strait negotiations that deadlocked after 1998. Unfortunately, his MAC chairperson Tsai Ing-wen soon contradicted his goodwill and friendly gesture toward China on the next day.[11] She set a bad precedent for the future, in a sense, because it was the first time that an lower level official had gone back on what the national leader advocated in his policy statement.

After meeting with a retired American official, President Chen once decided to propose the "1992 spirit" as a basis for the resumption of the cross-Strait negotiations on July 31, 2000. Unfortunately, after he proposed the "1992 spirit" once again on the Double Tenth ceremony in 2000, it was no longer in use. In the year-end legislative election of 2001, Chen even labeled the 1992 Consensus an "act of surrender" or an "act of selling Taiwan." After a couple of months of observation, however, China decided to use the 1992 Consensus as a term that would be interchangeable with the "one-China principle" in late 2000.[12] Although the

---

11_Chi Su, *Weixian Bianyun (Brinkmanship: From Two-States-Theory to One Country on Each Side)*, (Taipei: Book Zone, 2004), 129.

12_Chi Su, former MAC Chairman in the KMT government, proposed the new formula of "1992 consensus" for the basis of the resumption of the cross-Strait negotiations at an international conference sponsored by Tamkang University on April 28, 2000,

"1992 Consensus" was a proposal that was supposed to be acceptable to the DPP, KMT, and the CCP, it was not well received by DPP leaders.

As a friendly gesture to extend an olive branch to his Chinese counterpart Hu Jintao, Chen Shui-bian suggested in a speech on October 10, 2004 that both sides of the Taiwan Strait could use the 1992 meeting in Hong Kong as a basis for the resumption of cross-Strait negotiations. It was the first time that Chen formally suggested that the 1992 Hong Kong meeting between Chinese and Taiwanese officials could form the basis for the two sides of the Taiwan Strait to return to the negotiation table.[13] He proposed that both sides use the basis to seek a possible formula that would be "not necessarily perfect but acceptable," as a step toward resuming the long-stalled negotiations.

In an about face, he said that the two sides should resume dialogue based on a 1992 informal understanding on the interpretation of Beijing's cherished "one-China" principle, raising the prospect of breaking a five-year deadlock on the horizon. In addition, he said that both sides of the Taiwan Strait should seriously

---

Weixian Bianyun, 130-133.

13_For English text of President Chen Shui-bian's Address to the National Day Rally, Presidential Office, October 10, 2004, see http://www.president.gov.tw/php-bin/prez/shownews.php4?_section=5&_rid=1784.

consider arms control and take concrete actions to reduce tensions and military threats across the Taiwan Strait. He announced: "We should review the armament policies of both sides and seek to establish a code of conduct across the Taiwan Strait as the tangible guarantee of permanent peace in the Taiwan Strait."[14]

In the face of Chen's changing position, Beijing could hardly place its trust in him due to his record of policy fluctuation. Chen once said that both sides of the Taiwan Strait could go back to the so-called 1992 Consensus in 2000 when he was elected president. Unfortunately, he soon retreated from that position as a result of strong opposition within his own camp. Now he proposed to use the "1992 Hong Kong meeting basis" or "1992 basis" for the resumption of cross-Strait negotiations. Certainly, his proposal was no longer acceptable to Chinese leaders. Substantial cross-Strait negotiations require not only a good atmosphere but also enduring goodwill and mutual trust on both sides. Given the cross-Strait tensions and the lack of mutual trust, all his appeals for a better environment for cross-Strait negotiations will fell on deaf ears. Due to the lack of mutual trust between the pan-Blue camp and

---

14_Staff, "Chen Seeks Cross-Strait Code of Conduct," *The China Post* (Taipei), October 10, 2004, http://www.chinapost.com.tw/detail.asp?ID=53205&GRP=A; and Huang Tai-lin, 'President Calls for Cross-Strait Dialogue,' *Taipei Times*, October 11, 2004, http://www.taipeitimes.com/News/front/archives/2004/10/11/2003206417.

the pan-Green camp within Taiwan, between Taipei and Beijing, between Taipei and Washington, and between Beijing and Washington, a quick resumption of cross-Strait negotiations was not on the the horizon.

4. Cross-Strait Relations from 2008 to 2012

In the face of Chen's changing policy, Beijing could hardly place its trust in him due to his record of policy fluctuation. During the campaign period of 2007-2008, KMT presidential candidate Ma Ying-Jeou proposed a "modus vivendi" approach, a "mutual non-denial" formula, and the so-called "Three-Noes" policy, namely, "no unification, no independence, no use of force." First, according to Ma himself, the "modus vivendi" approach is that the KMT government is seeking a practical arrangement by which Taiwan and China, after quarreling for nearly 60 years, can continue to coexist or work together while waiting for their disputes to be eventually settled. Putting aside the dispute of sovereignty for the time being, it is hoped many consensuses and settlements can be reached.[15] Second, in preparation for possible

---

15_Dimitri Bruyas, "Ma Seeks 'Mutual Non-Denial' Across the Strait," *The China Post* (Taipei), March 24, 2008, http://www.chinapost.com.tw/taiwan/national/presidential%20 election/2008/03/24/148519/Ma-seeks.htm.

cross-Strait negotiations on Taiwan's international space, a "mutual non-denial" formula is proposed. It is contended that there will be benign mutual interaction between Taiwan and China if they do not deny each other. While it is impossible for them to recognize each other at the current stage, it is unnecessary for them to deny each other either. Third, the "Three-Noes" policy is proposed to accommodate future negotiations with China on a cross-Strait peace agreement.[16]

Unification is not acceptable to the overwhelming majority of Taiwanese people, whereas independence will only be a disaster to both sides of the Taiwan Strait. So long as Taiwan does not go independent and China does not seek unification, then coercion from China against Taiwan is unnecessary. Therefore, the only way to put the Chinese leader at ease is to go back to the normal track of cross-Strait relations under the consensus of "one China with respective interpretations," or what Dr. Chi Su called the "1992 consensus."[17]

16_News Staff, "Ma's 'Three-Noes' Policy Viable," *The China Post* (Taipei), April 3, 2008, http://www.chinapost.com.tw/editorial/taiwan%20issues/2008/04/03/150090/Ma%27s-%273-noes.htm.

17_Due to the DPP government's strong opposition to the use of "one China" in its relations with Mainland China, Dr. Chi Su, then Chairman of the Mainland Affairs Council (MAC) under the leadership of former president Lee Teng-hui, proposed the term "1992 consensus" in lieu of "One China, respective interpretations" in an academic conference at Tamkang University in 2000, believing such an ambiguous term might

The United States, as informal ally of Taiwan, was actively engaged in the initial stage after Ma Ying-jeou's victory in the presidential election during the period March 22 to May 20, 2008. For example, Douglas Spelman, a Department of State (DOS) coordination chief in charge of Taiwan affairs, proposed the United States' "five expectations" of cross-Strait relations on March 25, 2008. First, US-Taiwan relations should go back to their normal track. Second, Taiwan should strengthen its military defense capabilities. Third, China should drop military coercion against Taiwan. Fourth, China should respect Taiwan's international space. Fifth, both sides of the Taiwan Strait should resume substantial dialogues.[18]

Reluctant to play the role of mediator in cross-Strait relations, Washington anxiously expressed its concerns over the cross-Strait negotiations one week after Ma's victory. Raymond Burghardt, Chairman of the Board of the American Institute in Taiwan (AIT),

---

be more acceptable to the pro-independence DPP government. Nonetheless, Chen Shui-bian not only refused to accept "1992 consensus," but also accused it of being a "surrender consensus," criticizing that its existence could never be found in the official cross-Strait documents and claiming that China never recognized or accepted its existence in public.

18_Liu Ping, "Five Expectations from Department of State after Ma's Victory," *Zhongguoshibao (China Times)* (Taipei), March 26, 2008, http://news.chinatimes.com/2007Cti/2007Cti-Focus/2007Cti-Focus-Content/0,4518,970326033+0+0+225606+0,00.html.

said on March 28, 2008 that he advised President-elect Ma to divide cross-Strait dialogues into three stages.[19] In the first stage, Taiwan and China can tackle the issue of cross-Strait charter flights and direct flights. Then, in the second stage, Taipei can enter into negotiations with Beijing on cross-Strait economic, trade, and investment issues. It is not until the third stage that the two parties can start the politically sensitive negotiations on a peace accord, confidence-building measures, and Taiwan's participation in non-governmental organizations (NGOs) and intergovernmental organizations (IGOs).

Nonetheless, since President Hu Jintao delivered a speech at a ceremony commemorating the 30th anniversary of the mainland's "Message to Compatriots in Taiwan" held in Beijing on December 31, 2008 to offer six proposals in promoting the peaceful development of the cross-Straits relationship, the role of the United States in cross-Strait affairs has no longer been as important as it used to be.[20]

19_Dimitri Bruyas, "U.S. Won't Play Mediator in Cross-Strait Issue: AIT Head," *The ChinaPost* (Taipei), March 29, 2008, http://www.chinapost.com.tw/taiwan/foreign%20affairs/ 2008/03/29/149336/U.S.-won%27t.htm.

20_"Six Proposals Offered for Cross-Strait Relations," *Xinhua*, December 31, 2008, ⟨http://www.chinadaily.com.cn/china/2008-12/31/content_7357490.htm⟩. Hu Jintao's six proposals are as follows: (1) Political mutual trust across the Taiwan Strait can be established through cross-Strait consultations under the One China principle; (2) Beijing is willing to sign the Comprehensive Economic Cooperation Agreement

The swift cross-Strait economic relations have had economic impact and restraints on the informal US-Taiwan Alliance system. The cross-Strait economic relations have by and large developed on a basis of "economy first, politics later" and "Easy first, hard later" since May 2008. With a single exception, a general trend is that the trade volume of Taiwan's exports to China has significantly increased since 2000. The amount of trade volume of Taiwan's exports to China increased from US$4.22 billion in 2000 to US$66.88 billion in 2008. Probably because of the uncertainty about the future of the ECFA, the amount of trade volume of Taiwan's export to China decreased from to US$54.25 billion in 2009. The trade volume of Taiwan's exports to China has increased steadily for the two consecutive years since the inking of the ECFA in late June 2009, jumping to US$76.93 billion in 2010 and US$71.204 billion in

---

(CECA) with Taipei and seek methods to link cross-Strait common development with Asia-Pacific economic integration; (3) Both sides of the Taiwan Strait can work together to promote common cultural heritage, stressing that Taiwanese sentiment is not equal to Taiwanese independence sentiment; (4) Beijing is urging the DPP to stop secessionist activities, stressing China will make a positive response to the party if independence moves are abandoned; (5) Beijing is willing to consult with Taipei on the proper and reasonable arrangements for Taiwan's participation in international organizations as long as this does not create a scenario of "Two Chinas" or "one China, one Taiwan;" and (6) Beijing is willing to step up cross-Strait contacts and exchanges on military issues and negotiate with Taiwan on military security mechanisms of mutual trust, ending cross-Strait hostility and reaching peace agreements under the One China principle.

2011.

On the other hand, a general trend is that the trade volume of Taiwan's exports to the United States, with a few exceptions, has by and large decreased since 2000. Trade volume of Taiwan's exports to China was US$76,93 billion in 2010 and US$71.2 billion in 2011, more than double that of Taiwan's exports to the United States – US$31.47 billion in 2010 and US$30.77 billion in 2011. It is thus reasonably expected that the US-Taiwan economic affinity will be increasingly less prevalent.

Taiwan has survived well and resurrected its economy since May 2008, when it started to improve relations with China. It has benefited from improved relations across the Taiwan Strait and recovered mutual trust with the United States. In the wake of Ma's victory in the 2012 two-in-one election, it is expected that the follow-up negotiations of the Economic Cooperation Framework Agreement (ECFA) and more cultural/educational exchanges will be conducted under the strategy of "making peace with China, making friends with Japan, and adopting a pro-US stance."

As early as mid-2011, in order to further strengthen US-Taiwan mutual trust, President Ma Ying-jeou decided to provide costly signals by highlighting the importance of US diplomatic and military assistance to Taiwan. In a Digital Video Conference with the Center for Strategic and International Studies (CSIS), a Washington-based think tank, he declared the three lines of defense at the presidential office in Taipei.[21] In his speech, the president promised to institutionalize cross-Strait relations and develop an international cooperative mechanism, while strengthening relations with the United States and Japan by establishing a national security network to integrate defense force and diplomacy. He called for the United States to help maintain Taiwan's ability to defend itself according to the Taiwan Relations Act (TRA).[22]

On the other hand, President Ma advocated that Taiwan should continue to adhere to its "Three-Noes" policy of "no unification, no independence, and no use of force" under the ROC Constitution in promoting relations with China. In addition, he adopted the "1992 Consensus" as the cornerstone for Cross-Strait negotiations. The 1992 Consensus, meaning "one China, respective interpretations," has proven crucial to paving the way forward.[23] It was under this Consensus that the seven rounds of Chiang-Chen Talks were able to take place, and the two sides were able to achieve so many breakthroughs. By "putting Taiwan first for the benefit of the people," Taipei and Beijing have thus far

---

21_Ma Ying-jeou, "Building National Security for the Republic of China," President Ma's Remarks in a videoconference with the Center for Strategic and International Studies, Office of the President, Republic of China (Taiwan), News Release, 2011/05 /12, http://english.president.gov.tw/Default.aspx?tabid=491&itemid=24284&rmid=23 55.

22_Ibid.

23_Ibid.

signed 16 agreements that tackle the issues of greatest concern to the people of Taiwan. It was only through this groundwork that the ECFA could be inked in June 2010. One econometric study shows that the ECFA will eventually add 4.4% to Taiwan's GDP, once the dynamic gains of structural adjustments have time to be fully implemented. And that is not even including other potential spillover benefits as a result of an improved services, trade and investment environment. This has changed the fundamental structure of, and created a "virtuous cycle" for, cross-Strait relations.

The eighth round of the negotiations between the ARATS and the SEF will be concluded in June 2012. Despite more and more difficulties, the ECFA follow-up negotiations will constantly proceed and more cultural exchanges will be positively conducted. It is expected that the cross-Strait Investment Guarantee Agreement will be inked at that time.

It is anticipated, particularly on the China side, that the inking of a cross-Strait cultural agreement or the so-called "Cultural ECFA" will be on the horizon in President Ma's second term. Nonetheless, whether Taipei will start to negotiate on the issue of the cross-Strait cultural agreement or the so-called "Cultural ECFA" remains a highly controversial issue in Taiwan due to the following four reasons. First, a cultural ECFA may involve a cross-Strait cultural identity which has not yet become a majority consensus among the people of Taiwan. Second, a cultural ECFA may involve the issue of who is the common ancestor across the Strait. While most of the pan-Blue supporters regard the Yellow Emperor of Huangdi as the common ancestor, the pan-Greens do not think so. Third, a cultural ECFA may involve the issue of the source of the nation across the Strait. Most pan-Blue supporters accept the "Chinese nation" as the only nation of the Chinese people across the Strait, whereas many of the pan-Green supporters believe they belong to the "Southern islands nation." Fourth, a cultural ECFA may involve the issue of national identity across the Strait in the long-run. While most of the pan-Blue supporters accept "Chinese" as one of their national identities (the other being "Taiwanese"), pan-Green supporters do not accept such an identity.

It goes without saying that more calculations and deliberations will be taken when promoting militarily and politically sensitive issues across the Taiwan Strait. One of the most difficult issues across the Strait is the one of Taiwan and China's respective positions. In the eyes of Chinese leaders and historians, the "Republic of China (ROC)," as a country, came to an end in 1949. Nonetheless, the ROC is more than the name of a nation; it also stands for a free and democratic way of life, and serves as a model for those living in other ethnic Chinese societies who yearn for freedom and democracy. For more than 60 years, the ROC has ensured the security of Taiwan, Penghu, Kinmen, and Matsu; safeguarded the viability of Chinese culture; and created an economic and a political miracle. In the eyes of the 23 million people of Taiwan, the ROC Constitution has long served as the bedrock of a society-wide consensus. The ideals that Dr. Sun Yat-sen sought in establishing the Republic were not achieved in the mainland during his lifetime, but they have come to full fruition here in Taiwan.[24] So long as the issue of Taiwan and China's respective political positions remains unsolved, none of the politically and militarily sensitive issues will be taken into consideration.

On January 15, 2012, President Ma pointed out he would make every effort to defend the sovereignty of the ROC and the security of Taiwan, as well as ensure dignity for the people of Taiwan.[25] He promised that he would not start negotiation on the issue of a "peace accord" with China during his second term; however, he believes it is something Taiwan has to face in the upcoming decade. President Ma contends that such a cross-Strait peace accord will be inked only when it is needed by the country, supported by the majority of Taiwan's people, and supervised by the Legislative Yuan.

24_President Ma Ying-jeou's National Day Address, Office of the President, Republic of China (Taiwan), News Release, 2011/10/10, http://english.president.gov.tw/Default.aspx?tabid=491&itemid=25514&rmid=2355.

25_President Ma Meets Delegation of Visiting American Scholars and Experts, Office of the President, Republic of China (Taiwan), News Release, 2012/01/15, http://english.president.gov.tw/Default.aspx?tabid=491&itemid=26368&rmid=2355.

If referendum voting is added as an extra prerequisite for a peace accord, then it suggests that there would not be any accord on the horizon because no political referendum would be approved under the current referendum law.[26] Another possibility is that, given the high degree of unlikeliness of a cross-Strait peace accord, it is proposed that Taipei and Beijing might negotiate a framework agreement of cross-Strait peaceful development.[27] Certainly, any cross-Strait politically and militarily sensitive agreement will proceed on an incremental basis with the blessing of the United States.[28] Therefore, even a cross-Strait cultural agreement will not on the horizon in president Ma's second term, much less a politically sensitive peace agreement or peace accord, give the respective positions across the Strait, and confidence building measures agreements.

26_Given the current referendum law, none of the political referenda would be passed, as shown in the case of 2004 when the pan-Blue camp passively opposed the two referenda on missile procurement and mainland policy proposed by President Chen Shui-bian by refusing to vote, and the 2008 case when the pan-Blue camp actively opposed President Chen's UN bid referendum by proposing another "Back to the UN" referendum.

27_The concept of cross-Strait negotiations on a framework agreement of cross-Strait peaceful development is still in the paperwork stage among pro-KMT think tanks in Taiwan.

28_Before a cross-Strait agreement is inked, there are three stages, namely, (1) respective studies, (2) common studies; and (3) negotiations.

III. Inter-Korean Relations

1. Inter-Korean Relations from 1988 to 1998

In the wake of the Korean War, Kim Il-sung, leader of Democratic People's Republic of Korea (North Korea), eliminated his main political adversaries at home on the one hand and embarked on a policy of economic reorganization on the other by adopting the Stalinist model of forced collectivization and centralized economic planning. In the international community, Pyongyang developed a policy of Juche (self-reliance), which extended to Kim Il-sung's Marxist-Leninist ideology and unsuccessful efforts at economic insufficiency. During the 1960s and 1970s, North Korean relations with Moscow and Beijing alternated between tensions and warmth as it attempted a deliberate balancing act under the rubric of Juche. In the early 1970s, encouraged by the more relaxed international political climate, Pyongyang decided to make large purchases of plant and equipment from the West and Japan. As a result of defaulting on payments, North Korea owed billions of dollars to foreign countries.[29]

In contrast, South Korea's political democratic experiment was

29_Borthwick, Mark (with contributions by selected scholars), *Pacific Century: The Emergence of Modern Pacific Asia.* Boulder, Colorado: Westview Press, 1992, 352-355.

not very successful in its early stage. Its initial democratic experiment failed as Syngman Rhee, a formerly exiled leader, assumed increasingly dictatorial powers. By the time of the presidential elections in 1960, the regime's unpopularity had become so great that a political eruption was inevitable. Massive student demonstrations broke out and won widespread support. After a brief resistance, Rhee had no choice but to step down. South Korea was thus ruled by the democratically elected Chang Myon for a short period. Unfortunately, Chang was indecisive and the government was soon divided. The government fell to a military coup d'état led by Major-General Park Chung-hee. His 19-year authoritarian rule ended in 1979 when he was assassinated by his own intelligence chief. By that time, the regime was facing increasingly rising public discontent over its intolerance of criticism. When army General Chun Doo Hwan stepped in to fill Park's vacancy, he forcefully and successfully quelled all opposition forces. His authoritarian rule endured for another seven years until democratic forces took over the government. Therefore, the transition toward democracy in South Korea was a slow and painful one, making it difficult for Seoul to extend an attractive, peaceful olive branch to Pyongyang during the period from 1960 to 1986.[30]

30_Ibid, 350-52.

It was not until 1987 that South Korea was in a dramatic struggle for democratic reform under the worldwide wave of democratization and the strong opposition at home. Roh Tae-woo, a former general and leader of Chun's Democratic Justice Party (DJP) became president in the election of 1987. By the early 1990s, Seoul had scored a series of diplomatic, economic, and political successes. Other than its burgeoning economic growth, South Korea commenced the process of democratization and hosted the 1988 Olympics in Seoul. Moreover, it established diplomatic relations with the Soviet Union and developed commercial relations with China.[31] Under the leadership of Roh Tae-woo, South Korea's policy toward communist states, including North Korea, became more conciliatory and accommodating than ever before. Known as pukpang chŏngch'aek (Northern Policy), South Korea's efforts to improve relations with the Soviet Union, China, and Eastern European countries were aimed not only at diversifying trading partners but also at ensuring peace, security, and stability on the Korean Peninsula. The South thus successfully compelled the North to counter its diplomatic initiatives. While its relations with the Soviet Union, China, and Eastern European countries significantly expanded in the spheres of trade, joint ventures, sports,

31_Ibid, 352-53.

and culture, inter-Korean relations made a few dramatic breakthroughs. There followed in 1990 three consecutive meetings between the prime ministers of the two Koreas as well as sports exchanges.[32] In addition, North Korea and Japan started negotiations on the normalization of their diplomatic relations.[33]

It was also in this context that Pyongyang occasionally demonstrated its diplomatic flexibility. For example, in February 1991, North Korea broke off inter-Korean prime ministerial talks to protest US-South Korean military drills conducted on a yearly basis. Nonetheless, South Korean Prime Minister Chung Won-shik suggested to his North Korean counterpart that the dialogue should be resumed.[34] At Seoul's request, Pyongyang subsequently rescheduled the talks from August 27 to October 22 in 1991.

Moreover, North Korea could not but respond to South Korea's application for a seat in the United Nations (UN). Kim Il-sung had persistently opposed the idea of both Koreas' application for UN membership, believing that such a move would lead to a permanently divided Korea. For many years, North Korea's diplomatic efforts focused on preventing South Korea from gaining separate

---

32_Koh, B.C. "Seoul's Northern Policy and Korean Security," *The Korean Journal of Defense Affairs* 1, no. 1 (Summer 1989), 127-143.

33_Borthwick (1992) 352-53.

34_"Koreans Agreed to Resume Prime Ministerial Talks," *International Herald Tribune*, July 12, 1991, 5.

UN membership. In 1991, South Korea announced its intention to apply for a seat in the UN, a possibility that had long been foreclosed by an assured Security Council veto from either the Soviet Union or China. This time, however, both Moscow and Beijing quietly informed Pyongyang that they would not block the request of Seoul. Left with little option, North Korea chose to apply simultaneously with South Korea.[35] As a result of Moscow's support for Seoul's application and Beijing's weakened support for Pyongyang's position, North Korea decided to concede to both Koreas' entering the UN.[36]

Furthermore, Pyongyang eventually agreed in 1992, in principle, to accept International Atomic Energy Agency (IAEA) inspections of its nuclear facilities.[37] North Korea's development of nuclear weapon capability was accelerated in the late 1980s, possibly because of a belief that neither the Soviet Union nor China was a reliable supporter of its own unification dream. Pyongyang might have thought that, with nuclear weapons at hand, it could not only deter an attack from South Korea and the United States but also use as bargaining leverage with its neighboring countries

---

35_Borthwick (1992) 353.

36_Ahn Byungjoon, "North Korea's Foreign Policy in the Post-Cold War Era," *East Asian Review* 3 (Summer 1991): 87-88.

37_Shim Hae Hoon, "The Inevitable Burden," *Far Eastern Economic Review*, August 22, 1991: 21-23.

and the West in gaining more economic support. Since then, the threat of an autonomous North Korean nuclear weapon capability has been the focus of concern by Pyongyang's friends and foes alike. Washington had exerted pressure on Pyongyang to accept IAEA inspections of its nuclear power facilities by threatening to postpone the drawdown of US forces from South Korea and by increasing the effectiveness of US-ROK military drills such as the annual Team Spirit. The autumn 1991 decision by Washington and Seoul to withdraw US tactical nuclear weapons from South Korea offered North Korea an opportunity to reciprocate through IAEA inspections without losing face. Moreover, President Roh Tae-woo promised North Korea that South Korea would never develop nuclear weapons on its own, a path was opened for both governments to permit IAEA scrutiny of their respective nuclear facilities. Furthermore, US President George H. W. Bush in his January 1992 visit to Seoul offered to cancel US-ROK Team Spirit military drills for that year as an additional incentive if Pyongyang opened its nuclear plants to international inspection.[38] Therefore, North Korea's concession to agree to IAEA inspections of its nuclear facilities was regarded as a significant breakthrough in US-led

---

38_Simon, Sheldon W. "Regional Security in Asia: the Question of Relevance," in his edited book *East Asian Security in the Post-Cold War Era*. New York: M. E. Sharp, 1993, 16-19.

non-proliferation efforts.

More importantly, major breakthrough in inter-Korean relations came in the early 1990s with the end of the Cold War. For the first time since the 1972 Joint Communiqué, the two governments held several rounds of ministerial meetings in shuttle diplomacy between Seoul and Pyongyang. In December 1991, they announced the Basic Agreement on Reconciliation, Nonaggression, and Exchanges and Cooperation between South Korea and North Korea. The Agreement even suggests replacing the present armistice system with a peace treaty in the future.[39]

2. Inter-Korean Relations from 1998 to 2003

Under the leadership of Kim Dae-jung, South Korea pursued a new North Korea policy, known as the "Sunshine Policy," to induce Pyongyang to the negotiation table to promote inter-Korean relations. President Kim announced three principles in his policy towards Pyongyang: "First, South Korea will never tolerate armed provocation [by North Korea] of any kind. Second, South Korea

39_Sheen, Seongho, "Inter-Korean Relations without the U.S.-ROK Alliance," paper presented at the KiFS/NBR Conference - "U.S.-ROK alliance: implications of an 'Alternative Future," Sponsored by The Korean Institute for Future Strategies and the National Bureau of Asian Research, Seoul, South Korea, September 10-11, 2007, 1-29.

does not have any intention to undermine or absorb North Korea. Third, South Korea will actively pursue reconciliation and cooperation between the South and the North beginning in those areas which can be made available to it."[40] In close consultation with Washington, Seoul examined various alternatives that could help create a permanent peace regime on the Korean Peninsula. On April 16, 1996, the United States and South Korea jointly proposed four-party Talks at a summit on Cheju Island. At the summit, it was stated that North and South Koreas were to be responsible for the Korean problem, whereas the United States and China were to play supporting and guaranteeing roles according to the "2 + 2" formula.[41]

In June 2000, the first-ever summit between South Korean President Kim Dae-jung and North Korean Defense Commission Chairman Kim Jong-il was held in Pyongyang. This landmark summit relit hopes for peace on the Korean Peninsula. Upon his return to Seoul, President Kim announced that a new peace process was ushered between South Korea and North Korea. The goal of South Korea's "Sunshine Policy" was to garner continued support at home and abroad. It is important to note that the summit oc-

40_"Text of Kim Dae-jung's Inaugural Speech," *Korea Herald*, February 26, 1998.

41_Koo, Bon-Hak "Challenges and Prospects for Inter-Korean Relations under the New Leadership," *The Korean Journal of Defense Affairs* 10, no. 1 (1998), 75-93.

curred without the intercession of a third party, suggesting that real dialogue between the two Koreas could take place as long as both sides are determined to engage one another seriously.[42]

From the inauguration of the Kim government, Seoul pursued its Sunshine Policy, resulting in a historical summit at which the two leaders agreed to work together. It did contribute significantly to the expansion of inter-Korean trade and contacts, including the reunion of separated families, ministerial meetings, defense ministers' meetings, and various working-level meetings. Despite increasing contacts on many levels, military tensions have not been reduced substantially. Though President Kim stated that the animosity between the two Koreas had come to an end, North Korea increased its forces along the DMZ and stepped up military drills. In addition, Pyongyang even stopped all inter-Korean dialogues after US President George W. Bush's inauguration in 2001. Although the summit helped the outside world understand more about North Korea and what it needed badly at home, bilateral relations between the South and the North were not mature enough for them to embark on serious talks to resolve mutual hostilities.[43]

42_Lho, Kyongsoo "Two Koreas' Post-Summit Foreign Policy and the Issue of Cross-Recognition," *The Korean Journal of Defense Affairs* 13, no. 1 (Fall 2001), 53-77.

43_Koo, Bonhak and Changhee Nam, "South Korea's Sunshine Policy and the Inter-Korean Security Relations," *The Korean Journal of Defense Affairs* 13, no. 1 (Fall 2001), 79-101.

As a result, the post-summit optimism was replaced by a more realistic assessment of Inter-Korean relations, and it is no longer expected that a genuine reconciliation between the South and the North will occur in the foreseeable future. Actually, the impasse was not because of President Bush's hard-line approach towards North Korea, but because of a lack of confidence between the two Koreas.

3. Inter-Korean Relations from 2003 to 2008

President Roh Moo-hyun, Kim Dae-jung's successor, continued to pursue the "Sunshine Policy" towards North Korea with the blessing of the United States, Russia, and China, with some fruitful outcomes. Inter-Korean trade increased substantially. South Korea became the second largest economic partner of North Korea with over US$1.35 billion of trade volume in 2006. South Korea's "sunshine policy" was often criticized by hawks in Washington, which regarded it as rewarding North Korea's bad behavior of nuclear defiance. After North Korea's first nuclear test in October 2006, Washington and Seoul expressed their differences over whether South Korea should continue the Kaesong Industrial Complex and the Mt. Kumgang Project amidst UN economic sanctions on North Korea. Although South Korea cast its vote in favor of the UN sanctions, it decided to continue the two projects which became important cash crops for North Korea, thus placing itself at odds with the United States.[44]

4. Inter-Korean Relations from 2008 on

When President Lee Myung-bak came to office, North Korean leader Kim Jong-il chose confrontation rather than cooperation towards South Korea. In April 2009, North Korea conducted its third test-launch of a long-range missile, and in June, its second nuclear test. Pyongyang took provocative moves such as an attack on the South Korean corvette Cheonan in March 2010, killing 46 sailors, and a bombardment on the Yeonpyeong Island in November of that year, killing two marines and two civilians. The Lee government position towards North Korea is no different from that of his predecessors in its fundamental principles and approach to reunification as a process of integration and not reunification through absorption. The major difference in the approach of the Lee government toward North Korea is a stronger emphasis on resolving their problems on a reciprocal basis. After the killing of a South Korean tourist at Mt. Kumgang resort, President Lee insisted on a promise that there would be no recurrence of similar acci-

44_Sheen, Seongho (2007) 6-7.

dent before tours could resume. The Lee government was determined not to reward North Korea's brinksmanship diplomacy, understanding that doing so would only encourage Pyongyang's provocations.[45]

Despite a relatively relaxed climate between the two Koreas, both sides have remained highly watchful and suspicious since the early 1990s. First, there exists an insurmountable gap between the two Koreas in terms of political systems. While South Korea has successfully democratized itself since the late 1980s, North Korea has continued to lay the groundwork for a communist dynasty from Kim Il-sung to Kim Jong-il, and now from Kim Jong-il to Kim Jong-Un.[46]

Second, there has long existed a security dilemma between the two Koreas as both sides have maintained large standing armies. North Korea's increase in its military budget and introduction of advanced weaponry will result in South Korea's fear or vice versa. North Korea has taken provocative moves toward South Korea as shown in the cases of its attack on the Cheonan on Yeonpyeong Island in March and November 2010, respectively. Especially trou-

---

45_Park, Won Gon "North-South Korea Relations under the Lee Myung-Bak Administration: The North's Provocations and the South's Principled Response," *The Korean Journal of Defense Affairs* 23, no. 3 (Fall 2011), 321-333.

46_"North Korea," *The New York Times*, January 12, 2012, http://topics.nutimes.com/top/news/international/countriesandterritories/northkorea/index.html.

bling to South Korea has been North Korea's development of its own nuclear weapon systems.[47]

Third, human and business exchanges between the two Koreas have increased markedly since South Korea started its Sunshine Policy towards North Korea.[48] Numerous NGOs, churches, and charities were allowed to offer aid, and businessmen were no longer asked to seek specific approval for a visit to Pyongyang to negotiate investment and trade agreements. Almost forty thousand people exchanges were made during the Kim Dae-jung administration, a more than twentyfold increase compared to 1,733 in previous administrations. This figure increased substantially under the presidency of Roh Moo-hyun, with more than one hundred thousand people exchanges in 2006 alone. Inter-Korean social exchanges showed constant progress in their content as well. People from various arenas including science, technology, academia, literature, arts, medicine, hospital, sports, media, journalism, and religion have had numerous exchanges. Meanwhile, only a select few North Koreans visited South Korea. In 2006, 870 North Koreans visited the South , while over one hundred thou-

---

47_Manyin, Mark E., Emma Chanlett-Avory, and Mary Beth Nikitin, *U.S.-South Korea Relations*, Congressional Research Service (CRS) Report for Congress, prepared for members and committees of U.S. Congress, November 28, 2011, 1-31.

48_Sheen, Seongho (2007) 13-14.

sand South Koreans visited the North. More importantly, North Korean visitors have not been allowed to contact their counterparts. Despite increased contacts and a rhetoric of national cooperation, there seems to be no fundamental changes in the North Korean regime, with its continued emphasis on the exclusive Juche ideology, military first policy, and the personality cult of Kim Jung-un.

IV. Cross-Strait and Inter-Korean Relations from a Comparative Perspective

Based on the analysis above, it is argued that the inter-Korean relations can be depicted as a top-down relationship, whereas cross-Strait relations are a bottom-up relationship. On the Korean Peninsula, the two Koreas have had a ministerial meeting, prime ministerial meetings, and even a summit between their top leaders. Taiwan and China have not had any meeting between high-level officials. During the Ma administration, there have been negotiations across the Strait in which officials up to deputy ministers are dispatched from both sides.

In December 1991, Seoul and Pyongyang declared a Basic Agreement on Reconciliation, Nonaggression, and Exchanges and Cooperation between South Korea and North Korea. The

Agreement even suggests replacing the present armistice system with a peace treaty in the future. Nonetheless, Taipei has not been ready to negotiate on the issue of cultural framework agreement, much less a politically sensitive peace accord, respective positions across the Strait, and confidence-building measures. Based on their fundamental mutual trust, Taiwan and China inked the Economic cooperation Framework Agreement (ECFA) on June 29, 2009, thus having a far-reaching impact on the cross-Strait relations. While cross-Strait relations are characterized by substantial people and business exchanges on a daily basis, inter-Korean relations are a rhetoric of national cooperation without face-to-face contacts among people.

The international factors seems more important in inter-Korean relations as the United States, China, Russia, and Japan all play certain roles on the Korean Peninsula. In contrast, only the United States is playing an important role across the Taiwan Strait. Indeed, the United States has played a very important role across the Taiwan Strait and in inter-Korean relations. The United States has been so adept at playing multi-dimensional roles that it always benefits most from interactions with both sides of the Taiwan Strait. For example, while the United States has played the role of an economic balancer across the Strait, it has also simultaneously played the role of a trade promoter. While it has played the role of a military balancer, it has also played the role of an arms broker.

While it has played the role of a political balancer, it has also played the role of a political interpreter. All these can be seen as the United States' desire for a balanced cross-Strait relationship, in which Taiwan maintains a necessary defense, but does not provoke the mainland, in which Taiwan maintains a certain political confidence in running its own government, but does not challenge the cross-Strait status quo, and in which Taiwan develops strong economic connections with China, but does not become excessively dependent on a single market. More importantly, in spite of the fact that the United States often pursues its own national interests at the cost of Taiwan and that there exists fundamental contradictions between China and the United States, both Beijing and Taipei often claim that their relationship with Washington "has never been so good" or "couldn't be better." The United States is so skilled in playing dual and even multi-dimensional roles that it benefits most from its interactions with both sides of the Taiwan Strait. If the United States is really more than willing to see the improvement across the Strait, it will sooner or later to take into serious consideration what kind of role it plays between Taipei and Beijing in the future.

Likewise, while the United States has played the role of a military balancer in inter-Korean relations, it has also played the role of supplying arms to South Korea. While America has played the role of a political balancer in inter-Korean relations, it has also played the role of a political interpreter. All this can be seen as the United States' desire for a balanced inter-Korean relationship, in which the South maintains a more than necessary defense, but is not strong enough to absorb the North, and in which North Korea maintains a certain political confidence in running its own government, but is not strong enough to change the status quo, and in which North Korea depends upon China's markets, but can still find alternatives elsewhere. More importantly, the United States is so skilled in playing dual and even multi-dimensional roles that it benefits most from its interactions with both sides on the Korean Peninsula. If an improvement in inter-Korean relations is desirable, Washington will play a kind of role between Seoul and Pyongyang in the future.

The lesson of German reunification for South Korea and North Korea is totally different. For most South Koreans, it was that the price of reunification is simply unaffordable. After the two Germanys decided to reunify themselves in 1991, they soon discovered how profound a division remained after forty years of divergent economic and political evolution. Most South Koreans have realized how difficult North Korea would be to assimilate. From the viewpoint of North Korea, the lesson might be that it would be a mistake to allow controlled yet extensive exchanges of personnel and information to pass between the two Koreas. The East Germans witnessed clearly the failure of their economic and political system after their government allowed such exchanges and flows to occur from the early 1970s. It was once Seoul that feared the expansion of North Korean communist ideology in South Korea, whereas it is Pyongyang that fears the attractiveness of South Korean capitalism and democracy and being absorbed in the manner of East Germany. It seems that the more attractive the South Korean economic and political system is, the more likely North Korea will withdraw from inter-Korean contacts and dialogues.[49]

There exist forces working towards national reunification. The outcome of reunification will be determined by relative national power, namely, diplomatic, economic, military and political power.[50] The polity with greater national power tends to absorb the polity with weaker national power, as shown in the case of German reunification. If national power is more or less equal between two polities with divergent ideologies, then relative military power may help determine the outcome, as shown in the case of Vietnamese reunification. Despite US support, South Vietnam became the loser in the struggle of national reunification. The only explanation for such an outcome is that the United States neither

---

49_Borthwick (1992) 353.

50_Oh, Kwan-Chi "Is There a Natural Process of National Reunification for the Two Koreas?" *Korean Journal of Defense Affairs* 9, no. 2 (Winter 1997), 93-111.

had the right military and political strategy to win the struggle between capitalism and communism, nor the sufficient political will in the defense of South Vietnam. The case of German reunification demonstrates that the greater the relative difference in national power, the more likely the process of reunification will be. South Korea gains the upper hand over North Korea in terms of relative national power; therefore, North Korea is fated to be absorbed into South Korea. Nonetheless, the natural and peaceful reunification process on the Korean Peninsula could be interrupted by North Korea's successful development of nuclear weapon systems, China's intervention in North Korea's internal affairs, and Pyongyang's imprudent or misjudged policies. North Korea's use of nuclear weaponry could determine the outcome of reunification on the Korean Peninsula. China's economic, military and political support could grant North Korea a new lease of life. North Korea's imprudent or misjudged policies could either delay or increase the costs of Korean reunification.

The same is by and large true for the process of reunification across the Taiwan Strait. China, as a polity, possesses much greater national power than Taiwan. Therefore, it is expected that the process of reunification across the Strait will be peaceful. Nonetheless, the natural and peaceful reunification process across the Strait could be interrupted by Taiwan's successful economic development through the improvement of cross-Strait relations, the United States' abandonment of Taiwan, and China's use of force against Taiwan.

V. Conclusion

A comparison between cross-Strait and inter-Korean relations is as fruitful as expected. Inter-Korean relations can be depicted as a top-down relationship, whereas the cross-Strait relations a bottom-up relationship. On the Korean Peninsula, the two Koreas have had ministerial meetings, prime ministerial meetings, and even summits between their top leaders. Taiwan and China have not had any meeting in which high-level officials are involved. During the Ma administration, there have been negotiations across the Strait in which officials up to deputy minister level have been dispatched from both sides.

More than twenty years ago, Seoul and Pyongyang declared the Basic Agreement on Reconciliation, Nonaggression, and Exchanges and Cooperation between South Korea and North Korea. The Agreement even suggests replacing the present armistice system with a peace treaty in the future. Unfortunately, such an important agreement does not guarantee a peaceful relationship on the Korean Peninsula. On the other hand, Taipei has not been ready to negotiate on the issue of a cultural framework agreement, much less a politically sensitive peace accord, respective positions across the Strait, and confidence-building measures. Based on their fundamental mutual trust, however, Taiwan and China inked the ECFA on June 29, 2009, thus having a far-reaching impact on cross-Strait relations. Cross-Strait relations are characterized by frequent and substantial people and business exchanges, whereas inter-Korean relations reveal a rhetoric of national cooperation without face-to-face contacts among people on a daily basis.

International factors seem more important in inter-Korean relations as the United States, China, Russia, and Japan all play certain kinds of role on the Korean Peninsula. In contrast, only the United States is playing a significant role across the Strait. If the improvement of relations across the Strait is desirable, it will be a matter of time for the United States to take into serious consideration playing a kind of role between Taipei and Beijing in the future. Likewise, if the improvement of inter-Korean relations is desirable in the eyes of Washington, the United States will sooner or later play a kind of role between Seoul and Pyongyang in the future.

The case of German reunification demonstrates that the greater the relative difference in national power, the more likely the process of reunification will be. South Korea gains the upper hand over North Korea in terms of relative national powers; therefore, North Korea is fated to be absorbed into South Korea. However, the natural and peaceful reunification process on the Korean Peninsula could be interrupted by North Korea's successful development of nuclear weapon systems, China's intervention in North Korea's internal affairs, and Pyongyang's imprudent or misjudged policies. On the other hand, the natural and peaceful reunification process across the Strait could be interrupted by Taiwan's successful economic development through the improvement of cross-Strait relations, America's abandonment of Taiwan, and China's use of its forces against Taiwan.

In conclusion, it is argued that the substance of cross-Strait relations seems more important than the formality of inter-Korean relations, whereas a bottom-up cross-Strait relations relationship seems more crucial than a top-down inter-Korean relationship. Therefore, cross-Strait relations are characterized by frequent and substantial people and business exchanges, whereas the inter-Korean relations are by and large a rhetoric of national cooperation without face-to-face contacts among people and business circles on a daily basis.

References

Ahn, Byungjoon, "North Korea's Foreign Policy in the Post-Cold War Era," *East Asian Review* 3, Summer 1991.

Author unknown, "Chen Seeks Cross-Strait Code of Conduct," *The China Post* (Taipei), 10 October, 2004.

------. "Koreans Agreed to Resume Prime Ministerial Talks," *International Herald Tribune*, 12 July, 1991.

------. "Ma's 'Three-Noes' Policy Viable," *The China Post* (Taipei), 3 April, 2008.

------. "North Korea," *The New York Times*, 12 January, 2012.

------. "President Ma Meets Delegation of Visiting American Scholars and Experts." Office of the President, Republic of China (Taiwan), News Release, 15 January, 2012.

------. "Six Proposals Offered for Cross-Strait Relations," *Xinhua*, 31 December, 2008.

Borthwick, Mark. (with contributions by selected scholars), *Pacific Century: The Emergence of Modern Pacific Asia*. Boulder, Colorado: Westview Press, 1992.

Bruyas, Dimitri. "Ma Seeks 'Mutual Non-Denial' Across the Strait," *The China Post* (Taipei), 24 March, 2008.

------. "U.S. Won't Play Mediator in Cross-StraitIssue: AIT Head," *The ChinaPost* (Taipei), 29 March, 2008.

Chen, Edward I-hsin. "Chinese Negotiating Styles: A Case Study of CAL-CAAC Talks," paper presented at the International Conference on Cross-Cultural Negotiations and Communication, sponsored by Soochow University at Grand Hotel in Taipei on September 29-30, 1987.

Chiu, Hungdah. "The Koo-Wang Talks and the Prospects for Building Constructive and Stable Relations across the Taiwan Strait," in Gerrit W. Gong and Bih-jaw Lin (eds.) *Sino-American Relations at a Time of Change*, Washington, D.C.: Center for Strategic and International Studies (CSIS), 1994.

Huang Tai-lin, 'President Calls for Cross-Strait Dialogue,' *Taipei Times*, 11 October, 2004.

Kim, Dae-jung. "Text of Kim Dae-jung's Inaugural Speech," *Korean Herald*, 26 February, 1998.

Koh, B. C. "Seoul's Northern Policy and Korean Security," *The Korean Journal of Defense Affairs* 1, no. 1, Summer 1989.

Koo, Bon-hak. "Challenges and Prospects for Inter-Korean Relations under the New Leadership," *The Korean Journal of Defense Affairs* 10, no. 1, 1998.

Koo, Bon-hak and Changhee Nam, "South Korea's Sunshine Policy and the Inter-Korean Security Relations," *The Korean Journal of Defense Affairs* 13, no. 1, Fall 2001.

Lho, Kyongsoo. "Two Koreas' Post-Summit Foreign Policy and the Issue of Cross-Recognition," *The Korean Journal of Defense Affairs* 13, no. 1, Fall 2001.

Ma, Ying-jeou. "Building National Security for the Republic of China," President Ma's Remarks at the Videoconference with the Center for Strategic and International Studies, Office of the President, Republic of China (Taiwan), News Release, 12 May 2011.

------. "President Ma Ying-jeou's National Day Address," Office of the President, Republic of China (Taiwan), News Release, 10 October, 2010.

Manyin, Mark E., Emma Chanlett-Avory, and Mary Beth Nikitin, *U.S.-South Korea Relations*, Congressional Research Service (CRS) Report for Congress, prepared for members and committees of U.S. Congress, 28 November, 2011.

Oh, Kwan-chi. "Is There a Natural Process of National Reunification for the Two Koreas?" *The Korean Journal of Defense Affairs* 9, no. 2, Winter 1997.

Park, Won Gon. "North-South Korea Relations under the Lee Myung-Bak Administration: The North's Provocations and the South's Principled Response," *The Korean Journal of Defense Affairs* 23, no. 3, Fall 2011.

Ping, Liu. "Five Expectations from Department of State after Ma's Victory," *Zhongguoshibao (China Times)* (Taipei), 26 March, 2008.

Romberg, Alan D. Rein In at the Brink of the Precipice: American Policy Toward Taiwan and US-PRC Relations. Washington, D.C.: Henry L. Stimson Center, 2003.

Sheen, Seongho. "Inter-Korean Relations without the U.S.-ROK Alliance," paper presented at the KiFS/NBR Conference – "U.S.-ROK alliance: implications of an 'Alternative Future," Sponsored by The Korean Institute for Future Strategies and the National Bureau of Asian Research, Seoul, South Korea, 10-11 September, 2007.

Shim, Hae Hoon, "The Inevitable Burden," *Far Easter Economic Review*, 22 August, 1991.

Simon, Sheldon W. "Regional Security in Asia: the Question of Relevance," in his edited book *East Asian Security in the Post-Cold War Era*. New York: M. E.

Sharp, 1993.
Su, Chi. *Weixian Bianyun (Brinkmanship: From Two-States-Theory to One Country on Each Side)*, Taipei: Book Zone, 2004.

Power Politics and Conflict Resolution

The Cases of Cross-Strait and Inter-Korean Relations

Tung-Chieh Tsai

(Professor, Graduate Institute of International Politics, National Chung-Hsing University)

Ⅰ. Introduction: Balance of Power in East Asia

As Michael Evans points out, for the first time since the beginning of the sixteenth century, the single largest concentration of global economic power will be found this century not in Europe, nor in the Americas, but in Asia.[1] The wheel of geopolitics has turned full circle over the past three decades, from the North Atlantic to the Western Pacific. Regardless of popular discussion on the issue of stability in East Asia, the combination of an unpredictable regime in North Korea (especially after the death of Kim Jong-Il) and fundamentally irreconcilable nationalist move-

1_Evans, Michael "Power and Paradox: Asian Geopolitics and Sino-American Relations in the 21st Century," *Orbis*, Winter (2011), pp. 85-113.

ments between Mainland China and Taiwan have created two highly combustible zones of perpetual crisis that could plunge the entire region into war and conflict.[2] Yet developments on the Korean Peninsula and across the Taiwan Strait cannot be simply examined from the view of isolated case studies. More objective predictions of future developments may perhaps be attained by putting the two hot points within the regional or global power structure.

1. US Decline and Its Impact on Regional Policy

Although both the Soviet Union's collapse and US victory in the Gulf War in 1991 suggest that the US has basically consolidated its sole leadership on the global stage, the material basis of Washington's unilateral power or in other words, US economic power, has been in obvious decline due to serious financial deficits and stagflation since the 1980s. In the summer of 1990, the US economy entered its ninth major decline since the 1940s, with the recession lasting until the eve of the presidential election in 1991. Signs of the United States' growing economic decline could be found as early as 1969. Under the newly proposed Nixon

2_Berger, Thomas "Set for Stability? Prospects for Conflict and Cooperation in East Asia," *Review of International Security*, 26 (2000), p .406.

Doctrine, the "self-determination of Asia" offered Washington the necessary legitimacy for leaving the region.[3] In addition, Nixon also sought to confront Asia's problems directly by seeking to transfer Washington's responsibilities over to the collective security regime in East Asia, releasing the United States from the shackles of the Cold War.[4]

Commencement of the post-Cold War period pushed Washington to reconsider its global strategy. Washington's strategic choices clearly underwent the bipolar debates of neo-realism versus neo-idealism and isolationism versus new globalism. The first debate brings up the question of whether the United States should seek to re-build a global alliance based on geopolitical interests or to serve as the defender of the democratic peace,[5] while the latter suggests pondering over a hands off policy towards international conflicts or the establishment of a new collective se-

---

3_Laird, Melvin R. "The Nixon Doctrine: From Potential Despair to New Opportunities," in Laird, ed. *The Nixon Doctrine* Washington, DC: Town Hall Meeting, 1972, 3; Department of State, *United States Foreign Policy, 1969-70* Washington, DC: US Government Printing Office, 1971, 36-37.

4_Jones, Alan Jr. "Nixon and the World," in Jones, Alan Jr. ed. US Foreign Policy *in a Changing World* New York: David McKay, 1973, p. 24; Spanier, John *American Foreign Policy since World War II* New York: Praeger, 1973, 276.

5_Brzezinski, Zbigniew *The Grand Chessboard: American Primacy and Its Geostrategic Imperatives* NY: Basic Books, 1997; Maoz, Zeev "The Controversy over the Democratic Peace," *International Security*, 22:1 (1997), 162-198.

curity system to prevent a world of chaos and violence.[6] From a certain point a view, the inability to reach a consensus due to heated debates has often caused US foreign policy to be filled with paradox and conflict while providing opportunities for other potential regional competitors to carry out foreign policy challenges. The development of the global balance of power towards multipolarity creates further difficulties for US management of international affairs.[7]

Due to the trend of relative decline in the United States' total power, the status of the United States as hegemon in East Asia also entered an adjustment stage in the post-Cold War period. In this stage, Washington's East Asia strategy is demonstrated as the "new containment policy" proposed by former Secretary of State James Baker. Baker proposed the security of US interests through human rights policy, economic cooperation and multilateral forums in the Asia-Pacific.[8] Following the containment proposal, Washington

---

6_Schlesinger, Arthur Jr. "Back to the Womb: Isolationism's Renewed Threat," *Foreign Affairs*, 74:4 (1995), 8.

7_Lynn-Jones, Sean M. and Steven E. Miller, eds. *The Cold War and After: Prospect for Peace* New York: The MIT Press, 1994, 281.

8_Baker, James "America in Asia: Emerging Architecture for a Pacific Community," *Foreign Affairs*, 70:5 (1991), 1-18. See also Layne, Christopher "From Preponderance to Offshore Balancing: America's Future Grand Strategy," *International Security*, 22:1 (1997), 86-124; Layne, Christopher "Less Is More: Minimal Realism in East Asia," *National Interest*, 43 (1996), 64-78; Posen, Barry R. and Andrew L. Ross, "Competing

broached the New Pacific Community initiative, hoping to depart from the United States' alliance with Japan and establish a new partnership of cooperation and engagement with East Asia.[9]

2. Power Shift in East Asia

Currently, East Asia harbors perhaps the largest and most dynamic economies in the world, as well as vigorous great power competition. The combination of economic and strategic importance encourages preoccupation with the East Asian balance of power among great powers. Even though the U.S. continues to possess relative advantage in many indicators of competition and other countries have little chance of overtaking Washington's lead in the short run, some countries such as China have shown traits of catching up.[10] According to some scholars, adjusted for purchasing power parity (PPP), China's gross domestic product (GDP) can be expected to rapidly catch up with the United States, a sign of its potential to emerge as the new challenger against US power.[11] More importantly, not only does China possess objective char-

---

Visions of U.S. Grand Strategy," *International Security*, 21:3 (1996/97), 5-53.

9_Clinton, William Jefferson "Building a New Pacific Community," *Dispatch*, 4:28 (1993), 485-488.

10_Vogel, Ezra F. *Living with China: U.S.-China Relations in the Twenty-first Century* New York: W.W. Norton, 1997, 143.

acteristics to challenge United States hegemony, it is also actively preparing to enter global competition through actions such as the "great power diplomacy" (daguo waijiao) that has been advocated since the 1990s.

Aside from China, it is worth noting that Japan's behavior also draws much attention. Since the mid-1980s, slogans such as "return to Asia" or "exit the United States and enter Asia" (tuoMei ruYa) constantly remind Japan to play a bridging role between the United States and East Asian regional integration.[12] After the 1990s, Japan has even set out the achievement of great power status (political power) as its goal. However, the shadow of Japanese militarism in World War II continues to linger among East Asian countries while the Japanese economy has plunged into long term recession since the 1990s. On the other hand, Japan seems to be unable to escape the diplomatic reality of being a client state of the United States. The foregoing realities directly influençe the transformation of Japan's role in East Asia. In addition, incalculable economic damage caused by the major earthquake in 2011 place further variables in Japan's future development.

11_Nye, Joseph S. Jr. *Bound to Lead* New York: Basic Books, 1990; Segal, Gerald "Does China Matter," *Foreign Affairs*, 78:3 (1999), 29-32.

12_姚文禮, 〈簡論冷戰時期日本對外政策調整〉, 《日本學刊》, 第1期 (1994), 頁 67; 梁雲祥與應霄燕, 《後冷戰時代的日本政治, 經濟與外交》 (北京: 北京大學出版社, 2000年), 頁 139-45.

The East Asian balance of power became multi-polar with the end of the Cold War: the USSR collapsed and the United States was in decline, while both Japan and China have grown into new poles, though the new powers are still much weaker compared to the United States and the USSR in the Cold War. Japan once possessed the largest economy in East Asia, but depends overwhelmingly on the United States for security. Even though China possesses the greatest territory and population and also the largest army in the region, its naval and air forces are still too poorly equipped to dominate East Asia. Therefore, in terms of changes to the hegemonic structure in East Asia in the post-Cold War period, despite arguments that the region is dominated by tense bipolarity between Japan and China, the structure may still be beneficial for regional stability while the triangle relationship between China, the United States and Japan continues to be the focus of the region.[13] Amidst the relationship, Washington exploits the so called "China threat theory" in hopes of drawing Japan's support and maintaining its regional hegemony. At the same time, Beijing also seeks to gain Japan's support and achieve competitive advantage by proffering massive business opportunities generated by a single market and the future of East Asian integration.[14]

13_Ross, Robert "The Geography of the Peace: East Asia in the Twenty-first Century," I*nternational Security*, 23:4 (1999), p. 114.

Between Washington and Beijing's tug and pull, Tokyo seeks to establish its independent status in the hopes of moving the China-US-Japan relationship towards the structure of an equilateral triangle.

3. Continuing Cold War in the Post-Cold War Era

The basic phenomenon of the postwar East Asian order is the remarkably fixed and enduring US-led system of bilateral security ties with Japan, South Korea, Taiwan and Southeast Asia. The hub-and-spoke system remains the most important anchor of regional stability.[15] In a way, the continued division and opposition across the Taiwan Strait and on the Korean Peninsula can be said to be the very few typical examples that demonstrate "the Cold War in the post-Cold War era" in the current international structure. Both these cases not only developed during the United States- and Soviet-dominant Cold War period, confined to the rigid global structure, both issues continue to occupy their place on the

---

14_Goldstein, Avery "An Emerging China's Emerging Grand Strategy: A Neo-Bismarckian Turn?" in Ikenberry, G. John and Michael Mastanduno, eds. *International Relations Theory and the Asia-Pacific* New York: Columbia University Press, 2003, 57-106.

15_Ikenberry, G. John "American hegemony and East Asian order," *Australian Journal of International Affairs*, 58:3 (2004), 353-367.

world stage even as the leading actors have officially called an end to the Cold War act.[16] More importantly, in contrast to Washington and Moscow's "chronic pretense" of a Cold War (which began to thaw after the initiation of SALT-I in 1969), both cross-Strait relations and inter-Korean relations not only remained hostile - both sets of relations have also long been deemed by strategic experts to be hot spots with the highest potential for the outbreak of conflict. It is surprising that even to this day, both issues have yet to establish operational frameworks for dialogue. While North and South Korea commenced the first inter-Korean summit in 2000 and produced a joint declaration, which set the tone for an ensuing series of ministry level meetings, cross-Strait relations entered a low point in 1999-2007 before the re-commencement of dialogue in 2008.

Nevertheless, it is worth noting the "conflicting but stable" interactions found in both cross-Strait and inter-Korea relations. In other words, despite the continued stalemate between parties on either side of the mid-line of the Taiwan Strait and the thirty-eighth parallel that seems to be short of resolution, in the past

16_Wines, Michael "Bush and Yeltsin Declare Formal End to Cold War; Agree to Exchange Visits," *New York Times*, February 2, 1992; http://www.nytimes.com/1992/02/02/world/bush-and-yeltsin-declare-formal-end-to-cold-war-agree-to-exchange-visits.html

half century, especially after the signing of the armistice that ended the Korean War in 1953 and the shelling of Quemoy in 1958,[17] large scale conflicts stopped between the opposing entities, while characteristics of an "ultra stable structure" began to emerge. For neo-classical realists, whether an international conflict will enter the last stage of war not only depends on the perception of the decision maker and the difference in power between parties, the distribution of power in the international system also has an influence on the developing process.[18] This author sees the enduring Cold War phenomenon in cross-Strait and inter-Korean relations as "structural fortuity," a situation where both the internal and external structures produce constraints on the outbreak of a war. Washington and Beijing's current competition in Korea and Taiwan are typical great power conflicts of the new age. Sino-US

17_The conflict took place between PRC and ROC in 1958 is also called "The Second Taiwan Strait Crisis." It started with the Artillery Bombardment on 23 August. Afterwards, both sides continued to bombard each other with shells containing propaganda leaflets on alternate days of the week. Then, this strange informal arrangement continued until the normalization of ties between the United States and PRC in 1979.

18_See Lobell, Steven E., Norrin M. Ripsman, and Jeffrey W. Taliaferro, eds. *Neo-Classical Realism, the State and Foreign Policy* Cambridge: Cambridge University Press, 2009; Rose, Gideon "Neoclassical Realism and Theories of Foreign Policy," *World Politics*, 51:1 (1998), 149-150; Taliaferro, Jeffery W. "Security Seeking under Anarchy: Defensive Realism Revisited," *International Security*, 25:3 (2000/2001), 131-132.

competition is also fast spilling over into other countries in East Asia and other parts of the world.

II. Cross-Strait Relations: the Basic Triangle Structure

Recalling the fact that both the United States and the USSR were often deemed superpowers in the Cold War period, not only does the title suggest a domineering influence to a certain extent, it also hints that interactions between the two superpowers would inevitably become the foreign policy focus for many countries, particularly countries such as China and Taiwan, and the two Koreas, which engrossed the attention of the superpowers. As generally believed and widely acknowledged, Taiwan's US policy has long seemed to be the equivalent of its foreign policy. United States influence over Taiwan is clear: not only is Washington's each and every move (especially in terms of relations with Beijing) magnified and closely examined by Taipei, Washington's support is often directly interpreted as Taipei's international space or co-efficient for survival.

1. The China Issue: Comparison with Western Views

Whether as an emerging power that can be embedded into the

post-Cold War international order,[19] an evil hegemony with ambition for restoring the Middle Kingdom,[20] or a seemingly prosperous regional economic entity that is about to collapse,[21] the West's dizzying content on China's future development reflect the latter's critical status in the international system. Within China, despite the existence of slightly pessimistic or conservative views, the concept of the so called "China Rising" has basically achieved a certain degree of consensus over time.[22] Based on military and economic indicators proposed by scholars, it is important to note that China certainly demonstrates trends of mitigating the difference in power with developed countries (especially the United States). However,

---

19_Patterson, Bradley Jr. *The White House Staff: Inside the West Wing and Beyond* (Washington D.C.: Brookings Institution Press, 2000), 52-57.

20_Marble, Andrew D. "Why the 'China Threat' Debate," *Issue & Studies*, 36 (2000), 1-18; Mosher, Steven W. *Hegemon: China's Planto Dominate Asia and World* New York: Encounter Books, 2000; and Gertz, Bill *The China Threat: How the People's Republic Targets America* New York: Regency Publisher, 2000.

21_See Chang, Gordon G. *The Coming Collapse of China* New York: Rndom House, 2001.

22_閻學通等, 《中國崛起: 國際環境評估》 (天津: 天津人民出版社, 1998年), 頁 58. Even though the West has yet to reach a consensus on China rising, the key to understanding the potential effects of the phenomenon is how to correctly evaluate such economic growth. See Perkins, Dwight H. "How China's Transformation Shape Its Future," in Vogel, Ezra F. ed. *Living with China: U.S.-China Relations in the 21th Century* New York: Norton Press, 1997, pp. 143-145; Khalizad, Zalamay M. et al. *The United States and a Rising China: Strategic and Military Implication* New York: Rand Corporation, 1999.

in contrast to tackling the issue from the traditional perspective of power politics, we think that China's growing power may be understood from a different angle.

Most western states' feelings for China are often very paradoxical. In terms of vested interest in the long run, Western Europe, the United States and Japan obviously do not wish to see China become excessively powerful in the future and threaten their international status, hence disparaging China at least provides ideas for calming the mind. However, in terms of economic interest in the short run, as the current production cycle of industrial products is cut short by the increased speed caused by new technology, if the trend persists and effective solutions cannot be found for dealing with the speed of capital reflow, counter cyclical actions (such as factory closures and large scale cutbacks in employment) intended for cost reduction may directly threaten the international status of great powers while impacting social and economic stability. According to the logic of capitalism, the problem may be resolved by the development of new markets. Market creation not only gave rise to the global wave of imperialism in the late nineteenth century, it is also the key to the corporate rush into the Chinese market in the past thirty years. In other words, the real reason that China rising has become a hot issue for discussion is not the distance China has closed on the United States and Europe, but the West's need for China's potential markets.

Compared with the late Qing dynasty, not only has China greatly increased its capability for self-defense, the West's need for the Chinese market can also be deemed as its vital interest (as failure to expand will lead to the horrendous outcome of economic collapse). China's important status is apparent.

2. Cross-Strait Ultra-stable Structure in the Cold War Era

Similar to the concept of ultra-stable structure mentioned previously, at least in the Cold War period, the domestic and external environment of cross-Strait relations certainly contained the outbreak of war. In contrast to the historic view that war is a rational policy choice, whether the thinking of the renunciation of war (peaceful resolution of conflicts) evoked by the two World Wars, or the influence of mutual deterrence under the bipolar system in the Cold War, the bold act of initiating war is always temporarily excluded from the policy menu. Even as one takes into account the fact that China launched several border wars in the 1950s to 1970s, attention can still be placed on the role of the United States. Washington naturally intervened in cross-Strait relations because maintaining division across the Strait clearly supports US hegemonic status in the region. Moreover, despite the fact that the governments on opposite sides of the Strait do not deny mutual hostility towards one another, geographic separation by the Taiwan

〈Table 1〉 Stability change in cross-Strait relations

	Policy of Hegemony	Global Environment	Domestic Stability	Mutual Interaction
Cold War Era	+	+	+	+
Post-Cold War Era	+ to −	+	+ to −	uncertain

Note: + means moving towards stable development, − means increased conflict

Strait and US intervention forced both entities to return rationally to the priority of domestic stability, delaying the outbreak of war. Finally, as the quasi-domestic quality in cross-Strait conflict is higher than its international quality, coupled with the influence of nationalism, the softer forces in hard interactions across the Strait provide considerable momentum against war that help to maintain peace between China and Taiwan until this day.

However, 〈Table 1〉 suggests that the pillars that provide support for the ultra-stable structure in the Cold War period have all become loose over time and even lean towards collapse. Whether uncertainty over United States hegemony hints at Washington's reduced energy towards conflict intervention and the disappearance of the safety valve in cross-Strait relations, or with China's development towards a capitalist economy, or whether the crisis of rising populism similar to what Taiwan experienced in its early period of political transition may emerge domestically, both suggest the possibility of shifting the domestic focus through reactions towards the external environment (part of the reason for the 1996 missile crisis in the Taiwan Strait comes from such manipulation). As for the deadlock between the One-China principle and independent sovereignty that has characterized cross-Strait relations since the 1990s, even though bilateral relations can be said to be currently relaxed, the ultra-stable structure is clearly slowly developing towards an unstable structure. Yet the current global environment remains in the interest of peace-making. Not only is the peaceful resolution of conflicts still the general consensus in the international community, the coming age of globalization has caused existing international norms such as the nation-state or sovereignty to undergo fundamental changes. In other words, if these concepts that served as the main reasons for international conflicts in the past no longer guide decision makers, the search for potential answers to cross-Strait relations may be continued under a new framework of thinking.

3. The Transformation of Washington's China Policy

At least until now, the United States inevitably continues to be the most crucial factor influencing cross-Strait relations. However, the key to whether Washington can stabilize the situation in the Taiwan Strait does not depend on whether Taipei can excel on its United States policy but on the former's strategic considerations based on its evaluation of power. As mentioned above, the United

States has gradually transformed from a hegemonic state into a pre-eminent great power since the Cold War period, the change in power naturally influences Washington's strategic plans, particularly in the case of China, which has transformed from an instrument to provide checks and balances to a target to be balanced by the United States.[23] Both optimists and pessimists of America's future all regard China as the most important source of threat for the United States, which explains the reason for the development in Sino-US relations from strategic partners to strategic competitors.[24]

At the beginning of the new century, Washington has also come to include Japan and Taiwan as a part of its balancing strategy against Beijing in order to maintain its influence in East Asia. Accordingly, the United States has continued to expand the interpretation of the US-Japan Security Pact to increase its applicability while giving support to constitutional reforms in Japan for the re-establishment of local military forces and deployment of troops abroad. At the same time, step-by-step Washington revised former president Clinton's policy stance of forgoing support for Taiwan's participation in international organizations while increasing the

---

23_Schulzinger, Robert D. *U.S. Diplomacy since 1900* New York: Oxford University Press, 2002, 379.

24_See Brown, Michael et al. *The Rise of China* Cambridge, MA.: MIT Press, 2000. Vice versa, the U.S. has also become China's foremost competitor. See Pomfret, John "U.S. now a Threat in China's Eyes," *Washington Post*, November 15, 2000, 1.

level of military exchanges between Taipei and Washington (for example, allowing Taiwan's minister of national defense to visit the United States). The direction of US policy is clear.[25]

Nevertheless, "power as the foundation of policy" remains the key for analyzing the triple relationship between Mainland China, the United States and Taiwan. In other words, the comparison of real power is often the final basis for the realization of policy. In this perspective, despite the fact that China does possess multi-layered structural adjustment problems in terms of its political system, economy and society, if unstable factors that arise in reforms may be effectively held under control while the Chinese economy continues to rise, reducing China's distance from the United States and pulling away from Taiwan, Washington's space for voicing its opinion will become more limited while Taipei may be forced to submit to Beijing due to its inability to keep up with the arms race across the Strait. However, as this author mentions in the opening paragraph, with the difference in power gradually reducing between the United States and China since 2000, Washington has begun to slowly adjust its regional security strategy. The implication of such shift is to reinvigorate cases that were contained by US in-

---

25_Cambone, Stephen A. "The United States and Theatre Missile Defense in North-East Asia," *Survival*, 39 (1997), 66; 楊志恆, 〈美日安保之沿革及其對台海安全之影響〉, 《戰略與國際研究》, 2卷 2期, 頁 1-30.

tervention in the Cold War (such as cross-Strait relations) and sow the seeds of uncertainty in the future. Developments on the Korean Peninsula in the same period are also linked with Washington's shift in strategy.

Ⅲ. Inter-Korean Relations: Under Potential Multi-polarity

In contrast to the relatively simpler triangular power structure that affects cross-Strait relations, the balance of power surrounding the Korean Peninsula seems much more complicated. China, the United States, Japan and Russia (fomerly the USSR) are all involved in the regional geopolitical structure to a certain extent. The four countries have also been the main parties to the Six-Party Talks since 2003.

1. The Great Powers in Modern Korean History

In the roughly half-century beginning from the end of the 1800s, three major international wars broke out on the Korean Peninsula: the Sino-Japanese War (1894-95), the Russo-Japanese War (1904-05) and the Korean War (1950-53). It is worth pointing out that the Korean Peninsula was never at the center of these wars, which hints at the complicated international geopolitical context of the region and China, Japan, the United States and Russia as the main players in the game over interests on the peninsula. Furthermore, similar to other peninsular regions in the world, the fact that the Korean Peninsula is both a bridge and springboard that connects land and sea is the key factor in deciding its foreign relations.[26]

If the above list of wars may be used as the foundation for dividing modern history into periods, as the center of the East Asian system, China naturally dominated interests on the peninsula before 1894; Japan then pushed back China's intervention after 1894 and consolidated its leadership role in Northeast Asia through the Russo-Japanese War.[27] After the end of the Second World War and the passing of a transition period (1945-50),[28] the Korean War

---

26_Oberdorfer, Don *The Two Koreas: A Contemporary History* New York: Basic Books, 2001, pp. 3-4.

27_According to the Treaty of Portsmouth signed between Russia and Japan in 1905, Moscow recognizes Tokyo's right to "enjoy the highest political, military and economic interests such as to provide guidance, protection and supervision" of Korea. Russia "shall not constrain or intervene" in any measures considered necessary by Japan.

28_The United Staes and the USSR originally reached the consensus of entrusting the Korean Peninsula to the joint control of China, the United States, Great Britain and the Soviet Union in April 1945. However, the Soviet Union's rapid takeover of the northern region of the Korean Peninsula after the declaration of war against Japan brought uncertainties to the region. The United States was forced to suggest the temporary proposal of designating the 38th parallel north as the line of division for receiving Japan's surrender. The event marks the starting point for the formal division

that erupted in 1950 drew a disinterested Washington into peninsular affairs and made the United States the third great power and the first global power to dominate geo-strategic interests on the Korean Peninsula after China (1637-1894) and Japan (1894-5) after the temporary termination of the Korean War in 1953.[29] In contrast to China (mainly concerned with national security interests) and Japan (mainly concerned with regional strategic development and planning), the reason for Washington's decision to lend support and intervene in a supposed domestic conflict when the Korean War broke out in June 1950 is its perception of the war in terms of global strategic planning. The United States wished to prevent competition between Washington and Moscow from spiraling into another great war.[30] On the other hand, perhaps another key consideration for the United States is its concern for the deteriorating situation on the peninsula in affecting the regional containment design based around Japan.[31] As former South Korean president Kim Dae-jung pointed out, "the Korean Peninsula is like

---

of Korea after 1948.

29_According to NSC-8 issued by the US National Security Council, the United States originally planned to retreat from Korea at the end of 1948. NSC-8, Position of the United States with Respect to Korea, 2 April, 1948, FRUS, Vol. VI, pp. 1163-1169.

30_See Truman, Harry *Memoirs by Harry S. Truman: 1945 Year of Decisions* New York: William S. Konecky Associates, 1999, 355.

31_五百旗頭真主編, 《戰後日本外交史》 (北京： 世界知識出版社, 2007年), 頁 51-52.

a tentacle that grows around other powers nervously, which makes it the thermometer for great power conflict or balance."[32] The statement concisely points out the Korean Peninsula's complicated geopolitical character.

Controversies surrounding North Korea's development of weapons of mass destruction (WMD) replaced inter-Korean relations as one of the most important threats to international security in the post-Cold War period. In 2003, the WMD issue gave rise to the establishment of the Six-Party Talks multilateral framework involving China, the United States, Japan, Russia and the two Koreas. After enduring four years, six sets and ten rounds of marathon negotiations, parties to the talks finally agreed on the Joint Statement on Second-Phase Actions for Implementation and put a temporary end to the potential crisis. It is worth noting that even though North Korea seems to be at the heart of the problem, Pyongyang itself may not be the source of the crisis. The delay in reaching a consensus in the Six-Party Talks after the entry of great powers suggests that strategic competition among the powers remains the crux of the North Korean issue. Great power competition behind the nuclear issue on the peninsula is the reason why an optimal balance of power is yet to be achieved in Northeast

32_金大中著, 馮世則譯, 《建設和平與民主》(北京: 世界知識出版社, 1991年), 頁 173.

Asia, and serves as a decisive factor on the future development of the region. In other words, as long as stability cannot be achieved in international relations in Northeast Asia (whether through United States hegemony or the establishment of a multilateral governing regime), the North Korean issue can only be prolonged.[33]

2. Transformation of the Inter-Korean Ultra-stable Structure

Similar to cross-Strait relations, despite the outbreak of war between the Koreas in the early periods of independence, the containing effect of the deterrence structure in the Cold War and the war renunciation thinking stimulated by the Second World War have jointly restrained the outbreak of large-scale military conflict on the Korean Peninsula since 1953. Even though scattered conflicts have never ceased, the United States great power role and strategic agenda in the region have effectively blocked the rise of conflicts while the demilitarized zone (DMZ) has forced both entities on the Korean Peninsula to rationally give priority to domestic development, prolonging the outbreak of conflict.[34] In addition,

33_蔡東杰, 〈朝鮮半島核武爭議潛藏衝突引信〉, 《青年日報》, 2008年 4月 27日, 4版.

34_According to the ceasefire agreement signed on July 27, 1953, the two Koreas would establish a demilitarized zone along the 38th parallel north that would span 248km in length and 4km in width. Both entities would station a large number of troops on either side of the DMZ.

〈Table 2〉 Stability change in inter-Korean relations

	Policy of Hegemony	Global Environment	Domestic Stability	Mutual Interaction
Cold War Era	+	+	+	+
Post-Cold War Era	+ to −	+	+ to −	uncertain

Note: + means moving towards stable development, − means increased conflict

from a certain perspective, the lack of interactions in inter-Korean relations during the Cold War took away the excuse for war and indirectly helped to maintain peaceful development on the peninsula.

However, as with cross-Strait relations, changes to various supporting variables since the end of the Cold War have also caused the ultra-stable structure that has lasted for half a century to begin to show different possibilities of development. The comparisons in 〈Table 2〉 suggest that uncertainty over United States hegemony has led to Washington's reduced energy in conflict intervention. Seoul regained non-wartime operational control of its military in 1994, after transferring its military command to Washington upon the outbreak of the Korean War in 1950, and is expected to achieve full command in 2015 after the Choenan Incident in 2010 pushed back the earlier expected date of 2012. United States military influence on affairs on the peninsula will inevitably be affected. On the other hand, since Kim Il-sung's death in 1994, even though Kim Jong-il held power until the end of 2011, North

Korea has chronically suffered from low economic development and food crises under the rule of the latter. One may conclude that domestic challenges not only bring about enormous pressure for the North Korean regime, but Pyongyang is also forced to maintain its legitimacy through constant military saber-rattling, which adds negative factors to inter-Korean interactions.

Finally, although the Sunshine Policy initiated by Kim Dae-jung and carried on by Roh Moo-hyun brought the potential dawning of peace to inter-Korean relations from 2000 to 2008, and after four years of extended dialogues, the Six Party Talks seem to keep a WMD-threatened Korean Peninsula under a state of general control, interactions between the two Koreas continue to be hindered by uncertainties. Pyongyang's decision to withdraw from the Six Party Talks in early 2009 and the Cheonan Incident and shelling of Yeonpyeong Island in 2010 all exacerbate tensions in inter-Korean relations. Kim Jong-il's sudden death in 2011 laid down further challenges for bilateral relations on the Korean Peninsula.

3. Peninsula Security under a Power Struggle

The previous description reveals that security on the Korean Peninsula is in a highly uncertain state. Yet analysis of the Korean problem should not only be based on events on the peninsula but should be placed in the greater context of the regional environment, or perhaps even the global geo-strategic environment. Despite the fact that China and the United States have gradually become the main sources dominating the current global strategic balance,[35] as the existing hegemon, the United States may find it hard not to check China's behavior when chance provides, including the convenience to exploit the geographic position of the Korean Peninsula. As mentioned above, the Korean Peninsula has become an important site of great power competition since the end of the nineteenth century. In other words, resolution of the North Korean nuclear issue will be highly symbolic, as the situation would suggest the emergence of a new balance of power in Northeast Asia and implications for the development of a new hegemonic structure in East Asia. Currently, as the host state of the Six-Party Talks and the most influential state on Pyongyang, China holds greater advantage over many other countries in the region. However, ensuing development of the United States' "return to

35_Sokolsky, Richard, Angel Rabasa and C. R. Neu, *The Role of Southeast Asia in U.S. Strategy toward China* Santa Monica, CA.: RAND, 2000; Economy, Elizabeth *China's Rise in Southeast Asia: Implications for Japan and the United States* New York: Council on Foreign Relations, 2005; Ferguson, Niall and Moritz Schularick, "Chimerica and the Global Asset Market Boom," *International Finance*, 10:3 (2007), 215-239; Karabell, Zachary *Superfusion: How China and America Became One Economy and Why the World's Prosperity Depends on It* New York: Simon & Schuster, 2010; Foot, Rosemary and Andrew Walter, *China, the United States, and Global Order* New York: Cambridge University Press, 2011.

Asia" policy will bring about uncertainties to the regional balance of power in the near future.

In terms of North Korean policy, even though on the surface, the United States may seem to seek improvement in bilateral relations through the provision of aid,[36] in terms of strategic planning in East Asia, the maim thinking revolves around the search for a response to the rise of China.[37] Under the Bush administration, Washington first adopted the strategy of soft containment against Beijing, before the Obama administration adjusted the strategic planning of US foreign policy with Secretary of State Hillary Clinton's visit to East Asia in 2009 and the declaration to "return to Asia" at the end of the same year.[38] However, the complexity of power relations in East Asia not only makes the establishment of a mechanism for conflict management a mandatory consideration in multilateral cooperation,[39] hard power policies that are based on

---

36_Graham, Bradley *Hit to Kill: The New Battle over Shielding American from Missile Attack* New York: Public Affairs, 2001, 353-354.

37_Banlaoi, Rommel C. "Southeast Asian Perspectives on the Rise of China: Regional Security after 9/11." *Parameters*, Summer (2003), 98-107; Economy, Elizabeth *China's Rise in Southeast Asia: Implications for Japan and the United States* New York: Council on Foreign Relations, 2005; Goh, Evelyn "Southeast Asian Perspectives on the China Challenge." *Journal of Strategic Studies*, 30:4 (2007), 809-832.

38_Clinton's trip was highly symbolic, as the visit was the first time since the 1960s that any US Secretary of State has made Asia the destination for their inaugural state visit abroad. See: 〈希拉蕊啟程出訪亞洲, 矢言加強美亞關係〉, 《奇摩新聞網》 (2011/12/20 瀏覽) ; http://tw.news.yahoo.com/article/url/d/a/090216/19/1ej1z.html

the traditional use of force have also become unfavorable as a choice for realizing integration. This may also be the context for the "harmonious policy" (*mulinzhengce*) in becoming China's main guiding principle in East Asia after 2002.

It is important to note that in spite of arguments that East Asia is currently dominated by a bipolar power balance between China and the United States that may be in the interest of regional stability,[40] the triangular relationship between China, the United States and Japan continues to be the undisputable focus of attention.[41] In the relationship, the United States seeks to maintain its hegemonic status by garnering Japan's support through the so called China threat theory; China seeks to seduce Japan through the enormous market potential of a single market and the future of East Asian regional integration; and Japan seeks to establish an autonomous policy and move the three-way relationship towards the structure of an equilateral triangle.

Meanwhile, under the Putin administration, Russia has shown

39_Dosch, Jörn "The Post-Cold War Development of Regionalism in East Asia," in Fu-Kuo Liu and Philippe Regnier, eds., R*egionalism in East Asia: Paradigm Shifting* London: RoutledgeCurzon, 2003, 45.

40_Ross, Robert S. 〈21世紀東亞的力量均衡: 兩極結構的穩定性〉, 收於張蘊嶺主編, 《21世紀世界格局與大國關係》 (北京: 社會科學文獻出版社, 2001年), 頁 99-109.

41 _時殷弘, 〈中美日三角關係〉, 《世界經濟與政治》, 第1期 (2000); 楊伯江, 〈中美日三角: 利益磨合與良性發展前景〉, 收於中國現代國際關係研究所主編, 《亞太戰略場: 世界主要力量的發展與角逐》 (北京: 時事出版社, 2002年), 頁 303-324.

interest in playing a greater role in resolving critical security issues in East Asia, while actively seeking to participate in a regional security dialogue mechanism of the Asia Pacific.[42] Moscow's participation would not only deeply embed another major power within the East Asian power structure; the future of the region would become more complicated as well (at least in terms of problems on the Korean Peninsula).

IV. Conclusion: Power Politics and Its Implication

As Aidan Foster-Carter points out, "inter-Korean relations are manifestly sui generis in obvious ways."[43] The same may well be said of cross-Strait relations. Based on the logic of power politics and this author's analysis concerning the Cold War cases of cross-Strait and inter-Korean relations that have continued to be flashpoints to this day, the following conclusions may be drawn:

42_Tsygankov, Andrei P. "Russia's Interests and Objectives in East Asia," in Kim, Hyung-Kook, Myongsob Kim, and Amitav Acharya, eds. *Northeast Asia and the Two Koreas: Meta-stability, Security and Community* Seoul: Yonsei University Press, 2008, 209.

43_Foster-Carter, Aidan "Inter-Korean Relations," in Koh, Byung Chul ed. *North Korea and the World: Explaining Pyongyang's Foreign Policy* Seoul: Kyungnam University Press, 2004, 286.

A. Difference in power affects the possibility of intervention by external force

In terms of the realist conception of power, the amount of power that each state possesses cannot be perfectly equal. As a result, the hierarchical phenomenon that develops from such differences not only implies that a few dominant powers hold the dominant voice and influence on the world stage, relatively weaker actors in the middle and lower level of the structure also do not possess the capability to make autonomous policies as suggested by the concept of sovereignty. Moreover, for the latter, external force is always an important factor to be considered. Sometimes the external factor may become the key source for policy.

B. Submissive character of cross-Strait and inter-Korean relations in Cold War Era

As Martin Wight points out, buffer states located between great powers may be established or maintained in order to reduce potential conflict between great powers. The buffer state is sometimes also referred to as a "power vacuum."[44] Naturally, sub-

---

44_Wight, Martin *Power Politics* London: Royal Institute of International Affairs, 1978, 160.

mission and the lack of autonomy are the main characteristics of the foreign policy of these states. At least during the entire Cold War period, the fragmented entities of China, Taiwan, South Korea and North Korea had somewhat limited control over foreign policy due to their relatively weak position in the international power structure. Moreover, located at the frontline of US-Soviet competition in East Asia, China, Taiwan, South Korea and North Korea submitted to the superpowers' demand for mutual deterrence and holding back conflicts. The submissive quality in East Asian entities seemed to strip away policy autonomy, leaving these entities to be passively and chronically embedded within the so called "ultra-stable structure."

C. Changes in the power structure will bring uncertainties to future development

Although the Korea Peninsula and the Taiwan Strait are often cited by observers as the two potentially explosive areas in Northeast Asia,[45] at least in the Cold War period, the ultra-stable

45_Kim, Woosang and Yongho Kim, "Korea and Taiwan under the Future Northeast Asian Security Structure," in Kim, Woosang ed. *Northeast Asian Regional Security Order and Strategic Calculus on the Taiwan Straits* Seoul: Yonsei University Press, 2003, 11.

structure offered some momentum for controlling the conflicts. However, the difference in power implied by the power structure is the main force driving the development of cross-Strait and inter-Korean relations. Once change occurs in the distribution of power, the previous case may take on different paths in the future.

In short, in the post-Cold War period, both the regional and global power structures have changed rapidly. Looking to the future of security across the Taiwan Strait and on the Korean Peninsula, one may continue to keep watch of developments on two different levels.

Short-term (2011-2020)

Regardless of whether China's foreign policy is becoming more active or not,[46] under the impact of the financial crisis in 2008, China became the spotlight of attention at the G-20 summit in 2009 and 2010, and Hu Jintao squeezed out Obama to top Forbes magazine's most influential person ranking at the end of 2010. At the same time, not only did the size of the Chinese economy surpass Japan in 2010 to become the second biggest in the world be-

46_Johnston, Alastair "Is China a Status Quo Power?" *International Security*, 27:4 (2003), 5-56.

hind the United States, according to estimates by Goldman Sachs in 2009, but the size of the Japanese economy will make up merely about a quarter of the Chinese economy by 2030. Perhaps such a shift in economic power may end the Sino-Japanese competition over regional leadership since the 1990s.[47] However, China's development is not without barriers or challenges, while the international environment does not always go along with China's wishes. Taking into account remnant influences of United States hegemony and Washington's increasingly active East Asia strategy, in the short term and comparable to the Cold War, the United States will continue to play the important role of directing cross-Strait and inter-Korean relations and stabilizing relations across the Taiwan Strait and the thirty-eighth parallel.

Mid-term (2021-2030)

Despite Washington's continued regional presence, taking into consideration persisting changes in power and status between China and the United States and uncertainties that may emerge due to power transition, in the mid-term, in terms of South Korea and Taiwan, long term diplomatic allies of the United States, it is

---

47_Meyer, Claude *Chine ou Japon: quell leader pour L'Asie?* Paris: Presses de la fondation nationale des sciences Politiques, 2010.

crucial for both countries to react to new developments through policy responses. Both Seoul and Taipei must include the issue in its long term strategic planning as soon as possible.

References

Baker, James. "America in Asia: Emerging Architecture for a Pacific Community," *Foreign Affairs*, 70:5 (1991).

Banlaoi, Rommel C. "Southeast Asian Perspectives on the Rise of China: Regional Security after 9/11." *Parameters*, Summer (2003).

Berger, Thomas. "Set for Stability? Prospects for Conflict and Cooperation in East Asia," *Review of International Security*, 26 (2000).

Brzezinski, Zbigniew. *The Grand Chessboard: American Primacy and Its Geostrategic Imperatives*. New York: Basic Books, 1997.

Cambone, Stephen A. "The United States and Theatre Missile Defense in North-East Asia," *Survival*, 39 (1997).

Chang, Gordon G. *The Coming Collapse of China*. New York: Rndom House, 2001.

Clinton, William Jefferson. "Building a New Pacific Community," *Dispatch*, 4:28 (1993).

Department of State, *United States Foreign Policy, 1969-70*. Washington, D.C.: U.S. Government Printing Office, 1971.

Dosch, Jörn "The Post-Cold War Development of Regionalism in East Asia," in Fu-Kuo Liu and Philippe Regnier, eds. *Regionalism in East Asia: Paradigm Shifting*. London: Routledge Curzon, 2003.

Economy, Elizabeth C. *China's Rise in Southeast Asia: Implications for Japan and the United States*. New York: Council on Foreign Relations, 2005.

Evans, Michael. "Power and Paradox: Asian Geopolitics and Sino-American Relations in the 21st Century," *Orbis*, Winter (2011).

Ferguson, Niall and Moritz Schularick, "Chimerica and the Global Asset Market Boom," *International Finance*, 10:3 (2007).

Foot, Rosemary and Andrew Walter. *China, the United States, and Global Order*. New York: Cambridge University Press, 2011.

Foster-Carter, Aidan. "Inter-Korean Relations," in Byung Chul Koh, ed. *North Korea and the World: Explaining Pyongyang's Foreign Policy*. Seoul: Kyungnam University Press, 2004.

Gertz, Bill. *The China Threat: How the People's Republic Targets America*. New York: Regency Publisher, 2000.

Goh, Evelyn."Southeast Asian Perspectives on the China Challenge." *Journal of Strategic Studies*, 30:4 (2007).

Goldstein, Avery. "An Emerging China's Emerging Grand Strategy: A Neo-Bismarckian Turn?" in G. John Ikenberry and Michael Mastanduno, eds., *International Relations Theory and the Asia-Pacific.* New York: Columbia University Press, 2003.

Graham, Bradley. *Hit to Kill: The New Battle over Shielding American from Missile Attack.* New York: Public Affairs, 2001.

Ikenberry, G. John. "American hegemony and East Asian order," *Australian Journal of International Affairs*, 58:3 (2004).

Johnston, Alastair. "Is China a Status Quo Power?" *International Security*, 27:4 (2003).

Jones, Alan, Jr. "Nixon and the World," in Alan Jones, Jr., ed. U.S. Foreign Policy *in a Changing World.* New York: David McKay, 1973.

Karabell, Zachary. *Superfusion: How China and America Became One Economy and Why the World's Prosperity Depends on It.* New York: Simon & Schuster, 2010.

Kim Woosang and Yongho Kim, "Korea and Taiwan under the Future Northeast Asian Security Structure," in Woosang Kim, ed. *Northeast Asian Regional Security Order and Strategic Calculus on the Taiwan Straits.* Seoul: Yonsei University Press, 2003.

Laird, Melvin R. "The Nixon Doctrine: From Potential Despair to New Opportunities," in Laird, ed. *The Nixon Doctrine.* Washington, D.C.: Town Hall Meeting, 1972.

Lobell, Steven E., Norrin M. Ripsman, and Jeffrey W. Taliaferro, eds., *Neo-Classical Realism, the State and Foreign Policy.* Cambridge: Cambridge University Press, 2009.

Lynn-Jones, Sean M. and Steven E. Miller, eds., *The Cold War and After: Prospect for Peace.* New York: The MIT Press, 1994.

Marble, Andrew D. "Why the 'China Threat' Debate," *Issue & Studies*, 36 (2000).

Meyer, Claude. *Chine ou Japon: quell leader pour L'Asie?* Paris: Presses de la foundation nationale des sciences Politiques, 2010.

Moaz, Zeev. "The Controversy over the Democratic Peace," *International Security*, 22:1 (1997).

Mosher, Steven W. *Hegemon: China's Planto Dominate Asia and World.* New York: Encounter Books, 2000.

Nye, Joseph S. Jr. *Bound to Lead.* New York: Basic Books, 1990.

Oberdorfer, Don. *The Two Koreas: A Contemporary History.* New York: Basic Books, 2001.

Patterson, Bradley Jr. *The White House Staff: Inside the West Wing and Beyond.*

Washington D.C.: Brookings Institution Press, 2000.

Rose, Gideon. "Neoclassical Realism and Theories of Foreign Policy," *World Politics*, 51:1 (1998).

Ross, Robert S. 〈21世紀東亞的力量均衡: 兩極結構的穩定性〉, 收於張蘊嶺主編, 《21世紀世界格局與大國關係》 北京: 社會科學文獻出版社, 2001年.

------. "The Geography of the Peace: East Asia in the Twenty-first Century," I*nternational Security*, 23:4 (1999).

Schlesinger, Arthur Jr. "Back to the Womb: Isolationism's Renewed Threat," *Foreign Affairs*, 74:4 (1995).

Schulzinger, Robert D. *U.S. Diplomacy since 1900*. New York: Oxford University Press, 2002.

Segal, Gerald. "Does China Matter," *Foreign Affairs*, 78:3 1999.

Sokolsky, Richard, Angel Rabasa, and C. R. Neu. *The Role of Southeast Asia in U.S. Strategy toward China*. Santa Monica, CA.: RAND, 2000.

Spanier, John. *American Foreign Policy since World War II*. New York: Praeger, 1973.

Taliaferro, Jeffery W. "Security Seeking under Anarchy: Defensive Realism Revisited," *International Security*, 25:3 (2000/2001).

Tsygankov, Andrei P. "Russia's Interests and Objectives in East Asia," in Hyung-Kook Kim, Myongsob Kim, and Amitav Acharya, eds. Northeast Asia and the Two Koreas: Meta-stability, Security and Community. Seoul: Yonsei University Press, 2008.

Vogel, Ezra F. *Living with China: U.S.-China Relations in the Twenty-first Century*. New York: W.W. Norton, 1997.

Wight, Martin. *Power Politics*. London: Royal Institute of International Affairs, 1978.

Wines, Michael. "Bush and Yeltsin Declare Formal End to Cold War; Agree to Exchange Visits," *The New York Times*, February 2, 1992; http://www.nytimes.com/1992/02/02/world/bush-and-yeltsin-declare-formal-end-to-cold-war-agree-to-exchange-visits.html

姚文禮, 〈簡論冷戰時期日本對外政策調整〉, 《日本學刊》, 第1期 (1994).

梁雲祥與應霄燕, 《後冷戰時代的日本政治, 經濟與外交》 (北京: 北京大學出版社, 2000年).

時殷弘, 〈中美日三角關係〉, 《世界經濟與政治》, 第1期 (2000).

楊伯江, 〈中美日三角: 利益磨合與良性發展前景〉, 收於中國現代國際關係研究所主編, 《亞太戰略場: 世界主要力量的發展與角逐》 北京: 時事出版社, 2002年.

五百旗頭真主編, 《戰後日本外交史》 北京 : 世界知識出版社, 2007年.

金大中著, 馮世則譯, 《建設和平與民主》 北京: 世界知識出版社, 1991年.
蔡東杰, 〈朝鮮半島核武爭議潛藏衝突引信〉, 《青年日報》, 2008年 4月 27日, 4版.
閻學通等, 《中國崛起: 國際環境評估》 (天津: 天津人民出版社, 1998年.
楊志恆, 〈美日安保之沿革及其對台海安全之影響〉, 《戰略與國際研究》, 2卷 2期.

Frustrated Alignment

The Pacific Pact Proposals From 1949 To 1954 and South Korea-Taiwan Relations

Jung-hyun Park
(HK Resarch Professor of Asian Research Institute in Korea University)

I. Introduction

Around 1950, when the global tension of the Cold War was escalating, South Korea and Taiwan sought to build a strong alliance. In December 1949, when the Nationalist Government of the Republic of China (ROC) fled Mainland China and secured its power basis on the remote island of Taiwan, the South Korean government (the Republic of Korea, or ROK) became the first state in the world to recognize the legitimacy of this provisional government vis-à-vis the communist People's Republic of China (PRC),

---

* This chapter was published on the *The International Journal of Asian Studies* Vol. 12, no.2(Cambridge University Press, July 2015).

and immediately moved its embassy from Mainland China to Taiwan. Six month later, in June 1950, when the Korean War broke out on the Korean Peninsula, Taiwan also immediately responded, suggesting that it would send troops to assist South Korea against the invasion of the communist regime of North Korea. This extraordinarily strong alliance between South Korea and Taiwan shows that they had officially discarded their two-millennia-long hierarchical relations and had jointly entered the newly established "modern" international arena. Why had these old but new states so quickly replaced long-standing hierarchical relations with rather practical and strategic ones, and what were the motives behind this exceptional move? One of the key markers in investigating South Korea-Taiwan relations around 1950 is the idea of a Pacific Pact.

The idea of a Pacific Pact first emerged in response to the establishment of the North Atlantic Treaty Organization (NATO) as a United States-centered collective security system in Europe in 1949. Following the Second World War, the capitalist world was reorganized under American leadership, and Asian countries also responded to this changed international setting. As a practical means of both containing the Soviet Union and maintaining the capitalist system, the United States promoted regional integration, thus rebuilding the devastated Western nations and binding non-communist nations to the capitalist world. In Europe, this master plan was executed through implementation of the Marshall Plan and the establishment of NATO.[1] The leaders of anti-communist countries in Asia also anticipated the growing role of the United States in regional security and envisaged an Asian version of NATO. However, the United States' policy of non-intervention in Asia drove them to seek alternative measures to fill the security vacuum in the region.

South Korea and Taiwan, which were situated on the frontline of the Cold War confrontation, were more desperate than any other Asian countries. This led them to develop a regional security system on their own initiative: a Pacific Pact. The Pacific Pact was one of the major parameters in structuring Asian international relations during the Cold War period. The primary goal of the present work is to offer an in-depth explication of the initial formation of South Korea-Taiwan relations by investigating their collaborative, but eventually unsuccessful, promotion of a Pacific Pact before and after the Korean War.

At present, scholarly interest in South Korea-Taiwan relations has been eclipsed by the rising importance of South Korea-China relations. Works on the international relations of East Asia in the

---

1_Rho, Kiyoung "The Development of Pacific Pact Policy and the Plan of Regional Security in the Syngman Rhee Regime," *The Journal of Korean History (Chiyuk Kwa Yuksa)*, vol. 11 (2002), 188.

1950s have also long focused on the roles of the United States and Japan. As a result, other Asian countries have been relegated to the periphery.[2] Moreover, studies on the relations of South Korea, North Korea, China, and Taiwan have been confined to the issues of division and unification. Therefore, the topic of South Korea-Taiwan relations still remains under-examined.[3]

Nevertheless, the historical evolution of South Korea-Taiwan relations is integral to understanding the Cold War system in Asia until the 1990s. Although diplomatic ties between South Korea

2_For this, see Cumings, Bruce "The Origins and Development of the Northeast Asian Political Economy: Industrial Sectors, Product Cycles, and Political Consequences," in Deyo, Frederic C. ed. *The Political Economy of New Asian Industrialism* New York : Cornell University Press, 1987; Bix, Herbert P. "Regional Integration: Japan and South Korea in America's Asian Policy," in Baldwin, Frank ed., *Without Parallel: The American-Korean Relationship since 1945* NY: Pantheon Books, 1974; Lee, Chongwon *U.S.-Korean Relations and Japan in East Asia's Cold War* Tokyo University Press, 1996. Recently, Su-Ya Chang has studied the United States' policies over Taiwan in relation to the Korean War. See Chang, Su-Ya *Did Korea Go to War to Rescue Taiwan?* Taiwan: Acropolis Publish, 2011.

3_South Korea-Taiwan relations are briefly mentioned in official works such as Guoshiguan bian, *Zhonghua minguo waijiaozhi* 中華民國外交志 (Sanminshuju, 2000). *Shihanhuiyilu* 使韓回憶錄 Biographical Literature Press, Taipei, 1980, authored by the first ROC ambassador to South Korea Shao Yulin is an important source. Research works on South Korea - Taiwan relations from the Korean perspective are almost nonexistent. Research works on foreign relations in South Korea and Taiwan are primarily concentrated on relations with the United States and Japan. South Korea-Taiwan relations are only subsidiarily discussed in discussing foreign relations with the United States and Japan.

and Taiwan were severed when South Korea normalized relations with the People's Republic of China in 1992, following the end of the Cold War tension, the two countries have not yet entirely escaped the Cold War's fetters in their continued confrontations with their socialist counterparts. Furthermore, the questions of division and unification remain unsolved . These issues are essential to unraveling today's international relations in East Asia. For these reasons, South Korea-Taiwan relations of the 1950s figure prominently in understanding East Asia's contemporary regional security landscape.

Many works already touch on the context and significance of the Pacific Pact, including several on the Asian People's Anti-Communist League (APACL) of 1954, South Korean President Syngman Rhee's foreign policy, and regional security.[4] However,

---

4_Rho, Kiyoung "The Development of Pacific Pact Policy and the Plan of Regional Security in the Syngman Rhee Regime" discusses the Pacific Pact. Choi, Youngho "The Syngman Rhee Regime's Ideas of Pacific Alliance and the Asian People Anti-Communist League's Birth" *Korean Journal of International Relations*, 39-2, 1999, analyzed the process of the Pacific Pact's transformation into the Asian People's Anti-Communist League. Park, Jin-Hee "Syngman Rhee's Recognition toward Japan and Pacific Pact" *Historical Criticism*, 76, 2006, and Kim, Jeong-Bae "The Nature of the 'Pacific Union' Discussions in the Light of American Global Strategy" Pusan National University MA thesis, 1990, analyzed Taiwan's relations with Japan and the United States around the Pacific Pact. Cho, Muhyung "The Establishment and Decline of APACL - Conceptualizing ROK-US Conflict based on Role Theory" *Journal of World Politics*, 29-2, 2008, analyzed the Asian People's Anti-Communist League from the

because these topics have been approached separately, these studies have failed to explain South Korea-Taiwan relations from the broader perspective of the regional order. That said, some studies have broadly but briefly approached the Pacific Pact from the perspective of how the United States envisioned an Asia-Pacific security system, including Australia and New Zealand.[5]

To fill this gap, the present work describes how the Pacific Pact proposal of 1949 developed into the APACL after the Korean War, and thus explains how South Korea and Taiwan both co-operated with and competed against each other to form an anti-communist bulwark in Asia. Thus this essay seeks to shed fresh light on South Korea-Taiwan relations from the international and regional perspectives.

One of the main reasons South Korea-Taiwan relations have been relatively neglected is the lack of sources. To date, studies have relied mostly on the official documentary historical record of major United States foreign policy decisions called Foreign

---

role and perspective of Syngman Rhee. In addition, Lee, Hojae *Hanguk Oegyo Jeongchaek ui Yisang kwa Hyunsil: Haebang 8nyeon Minjok galdeunggi ui Banseong* Bupmunsa, 1986, thoroughly analyzes the relations between South Korea, Taiwan, and the United States at the time the Pacific Pact's concept came up.

5_Limb, Ben C. "The Pacific Pact: Looking Forward or Backward?" *Foreign Affairs*, 29-4, July 1951; Mabon, David W. "Elusive Agreements: The Pacific Pact Proposals of 1949-1951," *Pacific Historical Review*, 57- 2, May 1988.

Relations of the United States (FRUS). South Korea preserves almost no diplomatic documents, so most Korean-language sources on the Pacific Pact and other diplomatic relations consist of material published in Korean newspapers. Recently, the Taiwanese government opened its diplomatic archive of the 1950s to the public. This archive includes documents not only on South Korea-Taiwan relations but also on the foreign policies of the United States vis-à-vis Taiwan and the foreign policies of Taiwan vis-à-vis. Up to this point, no study has used this important source in re-examining South Korea-Taiwan relations. Primarily using this unexplored source, Waijiaobu dangan ziliao 外交部檔案資料 (Taiwan Diplomatic Documents), stored in the Archives of the Institute of Modern History, Academia Sinica, this essay elucidates South Korea-Taiwan relations from 1949, when the concept of a Pacific Pact was first introduced, to 1954, when the APACL was formed. In addition, it examines the different strategic circumstances in which South Korea and Taiwan were placed as they promoted the idea of the Pacific Pact, along with the cycle of cooperation and conflict between the two countries at the time.

II. The Initial Promotion Of The Pacific Pact And Its Frustration: 1949-1950

At the end of the Second World War, the United States and the Soviet Union emerged as the two superpowers of the new international order, prompting other countries to seek a security umbrella provided by one or the other of these two powerful nations. Before the outbreak of the Korean War, the United States had a plan to economically reintegrate the Asian region and place Japan at the center of this new network. Yet it also adopted a policy of maintaining the status quo of the region in terms of military affairs, in order to avoid unnecessary confrontations with the Asian communist countries as well as the Soviet Union. In this context, most of the Asian countries belonging to the so-called Free World sought a strong alliance with the United States and also attempted to build up an independent, albeit not purely autonomous, regional security alliance with other Asian countries in order to fill the security vacuum. This effort, however, was not compatible with the United States' status-quo policy in Asia, so it turned out to be unfruitful. As discussed in the next section, the outbreak of the Korean War galvanized this drive for organizing a self-protective security system once again.

In the present section, I examine the background and process of the initial surfacing and eventual frustration of a Pacific Pact as a semi-independent regional security system. More specifically, I investigate the collaboration between South Korea and Taiwan in forging this regional security system, and its correlation with their strategic approaches to the United States during the pre-Korean War period between 1949 and 1950.

The idea of the Pacific Pact, first promoted in concert by South Korea, Taiwan, and the Philippines, stemmed from the political realities of the nations involved. After losing control of Mainland China and relocating to Taiwan in 1949, Chiang Kai-shek wanted to have a shot at expanding the Chinese Civil War into an international confrontation between the communist and capitalist blocs via the formation of a Pacific Pact. The withdrawal of United States military forces from the Korean Peninsula on June 29, 1949, strongly motivated Syngman Rhee to seek out an alternative security system. As detailed below, the Philippines also pushed forward the idea for the sake of its own security. Given the absence of strong foreign support, particularly from the United States, it is no exaggeration to say that the Pacific Pact was an inevitable choice for these countries.

The establishment of NATO in Europe encouraged Asian leaders to establish an Asian version of that collective regional security system with the support of the United States. Even before the official announcement of the formation of NATO on April 26, 1949, President Elpidio Quirino of the Philippines proclaimed the idea of a Pacific Pact on March 20, 1949, and on March 23, President Rhee responded to it, expressing his sympathy for Quirino's proposal.[6] The Philippines was for the pact, given its security concerns that if the United States would not provide it with sufficient military equipment under the military assistance agreement; it needed an extra measure to ensure its security.[7] Chiang Kai-shek, faced with the strong resistance of Mao's Communist Party at the time, was also naturally inclined toward this proposal.

The primary objective of forming a Pacific Pact was not, however, to construct an independent and autonomous regional security system. Chiang intended to avail himself of the discussions on the pact to induce change in the United States' policy on Asian regional security. In light of the US policy of non-intervention in the complex situations of China and Korea, it seems that Chiang strategically considered that a Pacific Pact –which would mean a certain degree of independence of Asian countries from the United States– could provoke the United States to actively engage in the regional order.[8] Inspired by the formation of NATO in Europe, Rhee also envisioned the Pacific Pact as a collective re-

6_*Collection of President Syngman Rhee's Statements* 大統領李承晩博士談話集 The Ministry of Information, 1953, 144.

7_*Foreign Relations of the United States* (FRUS) 1949, vol. 7 part 2, 1123-1125.

8_Lee, Hojae *Hanguk Oegyo Jeongchaek ui Yisang kwa Hyunsil: Haebang 8nyeon Minjok galdeunggi ui Banseong*, 303, 305.

gional security system under the leadership of the United States.[9] Due to the planned evacuation of United States forces from Korea by June 1949, Rhee had already requested military aid from the United States in order to replenish much-needed military equipment and create a power balance with North Korea.[10] Realizing that South Korea could barely maintain its domestic security with the assistance of the United States' planned military aid, the Rhee administration also tried to take advantage of the discussions on the Pacific Pact to induce the United States' written commitment to the defense of South Korea. Rhee believed that, in confrontation with the Communist Bloc in the Cold War system, the United States must take up responsibility as the commander in chief, policing every corner of the "Free World," and that the security of South Korea as well as the Asian region greatly depended on the United States' unflagging commitment.[11]

The design for the Pacific Pact, however, soon faced objections. Postwar Asian nations all had different interests in terms of security. Prime Minister Jawaharlal Nehru of India immediately dismissed the plan for a Pacific Pact as premature.[12] On

---

9_*Dong-a Ilbo*, September 3, 1949.

10_Rho, Kiyoung "The Development of Pacific Pact Policy and the Plan of Regional Security in the Syngman Rhee Regime," 189-190.

11_Oliver,Robert T. *Syngman Rhee and American Involvement in Korea, 1942-1960: A Personal Narrative*, Panmun Book Company Ltd, 1978, 310.

May 18, 1949, then US Secretary of State Dean Acheson also publicly announced that there was a long way to go before the formation of the Pacific Pact.[13] He argued that, unlike NATO, which had begun with the shared security goal of defending Europe against the Soviet threat, formation of a collective security system in Asia would not be fruitful until Asian nations were able to solve more pressing internal problems, such as liberation from Western and Japanese colonialism and domestic political instability. In response, India's Nehru also added that Asia was not prepared for an anti-communist alliance.[14] Due to the United States' policy of non-intervention, the Philippines, South Korea, and Taiwan were still exposed to the threat of communist expansionism, whereas Southeast Asian nations, which were geographically distant from the Cold War frontline, had less interest in the Pacific Pact.[15]

Under these circumstances, the Philippines, Taiwan, and South Korea willingly collaborated on materializing the idea of the Pacific Pact with all possible speed. Three months after Quirino's

---

12_Lee, Hojae *Hanguk Oegyo Jeongchaek ui Yisang kwa Hyunsil: Haebang 8nyeon Minjok galdeunggi ui Banseong*, 302.

13_Oliver, Robert T. *Syngman Rhee and American Involvement in Korea, 1942-1960: A Personal Narrative*, 310.

14_*Dong-a Ilbo*, May 17, 1949.

15_Rho, Kiyoung "The Development of Pacific Pact Policy and the Plan of Regional Security in the Syngman Rhee Regime," 191.

announcement, a summit meeting between Chiang Kai-shek and Quirino took place in Baguio in the Philippines, on July 10 and 11, 1949. The two leaders agreed that the Asian nations should form an alliance for the sake of national as well as regional security.[16] Syngman Rhee viewed the Baguio summit as a meaningful step toward organizing a regional anti-communist alliance. He also declared that South Korea was ready to be a part of this alliance and, in the same vein, requested both Quirino and Chiang to make a visit to South Korea.[17]

Chiang, desiring a speedy formation of the Pacific Pact, immediately responded to Rhee's request. Chiang visited South Korea on August 6, 1949, and had two rounds of meetings with Rhee in Jinhae, a southern coastal city, on August 7, 1949. On August 8, the two leaders issued a joint statement, declaring that they agreed to pursue the idea of a regional anti-communist security system and requesting that Quirino soon hold a preliminary meeting for it in Baguio.[18]

The nascent South Korea-Taiwan collaboration, however, encountered critical problems from the beginning. On August 4,

---

16_Shao, Yulin *My Mission to Korea: A Personal Record of Modern Sino-Korean Relations*, 116.

17_*Collection of President Syngman Rhee's Statements*, 144.

18_*Dong-a Ilbo*, August 9, 1949.

1949, two days prior to Chiang's visit to South Korea, the US Department of State published the China White Paper in which the department announced that Washington would no longer support the Chinese Nationalist government due to its rampant corruption and extreme inefficiency.[19] The publication not only delivered a devastating blow to the Nationalist government's struggle for self-preservation, but also made it clear that the United States had no intention of joining or backing up the Pacific Pact.[20]

This change in the United States' policy on Taiwan was linked to a new strategic approach in Sino-Soviet relations. The US Department of State predicted that despite the PRC's and the USSR's shared ideological foundation, Sino-Soviet relations were bound to deteriorate sooner or later, given several potential areas of conflict, such as territorial disputes and competition over leadership in the Communist Bloc. On this basis, the United States speculated that the PRC could become the next Yugoslavia, if the United States continued to promote friendly relations and provide necessary economic aid to it. Washington believed that this new China policy was a better alternative than the impracticality of

---

19_Shao, Yulin *My Mission to Korea: A Personal Record of Modern Sino-Korean Relations*, 122.

20_Lee, Hojae *Hanguk Oegyo Jeongchaek ui Yisang kwa Hyunsil: Haebang 8nyeon Minjok galdeunggi ui Banseong*, 273.

military intervention in this region.[21] According to the 1949 China white paper, Washington believed that the only way to restore the Nationalist government on Mainland China would be to provide enormous economic and military aid to it. The United States adopted a more diplomatic strategy, however, because it was convinced that providing such aid would prompt the Soviets to intervene, and also because the United States lacked economic and military resources on the scale that would be needed.[22]

Soon after the summit in Baguio, the United States officially stated that most Asian nations were not yet ready for this collective action.[23] In addition to its changed policy on Sino-Soviet relations, the more fundamental reason for this attitude was closely related to Washington's grand plan for an economic regional integration in Asia. The first step in this plan was to economically integrate non-communist Asian nations and place Japan at the center of this integration. The next step was to gradually develop this economic association into a collective security system. On the one hand, this strategy meant that the United States was determined to treat Japan not merely as one of many defeated countries but as

---

21_Lee, Hojae Ibid, 312-313.

22_Lee, Hojae Ibid, 312.

23_Shao, Yulin *My Mission to Korea: A Personal Record of Modern Sino-Korean Relations*, 122.

one of its strong allies.[24] On the other hand, the United States maintained democratization and non-militarization as the pillars of its Japan policy so as to avoid Chinese and Soviet suspicion that it might plan to use Japan as a military stronghold against the communist alliance.[25]

To forestall the formation of a collective military security system in Asia, the United States also drove a wedge between South Korea, Taiwan, and the Philippines right before the Jinhae meeting between Rhee and Chiang. To realize its new Asia policy instead, the United States promised Quirino military aid and urged him, in return, to persuade other Asian nations to turn their attention to its plan for an economic regional integration.[26] In response, on August 3, 1949, three days before Chiang's visit to Jinhae, Quirino released an official statement that the primary objective of the Pacific Pact should be the formation of a political and economic alliance among Southeast Asian non-communist nations. This statement not only put a damper on the upcoming Jinhae meeting between Rhee and Chiang, but also nullified the statements from the Quirino-Chiang summit back in July in

---

24_Rho, Kiyoung "The Development of Pacific Pact Policy and the Plan of Regional Security in the Syngman Rhee Regime," 192.

25_Lee, Hojae *Hanguk Oegyo Jeongchaek ui Yisang kwa Hyunsil: Haebang 8nyeon Minjok galdeunggi ui Banseong*, 317.

26_*Dong-a Ilbo*, August 6, 1949.

Baguio. Quirino again emphasized before his visit to the United States that the ultimate goal of such an alliance was to promote political, economic, and cultural cooperation, not to form a military coalition.[27]

The direction of pursuit of a Pacific Pact changed drastically with the United States' new policy on Mainland China and Taiwan, as well as with Quirino's sudden change in attitude toward the pact. A speculative report began circulating that the Chinese Nationalist government in Taiwan and the ROK in South Korea would be excluded from the future alliance for the pact. Initially, Rhee resolutely reacted to it by claiming that South Korea would take leadership in case the pact did not pan out.[28] As controversies over the pact intensified, Rhee also opted for a more open stance vis-à-vis the Pacific Pact's content, noting that the framework of the organization could be decided by the agreement of the nations directly concerned. He added that while he himself could not attend, he would certainly send representatives to conferences on the pact organized by other nations.[29]

Surprisingly, the changed environment of 1949 did not seri-

27_Shao, Yulin *My Mission to Korea: A Personal Record of Modern Sino-Korean Relations*, 122.

28_*Dong-a Ilbo*, September 10, 1949.

29_*Chosun Ilbo*, March 11, 1950.

ously damage the partnership between South Korea and Taiwan. Following the Jinhae summit, the two countries took a series of actions to put their close relations on view internationally. When the Republic of China publicly announced that it had moved its capital to Taipei on December 7, 1949, South Korea was the first to move its embassy to Taipei, on December 22, 1949. Shin Suk-woo 申錫雨 (1894-1953), the South Korean Ambassador to Taiwan, also visited Quemoy Island, the frontline battlefield between the PRC and Taiwan, and was accompanied on his visit by Shao Yulin 邵毓麟 (1909-1984), the Taiwanese Ambassador to South Korea. Such diplomatic activities by Ambassador Shin played a significant role in stabilizing the people of Taipei, by demonstrating that Taiwan was not completely isolated from the international community.

When Great Britain officially recognized the People's Republic of China of the Chinese Communist Party on January 7, 1950, Rhee again stood on the Taiwanese side. Britian's action astounded Taiwan and South Korea, because Britain was one of the leading members of NATO, which had been organized for the sole purpose of defending the Free World against the potential threat of the Communist Bloc. Rhee publicly criticized Great Britain's action as being irresponsible on the part of one of the Free World's major powers. He asserted that Great Britain was motivated solely by its desire to protect its commercial supremacy in Mainland

China.[30]

On May 26, 1950, President Quirino of the Philippines called for a preparatory meeting in Baguio under the influence of the United States, thus verifying previous reports about the exclusion of South Korea and Taiwan from the alliance. As expected, the agenda of the meeting focused on economy and culture, and military and anti-communist issues were left out. The meeting was attended by seven Asia-Pacific nations – the Philippines, Indonesia, Thailand, India, Pakistan, Ceylon, and Australia.[31] Despite the more flexible stance displayed by Syngman Rhee, South Korea and Taiwan were not invited. Believing that South Korea and Taiwan were likely to demand anti-communist and military agendas at the meeting, the United States government pulled strings to persuade the Philippines to exclude the two countries.[32] Despite consensus among the seven nations on economic, cultural, and social cooperation, however, differences in their other respective interests precluded future meetings.[33]

30_*Kyunghyang Shinmun*, January 9, 1950. Rhee's criticism of the Great Britain also had much to do with the fact that Great Britain limited the territory of South Korea to below the 38th parallel in its recognition of the South Korea government.

31_Shao, Yulin *My Mission to Korea: A Personal Record of Modern Sino-Korean Relations*, 123.

32_*FRUS* 1949, vol. 7, part 2, 1162.

33_*FRUS* 1950, vol. 7, part 2, 88.

The initial promotion of a Pacific Pact and its eventual frustration demonstrate that, in the rapid restructuring of the international order after World War II, the regional security of the Asian non-communist nations largely fell under the sway of the United States – a fact that also sheds fresh light on the genuine objective of the proposal for the Pacific Pact. Although the United States continued its non-involvement policy in Asia during this period, it availed itself of indirect diplomatic channels to impose its plan on the region instead, as is clear from its interference in the initial collaboration of the Philippines, Taiwan, and South Korea on the formation of the pact. This raises the question of whether the leaders of those three countries had the sincere intention to organize a security community independent of the United States in the first place. It is certain that, given the non-interventionist policy of the United States, which created a considerable security vacuum in the region, South Korea and Taiwan were desperate for an alternative way to defend themselves from the communist threat. This continued structure of Asian security relations, however, was easily dismantled by the outbreak of the Korean War.

III. The Resurfacing of the Pacific Pact After the Korean War

The Korean War fundamentally transformed international relations surrounding South Korea and Taiwan. These changes in the international situation, in addition to the war itself, hindered South Korea and Taiwan from making progress on the Pacific Pact and from strengthening their mutual alliance. On June 30, 1950, five days after the outbreak of the Korean War, Taiwan publicly announced that it would, as a first round, aid South Korea with three army divisions and twenty aircraft.[34] This offer, however, was declined both by the United States and South Korea, who worried that it could trigger PRC intervention in the war. Even after China joined the war, Rhee continued to refuse the involvement of Taiwan's military forces for fear that it could provide Japan with a pretext for remilitarization.[35]

The war also substantially altered perceptions about Asian regional security. First of all, the war made the United States government realize that it must modify its non-involvement policy, and it

34_Shao, Yulin *My Mission to Korea: A Personal Record of Modern Sino-Korean Relations*, 143.

35_Oliver, Robert T. *Syngman Rhee and American Involvement in Korea, 1942-1960*, 549.

also changed public opinion on the United States role in East Asia. According to a Taiwanese diplomatic report, which was based on an article published in the Christian Science Monitor on November 28, 1950, although the majority of Americans had objected to the United States' potential military attack against the People's Republic of China before the Korean War, once the war began, they started to agree that military action might be needed to solve problems in Asia. This report added that, given these changes in the United States, its resistance, as well as that of neighboring Asian nations, to the idea of a military alliance between Taiwan and South Korea, would not be as strong as it had been during the pre-Korean War period.[36]

Second, the Korean War showed that South Korea and Taiwan were natural partners. The war demonstrated that the establishment of a stronger regional or international security system in Asia was no longer a mere option for peace in the region. More specifically, the two countries' situational resemblances –the threat of their communist counterparts and the territorial division– induced both Chiang and Rhee to believe that the survival of each re-

36_"President Syngman Rhee visited Taiwan, and discussed the Pacific Pact 韓國李承晩大統領訪臺暨擬訂太平洋同盟" (Document No. 012.22/0054, *Taiwan Diplomatic Documents* 外交部檔案資料 *11* in Archives of Institute of Modern History, Academia Sinica in Taiwan), 118.

spective nation and the recovery of its "lost territory" were inseparable. This consensus led Chiang to agree with Rhee's policies, such as the objection to armistice and the northward advance at the end of the Korean War.[37]

Under these circumstances, when the Korean War entered a stalemate phase beginning in mid-1951, both Rhee and Chiang began to hark back to the previous discussions on the Pacific Pact.[38] The war made the primary objectives and scope of the pact clearer and more distinct than they had been in the pre-Korea War discussions.

Rhee, who reaffirmed that the Pacific Pact would be an effective alternative for South Korea's security, continued to work for the formation of the pact. In January 1953, a South Korean newspaper reported that a summit between South Korea, Taiwan, and the Philippines would soon take place in Taipei for the purpose of organizing a NATO-type alliance in the Pacific.[39] For Rhee, foreign aid was critical not only to national security but also to its economic recovery from the devastating Korean War. Chiang, in contrast, was actively seeking international cooperation with other

---

37_*Taiwan Diplomatic Documents 11*, 18.

38_Rho, Kiyoung "The Development of Pacific Pact Policy and the Plan of Regional Security in the Syngman Rhee Regime," 197-198.

39_*JOINT WEEKA*, January 17, 1953; *Chosun Ilbo*, January 11, 1953.

nations in order to escape Taiwan's international isolation since the early 1950s.

This time, Taiwan took the initiative in reorganizing the pact. Although no severe military collisions had broken out between Taiwan and the PRC during the Korean War, the international maneuvers of the PRC in 1951 and 1952 heavily pressed the Taiwan government to seek an alliance with other nations. The PRC responded to the Free World's "peace aggression" by carrying out the so-called Asia-Pacific Peace Conference. A preparatory meeting was held in Beijing from June 3 to 6, 1952, at which the PRC decided to invite representatives of 31 nations and the World Labor Union across the ideological divide.[40] The official conference was held on September 28, 1952 in Beijing. Ostensibly due to visa problems, many of the invitees, such as Japan, the United States, and Australia, did not attend. The agenda of the conference included the guarantee of independence, freedom, and peace for the Asia-Pacific nations, while the particular and central goal was the prevention of Japan's remilitarization.[41] This conference shows

40_*Taiwan Diplomatic Documents 11*, 231. The nations that sought to participate include the Soviet Union, Japan, North Korea, Thailand, the Philippines, India, Myanmar, Vietnam, Laos, Cambodia, New Zealand, Canada, Mongolia, Ceylon, Pakistan, Indonesia, Australia, the United States, Mexico, Guatemala, Colombia, El Salvador, Honduras, Chile, Peru, Ecuador, Panama, Nicaragua, and Costa Rica.

41_*Taiwan Diplomatic Documents 11*, 231-232, 234.

that, just as Asian nations were concerned with the communist threat, so the Chinese Communist Party was concerned with the threat of the Free World.

Since Taiwan was excluded from the security alliance provided by the United States to most other Asian nations at the time, it had to give more attention to the formation of the Pacific Pact. Taiwan thus sped up the revival and reformulation of the Pacific Pact. In the fall of 1953, it presented the draft of a mutual assistance treaty to Pacific Rim countries.[42] At the time, Pacific Rim countries lacked a regional security system, and nations such as the Philippines, Japan, and Australia were individually tied to a mutual defense treaty with the United States. After the Korean War, the United States expressed its ostensible agreement with the formation of a regional security system by the nations in the region themselves.[43] Given these conditions, the mutual assistance treaty proposed by Taiwan had a preventative character, in the sense that it was designed to forestall foreign invasions by means of securing military

---

42_*Taiwan Diplomatic Documents 11*, 23-26. The content included clauses for a collective response to the threat and attack of communism, exchange of information on military and political matters, and establishment of a united command for common defense. Ratification instruments were to be exchanged, and additional members could be added only by the unanimous agreement among member nations. Such terms indicate the formation of a strong offensive and defensive military alliance.

43_*Taiwan Diplomatic Documents 11*, 130.

aid among the countries that joined.

The discussions on forming a Pacific Pact had great importance not only for shaping a regional or mutual security system but also for meeting the domestic and international needs of both Taiwan and South Korea. As discussed above, soon after the Baguio summit of July 19, 1949 between Chiang and Quirino, Chiang and Rhee met at Jinhae on August 7. Chiang's visits to the heads of foreign states were critical to the ROC's domestic political stability as well as to international recognition of ROC legitimacy after its loss of Mainland China and resettlement on the comparatively isolated small island of Taiwan.[44] Following the Korean War, Rhee also needed foreign aid and international recognition.

After the outbreak of the Korean War, the two nations pursued a summit talk again, and eventually Rhee visited Taiwan, on November 27, 1953. This summit occurred just before the planned visit of Unied States Vice President Richard Nixon to Asia in December. It took place, however, only after a war of nerves. As just mentioned, in July 1949, before the Chinese Nationalists' full retreat from Mainland China, Chiang Kai-shek visited South Korea and had a summit meeting with Syngman Rhee at Jinhae. According to diplomatic protocol, Chiang expected a reciprocal

44_*Taiwan Diplomatic Documents 11*, 37.

visit, yet it was practically impossible for Rhee to leave South Korea for Taiwan during the Korean War. In the winter of 1953, when the armistice agreement had already brought an end to the Korean War, the South Korean government requested that Chiang again visit Korea, stating that a negotiation between the two nations before Nixon's visit was essential and that Taiwan was in a comparatively more stable condition.[45] Taipei, however, had recourse to the reciprocal principle in diplomatic protocols and insisted on Rhee's visit instead.

To break this stalemate, Taiwan's Ambassador to Japan Dong Xianguang 董顯光 (1897-1971) crossed the Korean Strait in October 1953 to have a personal conversation with Rhee. According to Dong's report after the meeting, Rhee was interested neither in visiting Taiwan nor in collaborating on Taiwan's proposal for the Pacific Pact as an offensive and defensive alliance. Dong added that Rhee had an underhanded scheme to avail himself both of Nixon's visit to Korea as well as of Chiang Kai-shek's prestige for his own sake.[46] Dong nevertheless persisted in requesting Rhee's visit to Taiwan in the meeting, and in the end, Rhee agreed to Dong's request.

When Rhee arrived in Taipei on November 27, 1953, Chiang

45_*Taiwan Diplomatic Documents 11*, 34.

46_*Taiwan Diplomatic Documents 11*, 38.

personally welcomed him at the airport. The media in Taiwan broadcast his visit widely, and the people of Taipei gave Rhee a grand welcome during his stay.[47] In fact, Rhee was the first foreign head of state to visit the ROC since its relocation to the island. After this summit meeting, South Korea and Taiwan again began to pursue formation of the Pacific Pact. Recognizing the difficulty of establishing a regional collective security system in Asia, Taiwan preferred to sign a bilateral treaty of alliance with South Korea before inviting other nations to join. Rhee, however, preferred the broader regional security option in order to avoid being entangled in the Chinese Civil War.

South Korea and Taiwan greatly diverged on the main objective of the pact. On October 29, 1953, when he had met with Rhee to discuss the South Korea-Taiwan summit, Dong Xianguang had proposed that South Korea and Taiwan sign the proposal for an offensive and defensive alliance first, and then extend its membership to other nations afterward. Rhee insisted instead that he and Chiang issue a joint statement advocating the Pacific Rim anti-communist alliance first, and then make a formal agreement with the nations that responded positively to this plan. Rhee also reminded Dong that the United States might oppose the South

---

47_*Chongyang Ribao* 中央日報, November 28, 1953.

Korea-Taiwan military alliance out of fear that it would stimulate South Korea to put its "Northward Advance" into practice. Rhee also indirectly refused Taiwan's proposal for the pact by arguing that a written commitment could not be as binding as the tacit understanding and commitment between the two nations from the heart.[48] In the end, they could not reach an agreement on the form and objectives of the Pacific Pact at the November 1953 summit meeting.

Both nations had publicly proclaimed that the purpose of the November meeting was to enhance the friendship between the two nations, and that no political motive was involved. Yet after the summit, newspapers reported as fact the agreement on an anti-communist military alliance between South Korea and Taiwan.[49] Despite the denial of the United States, the Communist Bloc also alleged that an agreement on the alliance had been signed with a silent nod from Washington.[50] Although the alliance never materialized, the Pacific Pact had in fact been one of the main agenda items of the November 1953 summit meeting between South Korea and Taiwan after the Korean War.

48_*Taiwan Diplomatic Documents 11*, 46.

49_*Taiwan Diplomatic Documents 11*, 69, 118.

50_*Taiwan Diplomatic Documents 11*, 118.

IV. Conflicts Between South Korea and Taiwan Over The Formation of the Post-Korean War Pacific Pact

As described in the preceding section, although South Korea and Taiwan maintained a close and cooperative relationship after the outbreak of the Korean War, they could not fully collaborate on shaping a new version of the Pacific Pact. In this section, I examine the reasons behind their sharp division in the post-Korean War reformulation of a Pacific Pact.

The November 1953 summit meeting did not bear fruit. In a discussion in October 1953, South Korea and Taiwan found that although they agreed on the need for a Pacific Pact, they had different ideas on its particular structure. The Taiwanese government believed that most Asian nations of the Free World feared becoming entangled in the frontline of the Cold War that it and South Korea already faced. Therefore, Taiwan proposed that South Korea and Taiwan should first form a Pacific Pact as a strong offensive and defensive alliance, and then induce other Pacific Rim countries to join the pact afterward.[51]

After the outbreak of the Korea War, South Korea and Taiwan faced many similar problems in terms of national security – loss of

---

51_*Taiwan Diplomatic Documents 11*, 21.

territory, national division, communist threat, need for international recognition vis-à-vis a communist counterpart, and so forth. Both sides were well aware that international cooperation and support were critical to overcoming these problems. In this situation, they each found the other to be a natural partner, and on the basis of this consensus, the two nations embarked on a campaign for the Pacific Pact once again.

At the time, South Korean politicians were divided on the question of forming an offensive and defensive alliance with Taiwan. Pro-Taiwan politicians believed that because South Korea and Taiwan had a common destiny, they had to strengthen their military ties.[52] Particularly those who had led the Korean provisional government during the period of Japanese colonialism argued that South Korea was indebted to the Chiang Kai-shek government for its enormous support in establishing and maintaining the provisional government. They made the National Assembly pass a bill supporting the pact unanimously, pressing the government to agree on it.[53] However, Rhee objected to a pact consisting

52_*Taiwan Diplomatic Documents 11*, 6.

53_"Hankuk Kwa Chunghwaminkuk ui Dongmaeng Chegyul e kwanhan Gyuleuan (Union Concerning the Resolution between South Korea and the Republic of China)," (*Proceedings for 6th session of the 16th plenary session of the Second National Assembly*, June 11, 1953, available at http://likms.assembly.go.kr/record/index.html), 3-8. South Korea's pro-Taiwan politicians were those who established the Korean

initially only of Taiwan and South Korea, and instead emphasized the necessity of broader international participation.

Rhee knew that such an alliance would join together the Korean and the Chinese confrontations with their respective national divisions into communist and non-communist nations, thus entailing the expansion of the frontline of the Cold War to all of Asia. In addition, because South Korea had already secured its homeland security through concluding the ROK-US Mutual Defense Agreement earlier in October 1953, Rhee found no reason to be involved in Chiang Kai-shek's fight to regain Mainland China. He also cast doubt on the feasibility of Taiwan's plan for a Pacific Pact in the form of an offensive and defensive alliance. Specifically, he predicted that the other Asian nations would not join the pact for fear of sharing the fates of South Korea and Taiwan, which had lost control of their own territories.[54]

Rhee had an alternative design for the Pacific Pact. He proposed holding a preparatory meeting with other Asian countries to collectively decide the principal forms of the alliance as well as its particular rules. At a meeting in January 1954 with Wang

---

Provisional Government in China during the Japanese colonial rule of Korea. When they were in China, the Chiang Kai-shek government provided various means of support to them. They felt indebted to the Chinese Nationalist Party, and they believed in the need to "pay back" what they owed to Chiang.

54_*Taiwan Diplomatic Documents 11*, 89.

Dongyuan 王東原 (1898-1956), Taiwan's Ambassador to South Korea at the time, Rhee explained his plan. As a first step, he suggested Taiwan send a group of people to South Korea for training in anti-communist propaganda and extended this program to the Philippines, Thailand, and Malaysia in order to galvanize the anti-communist consensus among the people of these nations. In doing so, he desired to spread the idea that South Korea was the leader of the anti-communist movement in Asia. He underlined that the anti-communist campaign in Asia must be organized and managed by Asians themselves, given the condition that they could not elicit from the United States government a full agreement on the proposal for a Pacific Pact.[55]

Taiwan's post-Korean War proposal for a Pacific Pact thus failed to win the endorsement not only of South Korea but also of most Southeast Asian nations. For example, due to its geographical proximity, the Philippines had a great interest in the security of Taiwan, yet did not want to get involved in the touch-and-go situation of the Korean Peninsula by joining a comprehensive military alliance with South Korea.[56] When Ramon Magsaysay was elected president of the Philippines in December 1953, he maintained an unclear position about the Pacific Pact for

55_*Taiwan Diplomatic Documents 11*, 135-136.

56_*Taiwan Diplomatic Documents 11*, 109.

reasons of domestic politics.[57] The Taiwanese government concluded that cooperation from the Philippines would not be forthcoming. Before his election, Magsaysay had taken a positive stance toward the Pacific Pact, prompting the Taiwanese government to officially invite him to visit after his election. But according to a UP news agency report on December 3, 1953, Magsaysay made it clear that he had no interest in visiting Taiwan and discussing the Pacific Pact with Chiang Kai-shek.[58]

The discrepancy between South Korea and Taiwan on the Pacific Pact was closely related to Taiwan's plan for recovering Mainland China. Taiwan had sought an opportunity to attack the mainland during the Korean War by offering to dispatch troops to Korea. Realistically speaking, the presence of a socialist regime on mainland China was a great threat to South Korea as well, so Seoul basically supported the Chinese Nationalists' claim to recover the mainland. In his meeting with Dong Xianguang on October 29, 1953, Syngman Rhee had stated that South Korea would attack Manchuria if Taiwan launched an invasion of Mainland China. Rhee, however, also stated that due to American opposition to the idea, he could not attack Manchuria first, thus making a preemptive attack from Chiang a condition for his own military

57_*Taiwan Diplomatic Documents 11*, 110.

58_*Taiwan Diplomatic Documents 11*, 106.

involvement.[59] He also mentioned the indispensability of US material aid for a Korean invasion of Manchuria. In sum, Rhee carefully avoided any commitment to Taiwan's anti-communist drive against mainland China, by demanding American intervention as a necessary condition of South Korea's involvement.[60]

This attitude was reaffirmed when Rhee visited the United States. In a speech to the United States Congress on July 28, 1954, Rhee asked for American military assistance in the South Korean forces' fights against North Korea and China. Rhee said that the ground forces for this attack would be entirely composed of South Korean troops, so that the US military forces would only need to commit their navy and air force. He also asked the United States government for a clear and long-term policy to save China from communism. Taipei carefully watched Rhee's speech in Washington. When this speech caused a stir, Rhee explained to reporters that he was not looking for an immediate war against China and that his words instead represented a long-term plan. Rhee then claimed that an anti-communist crusade should be organized to drive out communism from Asia. This shows that Rhee approached the issue of South Korea-Taiwan relations from a completely practical perspective; hence his denial of the offensive

59_*Taiwan Diplomatic Documents 11*, 37.

60_*Taiwan Diplomatic Documents 11*, 41.

and defensive treaty proposed by Taiwan can be understood in the same light.

The different stances of Chiang Kai-shek and Syngman Rhee on Japan also held back the post-Korean War drive for a Pacific Pact. Given the ROC's international isolation and domestic instability, Chiang opted for a strategy to strengthen Taiwan's position by concluding a peace treaty with Japan. To speed it up, he decided not to demand compensation for Japan's colonial rule of China and took the position of simply putting aside past affairs. The road to the peace treaty, however, was not smooth. The relocation of the Chinese Nationalist regime to Taiwan in 1949 had produced two regimes, which raised the question of which of the two should be recognized as the legitimate Chinese government in international relations. This generated a host of problems, including representation in the United Nations and the concluding of a peace treaty with Japan. Although the United States had recognized the ROC government in Taiwan in December 1949, things had become more complicated when Great Britain recognized the People's Republic of China in January 1950.

A peace treaty with Taiwan also made Japan's stance complicated. Domestically, Japan was divided into pro-Beijing and pro-Taiwan factions. The Liberal Democratic Party of Japan was split in the same fashion, and the opposition parties all supported the regime in Beijing, with the exception of the Japanese

Communist Party, which had severed its connection to its Chinese counterpart. The popular media tended to be more sympathetic to the People's Republic of China, given Japan's lingering sense of guilt after the war.[61] Following the suggestion of John Dulles (1888-1959), United States Secretary of State under President Dwight Eisenhower, Japan eventually concluded a treaty with Taiwan in the middle of the Korean War, on August 5, 1952. On its signing, however, Japan attempted not to recognize the Chinese Nationalist government in Taiwan as the representative government of the entire nation. Eventually, the Nationalists in Taiwan succeeded in persuading Japan to define the territorial scope of Taiwan as "the current and future territories administered by the Republic of China," but only on the condition that Taiwan not ask Japan for compensation for forced Chinese wartime labor for the Japanese Empire, as authorized by the Treaty of San Francisco.[62]

South Korea, however, was deeply concerned about the revival of Japan, and not simply because it was haunted by its own colonial experience. Rhee was not content with the American designs to make Japan the regional center of Asia, since it was highly possible that this plan would help Japan in its remilitarization as

---

61_Guoshiguan bian, *Zhonghua minguo waijiaozhi*, 343.
62_Guoshiguan bian, Ibid, 344-345.

much as in its economic recovery. Rhee firmly believed that once the Japanese recovered from the postwar devastation, Japan would resume its expansionist policies toward Asia.[63]

With respect to the Pacific Pact, Chiang Kai-shek contended that Japan's membership was necessary. He believed that all Asian nations should unite against communism to maximize the effect of the pact. Chiang therefore strongly urged an improvement of relations between South Korea and Japan. In response, Rhee stated that South Korea could allow Japan to join the Pacific Pact only if Japan would guarantee that it would permanently abandon its aggression toward Korea, return all plunder, and stop demanding the return of pre-1945 Japanese properties in Korea.[64]

Such points of dissension came to the surface as the two countries prepared for the second convention of the Asian People's Anti-Communist League (APACL), an alternative form of the pre-Korean War Pacific Pact, initially planned to be held in Taipei on October 20, 1954. Believing that the absence of Japan would severely weaken the league's effectiveness, Taiwan proposed changing the rule of that any new member had to be received by a unanimous vote of approval. This rule had been made at the first convention of APACL, held in Jinhae, South Korea, on June

---

63_*Taiwan Diplomatic Documents 11*, 44.

64_*Taiwan Diplomatic Documents 11*, 45.

15, 1954. South Korea rigidly stuck to the original rule, while Taiwan attempted to amend it so that a new member could join the organization if it could garner votes from two-thirds of the existing members. The result was that South Korea decided not to attend the second convention, which was pushed back to May 23, 1955, and eventually postponed indefinitely.[65]

Realizing that a Pacific Pact in the form of an offensive and defensive alliance among Asian nations would not work out in the near future, Taiwan turned its attention to concluding a mutual defense treaty with the United States, as well as to transforming the system of the Pacific Pact into a comprehensive form of economic, cultural, and political alliance. According to the memorandum of a confidential conversation between Chen Zhiping 陳質平 (1906-1984) in December, 1953, then Taiwan's Ambassador to the Philippines, and William Sterling Byrd Lacy (1910-1979), the United States Ambassador to the Philippines, Chen requested US endorsement of this new form of Asian alliance. He delivered a message from the Taiwanese government noting that, given the fact that Taiwan, South Korea, Japan, the Philippines, Thailand, and Vietnam all received economic and military aid from the United States, this comprehensive form of alliance would greatly

65_*Gongbochu jubo* (*Weekly Bulletin*, 公報處週報), no. 158 (May 18, the Ministry of Information. 1955), 20-23.

enhance cooperation and effectiveness in the areas of information exchange, anti-communism training, economic development, and commercial trade in the region. Chen also emphasized that such an alliance could be an efficient collective anti-communist organization by letting Asian nations solve minor problems by themselves, thus alleviating the United States' burdens in Asia.[66]

As Taiwan changed its concept of a Pacific Pact after the November 1953 summit meeting of Chiang and Rhee, South Korea began to lead the drive for a pact and redefine its main objective as being that of a Pacific Rim anti-communist alliance instead of an offensive and defensive alliance. Beginning in February 1954, the South Korean government began to give shape to the idea of a Pacific Rim anti-communist alliance as a non-governmental organization. Around that time, Rhee made an international move as well, dispatching a South Korean delegation headed by Baek Nakjun 白樂濬 (1895-1985) to Pacific Rim countries such as Vietnam, Indonesia, Myanmar, Malaysia, New Zealand, and Australia. The tasks assigned to the delegation were to propagate a cooperative anti-communist front in conjunction with local anti-communist associations, and to urge public leaders to these countries to organize mass assemblies to spread anti-communism.

66_*Taiwan Diplomatic Documents 11*, 130.

The Korean delegation was sent three times, but according to a report by the Taiwanese government, most nations that the South Korean delegation visited either openly opposed this idea or displayed a passive attitude.[67]

Taiwan indirectly displayed its basic agreement with Rhee's proposal. Within the nations that the South Korean delegation visited, the groups that echoed the South Korean claim for a Pacific Rim anti-communist alliance were the organizations of overseas Chinese in Southeast Asia, collectively called Southeast Asian Chinese (南洋華僑). Well aware of the influence of these organizations in Southeast Asian nations, the Taiwan Ministry of Foreign Affairs used its leverage with the Southeast Asian overseas Chinese, requesting them to support the activities of the South Korean delegation, particularly by having local influential figures and leaders of local overseas Chinese organizations participate in the anti-communist alliance.[68] This clearly shows that although South Korea and Taiwan could not reach a full agreement on the purposes and structures of a Pacific Pact, they did at least agree on the idea of creating an anti-communist alliance.

67_*Taiwan Diplomatic Documents 11*, 122; Kiyoung Rho, "The Development of Pacific Pact Policy and the Plan of Regional Security in the Syngman Rhee Regime," 206.

68_*Taiwan Diplomatic Documents 11*, 156, 186.

V. Conclusion

Weak states have fewer resources on the whole than do stronger nations, and are unable to resolve their defense problems entirely on their own. Therefore, on most occasions, external sources of available strength are more crucial to weak states and constitute a relatively greater part of their total strength than is the case for the great powers.[69] Thus, the weak states have no choice but to rely on the great powers for their own survival. Korea and Taiwan took advantage of this situation and obtained the cooperation of the United States.

Thus far, studies on the regional order of East Asia during the early Cold War period have focused on United States policies concerning East Asia and on the United States' relations with individual East Asian states. They have thus provided us with a macroscopic view on the shaping of a new East Asian regional order during the period. The leadership of the United States in reshaping the regional order is beyond question. Nevertheless, this approach has not paid due attention to the importance of the roles played by the East Asian states in this process, but has instead seen the new regional order only as the consequence of the im-

69_Handel, Michael *Weak States in the International System* Frank Cass and Company Limited. 1981, 69-70.

plementation of United States policies towards East Asia.

The simplest and most common way for a weak state to get a great power to commit to supporting its interests is to persuade that great power to sign a formal defense treaty with the weak state, or to make an unambiguous promise of support in case of military attack.[70]

Certainly, the primary purpose of a Pacific Pact was not to form an autonomous regional alliance independently of the United States. In post-Second World War Asia, the United States sought to reorganize a new regional order in Asia, with Japan at the center of this proposed new order. Under these circumstances, the Chinese Nationalist government in Taiwan and the South Korean government, which were standing at the frontline of the Cold War, fell short of becoming the United States' full-fledged security partners in Asia. As a result, they were desperate to attract the United States' attention. Once South Korea and Taiwan secured the military and economic aid of the United States, they no longer pursued their former aggressive and expansive diplomatic strategies. After the signing of the Sino-American Mutual Defense Treaty on December 2, 1954, Taiwan permanently discarded the Pacific Pact as an offensive and defensive treaty and concentrated

70_Handel, Michael Ibid, 122.

on APACL.

South Korea, for its part, lost its motivation to further pursue the Pacific Pact after the ROK-US Mutual Defense Agreement was concluded on October 1, 1953.

From a different angle, however, the similarities shared by Syngman Rhee and Chiang Kai-shek were one of the key factors in explaining the initial formation of a cooperative relationship between South Korea and Taiwan from the late 1940s on. The two leaders, despite their devastating losses in armed conflicts with their communist counterparts, maintained the integrity of their states, albeit in a reduced form. The two also had a similar view on the critical role of the United States in containing communism in Asia. Instead of a democratic process to gain popular support, both Chiang and Rhee relied on military and policy means, as well as on United States aid, to hold onto their power. By responding to international and domestic challenges throughout their rule in a similar fashion, they developed and maintained a deep sense of sympathy and cooperation.

From the standpoint of the United States, both Chiang's aggressive policy against mainland China and Rhee's calls for a northward advance were unwanted obstacles to its pre-Korean War status-quo policy in Asia. Chiang and Rhee's aggressive positions made the United States even more passive in response. For South Korea and Taiwan, however, rivalry and confrontation with

North Korea and the People's Republic of China, respectively, were critical to their security. When the much-needed American commitment to protection and intervention was not forthcoming, South Korea and Taiwan sought to elicit American interest in and intervention for their security by forming a collective security system – namely, a Pacific Pact.

From 1949 to 1953, the loss of Mainland China much intensified Chiang's aspirations to achieve a collective security regime. After the Korean War, Rhee's calls for a northward advance became even louder than before. Given the ongoing Cold War tension with the Soviet Union and China, stability in Northeast Asia was crucial to the United States. For the United States, the aggressive policies of Chiang and Rhee were one of the major factors that might destabilize the regional order. In this context, the United States used its leverage to forestall South Korea and Taiwan from drawing in some Southeast Asian states, including the Philippines, and thus creating an uncontrollable regional alliance. In other words, it was in the American regional interest in East Asia to protect and contain South Korea and Taiwan via bilateral mutual defense treaties, rather than allowing South Korea and Taiwan to assume an aggressive stance toward North Korea and China and increase instability in the region.

The ROC no longer held the power it had formerly wielded. Its fate was largely subject to the rapidly changing international environment. Its relations with the United States were not reciprocal but nearly unilateral. Under these circumstances, the ROC tried to elicit support from the United States by being compliant with US policies, which Michael Handel has called the "affiliation strategy."[71] In this vein, Taiwan also tried to reverse the United States' negative recognition of Chiang Kai-shek by portraying him as an anti-communist leader of Southeast Asian Chinese and the Southeast Asian region.

Taiwan took advantage of the Korean War to change its relations with the United States. The Taiwanese government was aware that the expansion of the Korean War could provide it with great advantages for its security. Its propaganda campaign against mainland China provoked the PRC into participating in the Korean War, thus impeding normalization between the United States and the PRC for a long time. Consequently, Taiwan became once again one of the most important allies of the United States, particularly with respect to curbing the growing influence of the PRC over the region.

The restoration of the partnership between the United States and Taiwan can be best explained by the altered polices of the United States on East Asia. However, it should not be overlooked

71_Handel, Michael Ibid, 144.

that Taiwan also played a significant role in this restoration by adopting timely domestic and foreign policies in accordance with the changing international relations in the region.

Nevertheless, South Korea and Taiwan maintained an exceptionally close relationship even after the conclusion of their respective treaties with the United States. At times the two nations did not hesitate to maximize their own national interests, and thus competed against each other to play a leading role in the international relations of Asia. Yet despite the fact that significant differences of opinion were uncovered during such processes, these differences did not go so far as to disrupt the ongoing cooperation between the two countries, at least until the collapse of the Soviet Union brought an end to the Cold War system. South Korea then normalized relations with the People's Republic of China in 1992.

References

Archival Materials

Collection of President Syngman Rhee's Statements 大統領李承晚博士談話集. The Ministry of Information. 1953.

Foreign Relations of the United States (FRUS). 1949. vol. 7. part 2; 1950. vol. 7. part 2.

JOINT WEEKA (Intelligence Report of the Ambassador of the United States to the Republic of Korea). 1953; photographic edition. Yŏngjinmunhwasa. 1993.

"President Syngman Lee visited Taiwan, and discussed the Pacific Pact 韓國李承晚大統領訪臺暨擬訂太平洋同盟." Document No. 012.22/0054. *Taiwan Diplomatic Documents* 外交部檔案資料 *11*. in Archives of Institute of Modern History. Academia Sinica in Taiwan.

"Hankuk Kwa Chunghwaminkuk ui Dongmaeng Chegyul e kwanhan Gyuleuan (Union Concerning the Resolution between South Korea and the Republic of China)." *Proceedings for 6th session of the 16th plenary session of the Second National Assembly*. June 11. 1953. available at http://likms.assembly.go.kr/record/index.html.

Newspapers

Chongyang Ribao 中央日報. 1953

Chosun Ilbo. 1949-1953.

Dong-a Ilbo. 1949-1953.

Gongbochu jubo (Weekly Bulletin) 公報處週報. no. 158. May 18. the Ministry of Information. 1955.

Kyunghyang Shinmun. 1949.

Secondary Literature

Bix, Herbert P. "Regional Integration: Japan and South Korea in America's Asian Policy." in Frank Baldwin. ed., *Without Parallel: The American-Korean Relationship since 1945*. New York: Pantheon Books. 1974.

Chang, Su-Ya. *Did Korea Go to War to Rescue Taiwan?* Taiwan: Acropolis Publish. 2011.

Cho, Muhyung. "The Establishment and Decline of APACL—Conceptualizing ROK-US

Conflict based on Role Theory." *Journal of World Politics*. vol. 29. no. 2. 2008.

Choi, Youngho. "The Syngman Rhee Regime's Ideas of Pacific Alliance and the Asian People Anti-Communist League's Birth." *Korean Journal of International Relations*. vol. 39. no. 2. 1999.

Cumings, Bruce. "The Origins and Development of the Northeast Asian Political Economy: Industrial Sectors, Product Cycles, and Political Consequences." in Frederic C. Deyo. ed., *The Political Economy of New Asian Industrialism*. New York: Cornell University Press. 1987.

Guoshiguan bian 國史館中華民國史外交志編纂委員會編. *Zhonghua minguo waijiaozhi* 中華民國外交志. *Sanmin shuju*. 2000.

Handel, Michael. *Weak States in the International System*. Frank Cass and Company Limited. 1981.

Kim, Jeong-Bae. "The Nature of the 'Pacific Union' Discussions in the Light of American Global Strategy." Pusan National University MA thesis. 1990.

Lee, Chongwon. *U.S.-Korean Relations and Japan in East Asia's Cold War*. Tokyo University Press. 1996.

Lee, Hojae. *Hanguk Oegyo Jeongchaek ui Yisang kwa Hyunsil: Haebang 8nyeon Minjok galdeunggi ui Banseong. Bupmunsa*. 1986.

Limb, Ben C. "The Pacific Pact: Looking Forward or Backward?" *Foreign Affairs*. Vol. 29. No. 4. July 1951.

Mabon, David W. "Elusive Agreements: The Pacific Pact Proposals of 1949-1951." *Pacific Historical Review*, Vol. 57. No. 2. May 1988.

Oliver, Robert T. *Syngman Rhee and American Involvement in Korea, 1942-1960: A Personal Narrative*. Panmun Book Company Ltd. 1978.

Park, Jin-Hee. "Syngman Rhee's Recognition toward Japan and Pacific Pact." *Historical Criticism*. 76. 2006.

Rho, Kiyoung. "The Development of Pacific Pact Policy and the Plan of Regional Security in the Syngman Rhee Regime." T*he Journal of Korean History (Chiyuk Kwa Yuksa)*. vol. 11. 2002.

Shao, Yulin. *My Mission to Korea: A Personal Record of Modern Sino-Korean Relations* 使韓回憶錄. Biographical Literature Press. Taipei. 1980.

A Comparative Study on Inter- Korean Relations and Cross-Strait Exchanges after the 2000s

Kwangkyu Nam (ARI, Korea University)

I. Introduction

This article comes during a period of transition on the Korean Peninsula, on December 17th 2011, Kim Jong-il died and was replaced by his son Kim Jong Un as the new leader of North Korea. Thus far this has meant more of the status quo on the Korean Peninsula. Park Geun-hye was also elected president earlier this year, what this will mean for inter-Korean relations is as yet not clear.

The present President of Taiwan, Ma Ying-jeou, of the

---

* This chapter was published on the *The Journal of Peace Studies,*" Vol. 14, no 2(2013).

Kuomintang, won his reelection bid. Thanks to this, Ma has been able to continue to pursue his policy of cross-Strait exchanges; the election has also meant potential tensions had the opposition candidate been elected have been avoided. As is widely known, Taiwan has been able to secure its economic development through economic exchanges with China.

The two Koreas, and Taiwan and China were divided at similar times, and all maintain that their main goal is national unification. At the same time, the Cold War which constituted their separations has now ended. As a result of this, various exchanges began in the 1990s.

Compared to relations between the two Koreas, cross-Strait relations have been characterized by a high level of exchanges in the private sector. In recent years relations have started to be legally recognized and institutionalized with a raft of laws related to transport, economic and cultural exchange being passed or currently being prepared.[1]

This article compares and contrasts relations between the two Koreas and relations between Beijing and Taipei. The article attempts to understand why exchanges have developed and expanded in the case of the latter but not in the case of the former.

1_Ministry of Justice in Korea, *A Study on the Law of Exchange Cooperation in China and Taiwan*, Ministry of Justice in Korea (2008), pp. 3-5.

Both the two Koreas, and Taiwan and Mainland China have identical peoples who shared a common history and culture, and in spite of division and ideological discord, they both seek integration and reunification. Relations between the two Koreas are very different to those between Taiwan and the mainland are different in historical terms, political and economic terms, the international status of Taiwan is also very different to that of the two Koreas and the mainland.[2] Therefore, it is not possible for South Korea to merely copy the Taiwanese approach in dealing with its own communist cross-Strait neighbor.[3]

Generally speaking, in both inter-Korean interaction and cross-Strait interaction, domestic politics and the international system constitute the basic focuses of academic study. As explained by Yu-Shan Wu's account of Cross-Strait exchanges, those three variables can be subdivided into nine approaches. There are a number of models that attempt to explain cross-Strait relations,

---

2_Jun, Byoung-Kon, "Implication of the Cross-Strait Exchanges and Cooperation to inter-Korean Relations," *Journal of Korea-China Social Science*, Vol. 6, No. 1 (2008), p.2.

3_Cho, Myongchul and Park Hyunjung, "Enlargement of economic cooperation in Cross-Strait and It' Implication in Korea," *Country*, Vol. 311 (Korea Research Institute for Human Settlements, 2007); Shin, Sangjin, "The Prospect of Cross-Strait Relations and Maneuver of Korea," The Federation of Korean Industries (2005); Moon, Heungho, "Comparison of Internal and External Factors of China-Taiwan Relations and South-North Korea Relations," APRC, *Journal of Sino-Russia Studies*, Vol. 25, No. 3 (2001).

they are the 'divided-nation model', 'integration theory', and the 'power asymmetry model'. In the domestic political sphere, thee are a number of models as well, namely the 'vote-maximizing model', the 'developmental state paradigm', and the 'political psychology theory'. When discussing cross-Straight relations from an international standpoint, the 'triangle theory', the 'systems theory', and the 'cognitive approach' are often applied.[4]

In my opinion, the integration theory, vote-maximizing model, and the systems theory can be useful in explaining the differences and similarities between inter-Korean relations and cross-Strait exchanges after the year 2000. At the same time, there is another concept that helps to explain why Taiwan was so successful in avoiding conflict with the Mainland; this is the 'power-transition theory'. The power-transition theory states that as China has risen, Taiwan has sought to change its relations with the Mainland in a positive way in order to avoid conflict with the Mainland.

International factors are certainly important, but explanations that center on Taiwanese and Mainland internal politics have more explanatory power. The mainland has also responded positively to Taiwanese interest in cooperation. Economic cooperation has been beneficial to both sides, especially Taiwan, and has allowed

4_Wu, Yu-Shan "Theorizing on Relations across the Taiwan Strait: nine contending approaches" *Journal of Contemporary China* Vol. 9, No. 25 (2000), 409.

both sides to avoid potentially explosive political issues and sources of conflict.[5] Groups who have economic interests in the mainland have emerged within Taiwan. Naturally, these groups oppose confrontational cross-Strait relations. In fact, lots of Taiwan's people recognize that there is a real possibility of maintaining stable and peaceful relations between the two states through the maintenance of the status quo rather than through seeking Taiwanese independence.[6]

Concurrently, despite several crises in the Taiwan Strait and numerous occasions where war seemed to be an imminent possibility , there has been no major armed conflict between Beijing and Taipei since the 1950s. We can explain this puzzle by looking at the relations through the 'military balance of power' approach and neo-liberal argument of economic integration. Other scholars like Shiping Zheng stress the importance of "ethnicity." Zheng argues that "ethnicity" may provide a more convincing explanation of why a military conflict has not happened in the Taiwan Strait in

---

5_Goldman, Merle and Andrew J. Nathan, "Searching for the Appropriate Model for the People's Republic of China," *Historical Perspectives on Contemporary East Asia*. Harvard University Press, 2000, pp. 270-320, cited in Kim, Yeikyoung and Min Ji Kim, "Improved Cross-Strait Relations under the Ma Ying-jeou Administration and its Intrinsic factor," HUFS, *Journal of China Studies*, Vol. 50 (2010), p. 320.

6_Kim, Yeikyoung and Min Ji Kim, "Improved Cross-Strait Relations under the Ma Ying-jeou Administration and its Intrinsic factor," HUFS, *Journal of China Studies*, Vol. 50 (2010), pp. 320-321.

the past four decades.[7] Because Mainland China is the one state that has an interest in launching a war against Taiwan, the Chinese ethnic identity may still serve as an important constraint on Chinese decision-makers, that is so long as the Mainland Chinese continue to view people in Taiwan as their "compatriots," "brothers" and "their own flesh and blood."[8]

By contrast, Chengxin Pan argues that in Taiwan, the emergence of "Taiwaneseness", which is "largely conditioned on 'de-Sinofication'" and "often set against Chineseness," testifies to a focus on the island's difference or distinctiveness from the mainland. Thus, for some, the Taiwan conflict is "not about power but about identity," or more precisely, about two competing visions of national identity.[9]

Internationally, the United States is a crucial factor in cross-Strait relations. The United States has two positions regarding cross-Strait relations. It both supports Taiwanese independence in its Taiwan Relations Act and at the same time it is also recognizes "The principle of One China" as expounded by the

---

7_Zheng, Shiping "Ethnic Peace in the Taiwan Strait," *Journal of Chinese Political Science*, Vol. 15 Association of Chinese Political Studies, 2010, p. 413.

8_Zheng, Shiping p. 426.

9_Pan, Chengxin "Westphalia and the Taiwan Conundrum: A Case against the Exclusionist Construction of Sovereignty and Identity," *Journal of Chinese Political Science* Association of Chinese Political Studies, 2010, 372.

government of the Mainland. Throughout the years, the United States has been ambiguous over the question of Taiwan's legal status. Though the United States has never been ambiguous about its commitment to supplying Taiwan with weapons and defense technologies, periodic talk of "freezing" arms sales has caused great anxiety within Taiwan.[10] Maintaining Taipei's military power vis-à-vis the Mainland, especially with the continued purchase of US arms, plus maintaining the possibility of intervention by the United States in the event of an actual military conflict, are thus believed to have served as effective deterrents against military action by the People's Liberation Army (PLA).

Washington could either facilitate or hinder the rapprochement between Beijing and Taipei particularly when Cross-Strait relations move from 'low politics' to 'high politics' to deal with more difficult political and military-security issues. Indeed, while Beijing-Taipei rapprochement is still in its early stages, the two sides are still dealing with "easy issues" such as the so-called "three direct links". Washington may indeed feel relatively comfortable with the thawing in Cross-Strait relations. But, when the relationship begin to touch on more sensitive political and security issues that have implications for US interests and future US-China-

10_Hsiao, Bi-khim "A DPP Perspective on Domestic and Cross-Strait Challenges for Taiwan," *American Foreign Policy Interests*, Vol. 31 (2009), 43.

Taiwan relations, not only will Beijing and Taipei need to overcome many more hurdles, but Washington may also find it more challenging to adjust to the changing reality in cross-Strait relations.[11]

II. Characters of inter-Korean Relations and Cross-Strait Exchanges: Focused on 1991 Communique and 1992 Consensus

Amidst international changes resulting from the end of the Cold War in the early 1990s, the two Koreas drew up and signed the *1991 Communique: the Basic Agreement of the South-North Korea*. At around the same time, Mainland China and Taiwan also concluded their own *1992 Agreement*. The common ground enabling both of these agreements to be concluded was firstly the end of the Cold War; this strongly influenced the two sets of relations. Secondly, the 'democratization' of South Korea and Taiwan beginning in the late 1980s led domestically to significant changes in the approach to relations with the Mainland and North Korea in Taiwan and South Korea, respectively. Third, following

11_Wang, Jianwei "Is the Honeymoon Over? Progress and Problems in Cross-Strait Relations" *American Foreign Policy Interests*, Vol. 32 (2010), 164.

the end of the Cold War, the role of the United States has changed, that is, the United States has not been involved in reconciliation and cooperation between the two Koreas. In cross-Strait relations, the US has stood its ground on its opposition to China's military demonstrations of force, and its support for both Taiwanese independence and recognition for the principle of 'One China' have been maintained.

The two Koreas signed the *Inter-Korean Basic Agreement*, its full title being "The agreement on the Inter-Korean Reconciliation and Nonaggression and Exchange Cooperation" at the two nation's 5th round of high level talks in Seoul, on December 13th 1991. The Agreement, consisting of a preface, four chapters and 25 clauses, specified the swift implementation criteria in three fields, namely reconciliation, nonaggression and exchange cooperation. And the two Koreas agreed to halt slanderous language in official discourse and to not engage in military actions designed to redraw the de facto boundary between the two countries, the military demarcation line. They also agreed on resource sharing-development, to allow trade between the two countries, to allow the exchange of letters between families separated by the Korean War and also reunions of those families.

The Inter-Korean Basic Agreement is significant in that it marked a great improvement in inter-Korean relations. The framework for peaceful reunification contained within the agreement is the first official statement effected through open conversation between the countries without a third country's intervention. The December 1991 Communique between the representatives of South and North Korea almost wholeheartedly adopted the concept of "multi-system nations" as its basis. It furthermore clearly defined the situation on the Korean Peninsula as two political systems co-existing in one Korean nation. As a result, relations between the two Korean political systems are not international relations, but unique relations to be regulated by specific agreement between the South and North.[12]

There have not been real interactions or active contact between the peoples of North and South since the agreements – with the exception of special zones like Kaesong. In contrast, although the authorities in Beijing and Taipei have not arrived at a commonly accepted framework for reunification, the flow of people and goods across the Taiwan Strait has been far more intensive and extensive than between the two Koreas.[13]

In 1992, representatives of the semi-official Strait Exchange Foundation (SEF) and the Association of Relations Across the

---

12_Ministry of Unification in Korea, *1992 White Paper* Ministry of Unification, 1992.

13_Wei, Yung "From Functional Integration to Structural Readjustment: Taipei - Beijing relations and the role of the United States," Journal of Contemporary China, Vol. 13, No. 40 (August, 2004), 438.

Taiwan Straits (ARATS) reached a deadlock over the issue of "one China," which Beijing required as a prerequisite for cross-Strait dialogue. The two sides reached a compromise of sorts, agreeing to disagree. The 1992 consensus has been a political base for co-operation and dialogue between the two sides and of course, it is also a base for political negotiations. Following this consensus, in an exchange of letters, Beijing stated that "Both sides across the Straits insist on the one-China principle, and are making efforts to reunify the country, but in routine diplomatic exchanges between the two sides, the specific contents of the 'one China' principle will not be discussed." Taipei expressed the consensus as follows: "In the process that the two sides across the Straits make joint efforts to pursue national unification, though both sides insist on a one-China principle, but regarding the content of one China, they have respective interpretations."

The two sides have evaded the issue of sovereignty and explain it differently when it is discussed internally and externally. Taiwan internally declares that "it is an independent, sovereign state," but claims externally that it is in 'one of two areas in one country'. Concurrently, the mainland proclaims internally that "Taiwan is a province of China," while it externally states that "the two sides belong to one China."[14] By the same token, Mainland China and Taiwan, in agreeing to "the Principle of Unified China" in 1992 have avoided unnecessary conflict by being flexible in their interpretations of "Unified" as meaning either "the People's Republic of China", or "the Republic of China".

Taiwan put forth its "National Reunification Doctrine" in February 1991. This became Taiwan's basic policy and position towards Mainland China. Taiwan, while officially maintaining its "Three-Noes Policies" (no contact, no compromise and no negotiation), accepted Mainland China's proposed "three Through Links", and suggested unification be achieved through the implementation of the three principles of the people, i.e. Sun Wenism, on 1 August, 1992. Through the above-mentioned Doctrine, Taiwan has acknowledged the divided reality of the Chinese nation, and also Taiwan has not secured de jure sovereignty, but has admitted the Chinese Communist Party's de facto dominion over the mainland. On the other hand, China has de facto recognized the Taiwanese government. Taiwan expressed its assent to China's position that they start with economic and cultural exchanges, and excluded political issues from their discussions. Taiwan also sought the improvement of actual cross-Strait relations on substantial issues like travel rights through conversation with Beijing.[15]

14_Nianchi, Zhang "The Current Status, Problems, and Prospects of Cross-Strait Relations After the Turnover of Power From One Taiwanese Party to Another," *American Foreign Policy Interests,* Vol. 31 (2009), 49.

15_Park, Kwang-deuk, "Study of 2008 Presidential Election in Taiwan and Cross-Strait Relations," *Journal of Korean Political Science Association,* Vol. 16, No. 3 (2009), 153.

Under Chen Shui-bian, Taiwan proposed that cross-Strait relations be based on "one country on each side of the Taiwan Straits," stressing that Taiwan should "remake its constitution" in order for Taiwan to enter the UN as a nation state through a referendum.[16]

Many of Taiwan's people continued to support the status quo policy of 'Non-Through, Non-Isolation', and this was a constraining influence on the radical policy of Taiwan's leadership. Under Chen Shui-bian , Taiwan sought to internationalize the Taiwan issue through attempts to enter the UN and other international institutions.[17]

Political exchange has been more animated between the two Koreas , and non-political cooperation far less active. To be precise, cross-Strait political exchanges have been rare because of massive asymmetries between the two states in terms of territory, population, power, etc. Mainland China, in seeing Taiwan merely as a province of its own territory, has been a large impediment to political cooperation and exchange between the two sides, Mainland China's government does not perceive Taiwan as a state worthy of being negotiated with.

16_Hu, Lingwei, "The Basic Features and Challenges of Cross-Strait Relations in the New Era," *American Foreign Policy Interests*, Vol. 32 (2010), 8-9.

17_Oh, Seung-yul, Shin Sang-jin and Moon Heung-ho, *Inter-Korean Cooperation and the Change of North Korea : Focuses on the Cross-Straits Experiments*, Education Center for Unification (2003), 118-119.

China's lack of recognition of Taiwan as a state (legitimate or otherwise) has been the principle reason why political agreements and cooperation have not progressed further. Conversely, the two Koreas have held two rounds of summit talks, in 2000 and 2007, and have several rounds of talks yearly, reaching agreements every year (from 2000-2007). This demonstrates that the level of asymmetry between the two Koreas is not as high as between Beijing and Taipei. North Korea's development and possession of nuclear weapons have helped it offset the gap between the two Koreas' in terms of geopolitical power and relative international position in general.[18]

In terms of institutional developments, both Taipei and Beijing have established ministry-level agencies to handle policy-related issues. They have also established nominally 'non-governmental' offices to serve as 'white gloves' to facilitate contact and negotiate on concrete problems. Taiwan has also setup the Mainland Affairs Council in the Executive Yuan (ROC Cabinet) and it has permitted the establishment of the non-official contact organization Strait Exchange Foundation. This organization has also plays a significant role in both policy-making at the central government level and the handling of concrete problems at the cross-Strait level.[19]

18_Jun, Byoung-Kon, 11-12.

19_Yung Wei, 453.

III. Inter-Korean Relations under Kim Dae-jung and Roh Moo-Hyun and Cross-Strait relations in the Chen Shui-bian Era.

Kim Dae-jung's victory in 1997 and Chen Shui-bian's election in 2000 were the first real power rotations under the newly democratized South Korean and Taiwanese political systems. The similarities between Kim Dae-jung and Roh Moo-hyun governments, and the Chen government were first that the peaceful nature of the democratization process greatly influenced the two governments' relations with their respective antagonist states – both governments were markedly different in their handling of these states. Second, the successor to the Kim government, the Roh government, expanded the Sunshine Policy of the Kim government to include the Peace and Prosperity Policy. Conversely, the stated desire for Taiwan's independence by the Chen government raised the possibility of a serious military crisis with Mainland China.

Third, during this era, the Clinton administration, while supporting the Sunshine policy, experienced both conflict and cooperation with both North and South Korea due to North Korea's nuclear ambitions. At the same time, however, the United States government under Clinton tried to restrain Taiwanese ambition for independence and was broadly supportive of the Mainland's status quo policy.

Kim Dae-jung and Kim Jong-il stated in their June 15th Declaration that they intended to deepen the Sunshine Policy through North-South cooperation. Roh Moo-hyun and Kim Jong-il went further still in their October 4th Summit Declaration, in which they outlined the sweeping South-North Action Plan.

The principles of the Sunshine Policy were as follows. Firstly, any military provocation by North Korea would not be accepted. Secondly, reunification by absorption was no longer an option. Thirdly, South-North reconciliation and cooperation should be actively promoted.

The 'sunshine policy' suffered from a number of defects. First, South Korean views of North Korea were (and still are) contradictory; on the one hand, North Korea is seen as an adversarial military power, while on the other it is seen as the object of future unification. Second, the policy was not transparent - it was not clear what the South Korean government was spending its money on with regard to the Sunshine Policy. Third, there was no underlying mass political concession to underlie and reinforce the policy - it was highly controversial and polarizing (far from unifying!).[20] In spite of South Korean aid, the North Korea people continued to be malnourished and the North's military continued to

20_Youn, Jae-moon, *Kim Dae-jung Government's Reconciliation and Cooperation Policy toward North Korea : Outcomes and Limitations*, Chosun University, 2005, 9.

carry out provocations, such as the First and Second Battle of Yeonpyeong (in the Yellow Sea) and missile tests. The Sunshine Policy's core principle was the separation of politics from economics. With continued North Korean aggression and provocation however, the principle came under ever increasing criticism. The two Battles of Yeonpyeong, which occurred in June 1999 and June 2002, further damaged the beleaguered policy.

The Bush administration's hardline policy toward North Korea brought about cracks in the US-South Korea alliance. As a result of a visit to Pyongyang by James Kelly, then United States Presidential envoy, in October 2002. the second North Korea's nuclear crisis occurred. The Perry Process, the name for the Clinton era policy of cooperation and negotiation with the North, was scrapped. In 1994, the North, with the ascension of Kim Jong-il as the new leader of the country after the death of Kim Il-sung, pushed ahead with the development of nuclear weapons under its "military-first politics." The North took full advantage of the Sunshine Policy in the form of unconditional aid and preferential trade, while at the same time pursuing a policy of brinksmanship and tension.

Taiwan's Democratic Progressive Party (DPP), triumphant in its electoral victory, adopted Taiwanese independence as official party doctrine. Although the Chen Shui-bian government did not officially abandon national reunification, it adopted a stance favoring independence through the principle of 'one country on each side of the Strait'. In August 2002, Chen proclaimed this stance, which in effect reiterated former President Li Teng-hui's remark in 1999 of a "special state-to-state relationship" between Taiwan and Mainland China. Chen Shui-bian maintained that he could not find any reference to the 1992 Consensus in the negotiation records. He said that his government would agree to talk with China about "one China" as a topic, but would not accept it as a precondition. There was thus no semi-official dialogue –such as SEF/ARATS– during the Chen administration.[21] Chen then began pushing for a new constitution for Taiwan through a public referendum slated for 2003, and then proceeded to tie it to the presidential election in 2004. Both candidates stated their concerns about the risk of Taiwan becoming too economically dependent on the mainland.[22]

To calm the tensions in the Taiwan Strait, Chen was pressured by the Clinton administration. The United States wanted Chen to pledge in his 2000 inaugural address the "four noes: no declara-

---

21_Wang, Vincent Wei-cheng "The Chen Shui-bian Administration's Mainland Policy: Toward a Modus Vivendi or Continued Stalemate?" *American Asian Review*, vol. 20, No. 3 (Fall, 2002), 91-124, in Wang, Wei-cheng "The Impact of Taiwan's 2008 Election on Cross-Strait Relations: A Game-Theoretical Analysis," *Asian Perspective*, Vol. 32, No. 2 (2008), 169.

22_Zhao, Quansheng "Beijing's dilemma with Taiwan: war or peace?" *The Pacific Review*, Vol. 18, No. 2 (June 2005), 223.

tion of independence, no changing Taiwan's formal name of the ROC, no enshrining 'state-to-state' Mainland-Taiwan relations in the Constitution, and no holding a referendum on formal independence." Chen stated in his presidential inaugural address in 2004 that he would follow the following principles: ① No declaration of independence within his term, ② No change of the national name ③ No pushing ahead with the constitutional two nation theory, ④ No reunification referendum, ① Maintaining the existence of the national reunification committee and the compliance of the national reunification doctrine. This set of policies was called "four Noes and one Without". The final being 'without,' insofar as it was merely a promise to maintain an existing institution and a policy 'without' anything new to add.

In the summer of 2004, there were three military exercises around the Taiwan Strait. The PLA conducted military drills on Dongshan Island on the western edge of the Taiwan Strait, involving about 18,000 troops. The purpose of these exercises was to demonstrate China's air and sea superiority over Taiwan.[23] After the Cold War the Taiwan Strait has witnessed two military crises, in 1995-1996 and 1999-2000. In both crises, China conducted military exercises and missile tests in the Taiwan Strait in order to sig-

23_"Military exercises in the Taiwan Strait," *Far Eastern Economic Review*, July 29 (2004), 26.

nal its opposition to Taiwan's pro-independence movement. Following Chen Shui-bian's election as the new President of Taiwan in 2000, Beijing gradually changed its policies in dealing with Taiwanese independence. It has begun to rely far more on political and diplomatic pressure instead of military shows of force. Of late, tensions in the Taiwan Strait have been limited to non-military intimidation and verbal attacks between China and Taiwan.[24]

The use of diplomatic and political pressure is evident in Hu Jintao's Four Points enunciated in February 2005; the points were designed to restrain perceived Taiwanese moves toward 'separatism'. The Mainland went still further with the passage of the Anti-cessation law at the 10th National People's Congress of the China, 14 March, 2005. The law aimed to stop Taiwanese secession, but also to encourage moves toward eventual unification. However, as a result of the passage of the law, relations between the two sides entered a deep freeze.

The United States factor has played a significant role in the cross-Strait situation from its beginning. When the Mainland and Taiwan were going through a period of hostility, the existence of

24_He, Kai and Huiyun Feng, "Leadership, regime security, and China's policy toward Taiwan: prospect theory and Taiwan crises," *The Pacific Review*, Vol. 22 No. 4 (September 2009), 502.

the US factor helped maintain the peace and Taiwan's existence. In the Chen Shui-bian era especially, the US factor played a positive role in maintaining cross-Strait peace and the status quo of the Taiwan Strait.[25] In a December 2003 meeting with Chinese Premier Wen Jiabao, President George W. Bush made a clear statement of America's position on the Taiwan issue: "We oppose any unilateral decision, by either China or Taiwan, to change the status quo of Taiwan's relationship with the mainland." President Bush, for the first time, criticised Chen's referendum proposal as a move that would change the status quo. After Bush's criticism, Chen Shui-bian revised the question for his proposed referendum. At the same time, he warned Beijing that the United States would intervene if the Mainland attacked Taiwan.[26]

Washington's objection to Chen's initiative proved crucial in the outcome of the UN entry referendum. the turnout rate of 35.82 percent, below the required 50 percent of all eligible voters, was largely due to United States intervention.

China and the United States have found a common interest on the Taiwan issue, which has served as the foundation for policy coordination between Beijing and Washington to rein in the perceived attempts of Chen Shui-bian to "change the status quo."[27]

25_Hu, Lingwei, 11.

26_Zhao, Quansheng, 218-219.

Chen's Democratic Progressive Party (DPP) captured only 89 of the 225 seats in the 2004 Legislative Yuan election, failing to secure a majority necessary to pass Chen's initiative for a new constitution. In the wake of Lien Chan's 2005 meeting with Hu Jintao, his Kuomintang (KMT) signed a series of agreements with Beijing on expanding cross-Strait economic, trade, and cultural exchanges, thereby boosting its popular support substantially.[28]

The United States, remaining the major guarantor of Taiwan's security as of now against China's threat, has been and will continue to be an external influence on Taiwanese affairs.

US influence serves as the indispensable 'cue' to assist Taiwan's electorate in making sure about whether and when the pursuit of independence might give rise to an unbearable cost. The United States serves as a bulwark against impractical political choices and demagogy by some more irresponsible elements within Taiwanese politics. US pressure turned initiatives that had grown out of a search for Taiwanese identity into a potentially very dangerous

---

27_Wang, Jianwei "Hu Jintao's "New Thinking" on Cross-Strait Relations," American *Foreign Policy Interests*, Vol. 29 (2007), 26.

28_Ross, Robert S. "Taiwan's fading independence movement," *Foreign Affairs*, Vol. 85, No. 2 (March/April, 2006), 141-149. in Hsu, S. Philip "Between Identity Quest and Risk Aversion: lessons from the Chen Shui-bian presidency for maintaining cross-Strait stability," *Journal of Contemporary China*, Vol. 19, No. 66 (September, 2010), 697-698.

political choice. Risk aversion and practical considerations ultimately prevailed, even in the absence of Mainland Chinese pressure.[29]

In sum, the differences between the Kim Dae-jung and Roh Moo-Hyun governments, and the Chen government were that first, through the Sunshine policy, the Kim and Roh governments carried out a policy that emphasized inter-Korean cooperation, strengthening North-South cooperation and aid to North Korea. Through the 'One Country on each side' principle, Taiwan under Chen favored independence rather than reunification. This led to a great deal of tension between Taiwan and the Mainland. Secondly, the opposition party and the conservative political forces in general in South Korea denounced the Sunshine policy, criticizing the unconditional aid that was offered on opaque terms, even as North Korea continued to develop its nuclear weapons capability – the fact that the country continued to suffer from famine conditions further enraged the political right in South Korea. Chen's government also clashed with the approach of the opposition Kuomintang trying to establish a favorable relationship with the Mainland. Third, the Bush administration took a tough stance toward North Korea, while the Kim and Roh governments clashed

29_Hsu, S. Philip 2010, 716-717.

with the Bush administration over North Korea policy. The Bush administration became increasingly nervous about what they perceived as Kim and Roh favoring South-North Korea cooperation over the US-South Korea alliance. The Bush administration tried to maintain stability in cross-Strait relations while also responding toughly to talk of Taiwanese independence by the Chen government, and went so far as to publicly criticize the referendum on Taiwan joining the UN.

IV. Inter-Korean Relations in Lee Myung-bak Era and Cross-Strait Exchanges in Ma Ying-jeou Era

In 2008, the candidates' of the Grand National Party (GNP) in South Korea and the Kuomintang (KMT) in Taiwan won their respective presidential elections. The Lee administration advocated solving the North Korean nuclear issue through multilateral means rather than bilateral cooperation alone. The Ma government renounced the Chen government's policy of Taiwanese independence, and strengthened and deepened economic and political cooperation with the Mainland. At the same time, the US role in the region changed. US-South Korea relations were restored to that of a traditional alliance – the economic aspect of the alliance was further enlarged and developed by the ratification of the KORUS FTA. Conversely, while the Ma administration continued to import US weaponry, its overall reliance on trade with the United States has shrunk as a result of deepening ties with the Mainland. Thus the US has seen its influence over cross-Strait issues diminish.

The Lee Myung-bak government favored the principle of reciprocity and international cooperation centered on the US-South Korean alliance. Advocating a policy of peaceful coexistence with the North, the Lee government also pressed for denuclearization and North Korea's opening, the ultimate aim to create a common North-South economic community. The Obama administration's North policy has prioritized denuclearization. [30]

Since Ma Ying-jeou was elected president of Taiwan in March 2008, Cross-Strait relations have experienced a huge change. Economic, cultural, human, and other functional interactions and exchanges across the Taiwan Strait have reached unprecedented levels. Beijing and Taipei have resumed semi-official dialogues through the Association for Relations Across the Taiwan Strait (ARATS) and the Straits Exchange Foundation (SEF), which had been suspended for the previous nine years. Direct air and shipping services between the two sides, a long-time issue between

30_Paik, Hak Soon, "The North Korea Policy of Obama Administration," *Current Issues and Policy* (Jun, 2009), 15.

the two sides, has been solved, greatly promoting cross-Strait relations.[31]

Ma campaigned on "Three-Noes": If he was elected, he pledged that there would be no unification, no independence, and no war in his term. The United States and the Mainland were pleased by Ma's choice of policies.

The main reason for these policies was of course, to tap further into the huge mainland market, thus helping to boost the weak Taiwanese economy, which was in the most serious recession since the 1960s. But equally significant is Taiwan's interest in using the ECFA to pave the way for signing FTAs with South Asian and other countries and avoid being excluded from the ASEAN FTA, which was established in January 2010.[32] Mainland China remains Taiwan's largest export market, accounting for more than 28% of its exports. By virtue of the fact that Taiwan's current economic fortunes are very much tied to China, a reversal in the cordial cross-Strait relations that have developed over the past few years is unlikely.[33]

31_Chen, Qimao, "The Taiwan Straits Situation since Ma came to Office and Conditions for Cross-Straits Political Negotiations: a view from Shanghai," *Journal of Contemporary China*, Vol. 20, No. 68 (January, 2011), 153.

32_Zhu, Songling, "Why Are the Ma Ying-jeou Authorities So Eager to Sign ECFA?" (July 16, 2009), on *www.huaxia.com*. (2012/02/14).

33_*China & North East Asia* (September, 2011), 7.

According to a noted scholar, the Ma administration "has adopted a more moderate stance but has stopped well short of a thorough repudiation of his predecessors" positions. Ma too has pledged to safeguard the nation's sovereignty, sought to maintain formal relations with the ROC's remaining partners, rejected near-term political unification with the mainland, and brought to fruition moves begun under Chen to secure observer status at the UN-linked WHO and the nearest equivalent possible of accession to the two principal UN human rights covenants.[34]

On the eve of 2009, Hu Jintao delivered a speech commemorating the 30th anniversary of the "Message to Compatriots in Taiwan". Hu's speech revealed what the PRC means by the 'reunification of China' - namely, unification under the People's Republic of China. He added that the speech was aimed at the KMT and is pressuring the Ma administration to fast-track negotiations for political reunification under the 'One-China' principle.[35] Nonetheless 'Beijing's policy toward Taiwan under Hu Jintao has refocused its priority on preventing independence rather than forcing unification, adopting more conciliatory rhetoric and prag-

34_de Lisle, Jacques "Soft Power in a Hard Place: China, Taiwan, Cross-Strait Relations and U.S.Policy," Orbis (Fall, 2010). 515.

35_Park,, Kwang-Deuk, "Study of "Hu-Jintao's Four-Point" to "Hu-Jintao's Six-Point" in Cross-Strait Relations," *Journal of Politic-Information*, Vol. 12, No. 1 (2009), 163.

matic tactics but maintaining essentially the same policies'.[36]

The DPP is becoming increasingly anxious about the asymmetric vulnerabilities of Taiwan's negotiating positions in economic, security, and international arenas. Therefore, the DPP and its supporters demand that such an agreement with the mainland has to be approved by a referendum. It also promised that even with the ECFA, Taiwan would not open its market to farm products and laborers from the mainland.'[37]

In sum, the distinctions between Lee and Ma administrations are that first, whereas Lee has emphasized security over economic cooperation, the Ma administration has intensified economic cooperation and interdependence. Soon after the government came into office, the two Koreas' relationship and their economic cooperation drastically declined. This was further aggravated by the North's attack on the Cheonan warship and shelling of Yeonpyeong Island, both in 2010. On the other hand, cross-Strait exchanges under the Ma administration intensified as a result of policy changes.

Second, in South Korea, the domestic political debates sur-

36_Wang, Vincent Wei-cheng "The Impact of Taiwan's 2008 Election on Cross-Strait Relations: A Game-Theoretical Analysis," *Asian Perspective*, Vol. 32, No. 2 (2008), 167-168.

37_*CNA*, "The Bottom Line of ECFA: No Opening to Mainland's Farm Products and Laborers," (November 9, 2009).

rounding North Korea policy were characterized by opposition from the former ruling party. The pro-China policy of Taiwan's Ma administration also raised the political issue of 'Identity' in Taiwan – this issue has been discussed often in opposition discourse.

Third, the freezing of inter-Korean relations, and North Korea's military provocation continue to demonstrate that the Cold War has yet to end in Asia. On the other hand, the ambiguity of the United States' role in cross-Strait relations was further intensified under the Ma government. As a result of the conciliatory tone and policies of the Ma administration, the United States has found itself increasingly irrelevant, except as a supplier of military hardware.

V. CONCLUSION

This article has looked into the reasons why cross-Straits exchanges have expanded between the Mainland and Taiwan, but similar developments have not occurred between the two Koreas.

There are three variables that are of especial importance, they are as follows: (1) interactions between the Taipei and Beijing compared to those of Seoul and Pyongyang, (2) domestic political factors, and (3) the attitude of the United States. The deepening of South Korean democracy from around 2000, and the development of a separate Taiwanese identity are both also significant political factors.

In both the cross-Strait and inter-Korean cases there has been a general trend in the direction of increased exchanges. Secondly, domestically, both Taiwan and South Korea have begun to become post-ideological societies, with a far more practical and realistic attitude to their respective rivals. Third, Domestic political conflicts that surround cross-Strait policy in Taiwan and North Korea policy in South Korea have intensified as a result of changes in governments following elections. Fourth, while the United States remains a crucial partner of both South Korea and Taiwan, its influence in the region is diminishing.

On the other hand, the differences between the inter-Korean and the Cross-Strait are also numerous. First, security issues between the two Koreas have taken precedence other competing political and economic issues. Conversely, because cross-Strait relations have been advanced as a result of non-political interactions between Taiwan and the mainland, they have not as strongly affected by security concerns or political factors.

Another factor that has led to instability in North-South relations is a lack of institutionalization of those relations, the two Koreas do not recognize one another diplomatically, and therefore do not maintain formal or stable links. Such issues are further aggravated by the fact that there are two competing and antagonistic methods of dealing with issues related to North Korea in South

Korean politics; these methods are the 'internationalist approach', which seeks to build an international consensus to deal with North Korea, and the 'nationalist approach', which seeks to deal with North Korea-related issues through North-South dialogue.

Similarly, in Taiwan, there are two major approaches to dealing with the Mainland, the first is the One China approach – i.e. Chinese nationalism – the second is the Taiwanese identity approach – i.e. Taiwanese nationalism, or separatism.

International relations and the role of the United States cannot be ignore, either. Whereas in inter-Korean relations, the United States continues to play an important role because of North Korea's nuclear program, it has become a more peripheral player in cross-Strait relations.

References

1. Korean Scholars

Cho, Myong-chul and Park Hyun-jung, "Enlargement of economic cooperation in Cross-Strait and It' Implication in Korea," *Country*, Vol. 311, Korea Research Institute for Human Settlements, 2007.

Jun, Byoung-kon, "Implication of the Cross-Strait Exchanges and Cooperation to inter-Korean Relations," *Journal of Korea-China Social Science*, Vol. 6, No. 1 (2008).

Kim, Yei-kyoung and Kim, Min-ji, "Improved Cross-Strait Relations under the Ma Ying-jeou Administration and its Intrinsic factor," HUFS, *Journal of China Studies*, Vol. 50 (2010).

Ministry of Justice (Korea), *A Study on the Law of Exchange Cooperation in China and Taiwan*, Ministry of Justice, 2008.

Ministry of Unification (Korea), *1992 White Paper*. Ministry of Unification, 1992.

Moon, Heung-ho, "Comparison of Internal and External Factors of China - Taiwan Relations and South - North Korea Relations," APRC, *Journal of Sino-Russia Studies*, Vol. 25, No. 3 (2001).

-------. *Taiwan Issue and Inter-Strait Relations,* Politeia, 2007.

Oh, Seung-yul, Shin Sang-jin and Moon Heung-ho, *Inter-Korean Cooperation and the Change of North Korea : Focuses on the Cross-Straits Experiments*, Education Center for Unification, 2003.

Paik, Hak-soon, "The North Korea Policy of Obama Administration," *Current Issues and Policy* (Jun, 2009).

Park, Kwang-deuk, "Study of "Hu-Jintao's Four-Points" to "Hu-Jintao's Six-Points" in Cross-Strait Relations," *Journal of Politic-Information*, Vol. 12, No. 1(2009).

-------. "Study of 2008 Presidential Election in Taiwan and Cross-Strait Relations," *Journal of Korean Political Science Association*, Vol. 16, No. 3 (2009).

Shin, Sang-jin, "China-Taiwan Relation after Min Jin Party in Taiwan: Analysis and Prospect," *International Journal of Korean Unification Studies,* Vol. 9, No. 1 (2000).

-------. *The Prospect of Cross-Straits Relations and Maneuver of Korea.* The Federation of Korean Industries, 2005.

Youn, Jae-Moon, *Kim Dae-jung Government's Reconciliation and Cooperation Policy toward North Korea : The Outcome and Its Limitation*, Chosun University, 2005.

2. Taiwanese and Chinese Scholars

Chen, Qimao, "The Taiwan Straits Situation since Ma came to Office and Conditions for Cross-Straits Political Negotiations: a view from Shanghai," *Journal of Contemporary China*, Vol. 20, No. 68 (January, 2011).

de Lisle, Jacques, "Soft Power in a Hard Place: China, Taiwan, Cross-Strait Relations and U.S.Policy," *Orbis* (Fall 2010).

Ding, Yijiang, "Beijing's New Approach and the Rapprochement in the Taiwan Strait," *Asian Affairs* (2009).

He, Kai and Huiyun Feng, "Leadership, regime security, and China's policy toward Taiwan: prospect theory and Taiwan crises," *The Pacific Review*, Vol. 22 No. 4 (September 2009).

Hsiao, Bi-khim, "A DPP Perspective on Domestic and Cross-Strait Challenges for Taiwan," *American Foreign Policy Interests*, Vol. 31 (2009).

Hsu, S. Philip, "Between Identity Quest and Risk Aversion: lessons from the Chen Shui-bian presidency for maintaining cross-Strait stability," *Journal of Contemporary China*, Vol. 19, N0. 66 (September, 2010).

-------. "Reappraising the debate and practice of US strategic ambiguity/clarity in Cross-Strait relations," *The Pacific Review*, Vol. 23 No. 2 (May 2010).

Hu, Lingwei, "The Basic Features and Challenges of Cross-Strait Relations in the New Era," *American Foreign Policy Interests*, Vol. 32 (2010).

Hu, Shaohua, "Structural Constraints on the EU's Role in Cross-Taiwan Strait Relations," *European Journal of East Asian Studies*, IO. I (2011).

Pan, Chengxin, "Westphalia and the Taiwan Conundrum: A Case against the Exclusionist Construction of Sovereignty and Identity," *Journal of Chinese Political Science,* Association of Chinese Political Studies, 2010.

Wang, Jianwei, "Hu Jintao's "New Thinking" on Cross-Strait Relations," *American Foreign Policy Interests*, Vol. 29 (2007).

-------. "Is the Honeymoon Over? Progress and Problems in Cross-Strait Relations," *American Foreign Policy Interests*, Vol. 32 (2010).

-------. "United States and Evolving Cross-Strait Relations," *Journal of Chinese Political Science* (Association of Chinese Political Studies, Oct., 2010).

Wang, Vincent Wei-cheng, "The Impact of Taiwan's 2008 Election on Cross-Strait Relations: A Game-Theoretical Analysis," *Asian Perspective*, Vol. 32, No. 2 (2008).

Wei, Yung "From Functional Integration to Structural Readjustment: Taipei-Beijing relations and the role of the United States," *Journal of Contemporary China*, Vol. 13, No. 40 (August, 2004).

Wu, Yu-Shan, "Theorizing on Relations across the Taiwan Strait: nine contending approaches," *Journal of Contemporary China*, Vol. 9, No. 25(2000).

Xin, Qiang, "Beyond Power Politics: institution-building and Mainland China's Taiwan policy transition," *Journal of Contemporary China*, Vol. 19, No. 65 (June, 2010).

Zhang, Nianchi, "The Current Status, Problems, and Prospects of Cross-Strait Relations After the Turnover of Power From One Taiwanese Party to Another," *American Foreign Policy Interests*, Vol. 31 (2009).

Zhao, Quansheng, "Beijing's dilemma with Taiwan: war or peace?" *The Pacific Review*, Vol. 18, No. 2 (June 2005).

Zheng, Shiping, "Ethnic Peace in the Taiwan Strait," *Journal of Chinese Political Science*, Vol. 15 (Association of Chinese Political Studies, 2010).

3. Magazines, Newspapers, and Internet Resources

China & North East Asia (September, 2011).

CNA, "Ma Ying-jeou: ECFA Is a Must and Does Need a Referendum," (May 29, 2009).

CNA, "The Bottom Line of ECFA: No Opening to Mainland's Farm Products and Laborers," (November 9, 2009).

Epoch Times, "DPP Raised Economic Reasons against ECFA," (July 6, 2009).

Far Eastern Economic Review, July 29 (2004).

Joongang Daily Newspaper (2011/11/14).

The Economist Intelligence Unit Limited, *Monthly Review* (April 2011).

Zhu, Songling, "Why Are the Ma Ying-jeou Authorities So Eager to Sign ECFA?" (July 16, 2009), on *www.huaxia.com.* (2012/02/14).